Jacked Up and Unjust

Jacked Up and Unjust

*Pacific Islander Teens Confront Violent
Legacies*

———

Katherine Irwin
and
Karen Umemoto

UNIVERSITY OF CALIFORNIA PRESS

University of California Press, one of the most distinguished university presses in the United States, enriches lives around the world by advancing scholarship in the humanities, social sciences, and natural sciences. Its activities are supported by the UC Press Foundation and by philanthropic contributions from individuals and institutions. For more information, visit www.ucpress.edu.

University of California Press
Oakland, California

Some of the research included in this book was supported by an agency of the U.S. Department of Health and Human Services and private funding from two families in Hawai'i (through the Hawai'i Community Foundation). The contents of this book are solely the responsibility of the authors and do not necessary represent the official views of the funding agencies or agents. We are purposely not identifying which DHHS agency funded the violence prevention initiative as a step to protect the real names of the schools, communities, and people in this study.

Library of Congress Cataloging-in-Publication Data

Names: Irwin, Katherine, author. | Umemoto, Karen, author.
Title: Jacked up and unjust : Pacific Islander teens confront violent
    legacies / Katherine Irwin and Karen Umemoto.
Description: Oakland, California : University of California Press, [2016] |
    Includes bibliographical references and index.
Identifiers: LCCN 2016015751 | ISBN 9780520283022 (cloth : alk. paper) |
    ISBN 9780520283039 (pbk. : alk. paper)
Subjects: LCSH: Youth and violence—Hawaii—21st century. |
    Youth—Hawaii—Social conditions. | Pacific Islander American
    teenagers—Hawaii—Social conditions.
Classification: LCC HQ799.2.V56179 2016 | DDC 303.6083509969—dc23
LC record available at http://lccn.lov.gov/2016015751

Manufactured in the United States of America

25 24 23 22 21 20 19 18 17 16
10 9 8 7 6 5 4 3 2 1

Katherine Irwin: To Louis Ortiz, for being an extraordinarily supportive, encouraging, and inspiring partner

Karen Umemoto: To Kay and Hank Umemoto, for the loving foundation and guidance you always provided

CONTENTS

ACKNOWLEDGMENTS

Our utmost gratitude belongs to individuals who must remain anonymous and pseudonymous due to the nature of this work. They are the students, school administrators, counselors, teachers, security guards, community-based program leaders, youth workers, and juvenile justice system employees who generously shared their stories and time with us. We also want to thank the high schools we call Seaside and Cleveland and the neighborhoods we named Northward and Stevens Heights for literally and figuratively opening their doors to us. We are also grateful to the State of Hawai'i Department of Education for allowing us to conduct the research.

Maura Roessner, senior editor at the University of California Press, and the Press's faculty board deserve countless praises for encouraging this work. Barbara Owen and Barbara Bloom also deserve gratitude for introducing Katy to Maura and for taking part in dozens of productive conversations about critical criminology research. We extend many thanks to Jack Young, the editorial assistant for this project, for keeping us on track toward publication. Dianne Glei deserves appreciation for editing chapters and talking through this project with Katy. We also thank Laurie Schaffner, Jennifer Schwartz, and the anonymous University of California Press reviewers, who offered supportive and insightful suggestions to improve the book.

Because the initial research for this book was collected through grant funding from an agency at the U.S. Department of Health and Human Services (DHHS) there were many DHHS-based project managers who supported this research. Like the individuals at Northward and Seaside, they must remain anonymous. Karen and Katy, however, are thankful for their support.

Additionally, many University of Hawai'i-based researchers, professors, and students assisted this project, especially the coordination and completion of focus groups. We are indebted to Earl Hishinuma, who spent many hours reading and commenting on this book and assisting in the early research phases. Corey Adler, Bo Keopaseut, Jeanelle Sugimoto-Matsuda, Jane Chung-Do, Stephanie Nishimura, Janice Chang, Deborah Goebert, and Susana Helm were members of the many UH teams during the first phases of the research. We are thankful for their hard work. A special word of thanks goes to Tai-An Miao for her support and especially for her inspiration as someone who has shown such dedication to youth, their families, and to systems change.

Thanks to the philanthropic work of two families in Hawai'i, the lunch bunch program received generous funds. These philanthropists wanted to remain anonymous. We hope it is enough to say that we are extremely thankful to the Hawai'i Community Foundation for facilitating and coordinating the funding from these families. There were also numerous organizations in Northward and Stevens Heights that made this work possible. We sincerely thank them, but we cannot identify them by name. Carrie Shoda-Sutherland and RaeDeen M. Keahiolalo Karasuda were also lunch bunch champions, connecting Katy and Karen to funding sources. Katy is especially thankful for RaeDeen's keen scholarship and her friendship through the years.

This work was also made possible through years of friendship and collegueship at UH. Kalei Kanuha, William Wood, and Patricia Steinhoff served as chairs of the Department of Sociology at UH (Katy's department), and each encouraged this work. Thank you all for recognizing the importance of community-based research and service. Sanna King, a sociology graduate student, became a research partner and part of the lunch bunch team. We are thankful for all of her efforts. Penny-Bee Kapilialoha Bovard, Izzak Williams, Alexis Ibarra, Holly Sevier, Nick Gibson, Nick Chagnon, and Mari Kita always expressed interest in and support of the research. Izzak Williams and Nick Gibson deserve particular appreciation for attending camping trips with the lunch bunch teens. We hope that the games, campfires, and storytelling made up for the sleep that you lost at camp.

Katy's colleagues and friends were also enormously helpful. Her thanks go out to Meda Chesney-Lind, Lisa Pasko, Janet Davidson, Ashley Maynard, Katie Dragar, Lori Yancura, Jen Lois, Alice Fothergill, Adina Nack, Jennifer Darrah, Lisa Uperesa, Nandita Sharma, and Krysia Mossakowski, all of whom supported her as she completed chapters. She greatly appreciates all of their advice, comments, and views regarding this work. Kim Burnett, Stacia Murray, and Tammy Real kept Katy sane, active, and healthy throughout the book-writing process and she is so thankful for their steadfast support.

The support and incisive ethnographic insights of Patti and Peter Adler deserve special recognition. Katy is always thankful for the time that Peter and Patti take to talk through emerging ideas and ethnographic dilemmas. Thanks also to Brye and Jori Adler, Patti and Pete's adult children, who have listened with uncanny patience as Katy, Patti, and Pete discussed (and sometimes disagreed) about the art, science, and ethics of ethnography.

Katy's family—Fran Irwin, Marsha Rosenbaum, Johnny Irwin, Anne Rosenbaum Conger, James Conger, Jeanette Irwin, and Dave Mosick—deserve much gratitude for their support throughout this project. Fran Irwin, Katy's mother, was especially patient as Katy talked about her developing chapters during their many mother/daughter outings. Last but most important among Katy's supporters is Louis Ortiz, who lived through and supported every part of this project. A thousand thanks and Katy's dedication of this book to Louis are probably not enough to express the depth of Katy's gratitude to her husband.

This research was also made possible through the collegial support of the UH Department of Urban and Regional Planning (Karen's department). One could not ask for a more nurturing social and intellectual environment and Karen's thanks go to Dana Singer, fellow faculty, and the rest of the staff and student assistants for creating and sustaining it. Kem Lowry and Dolores Foley have been especially important mentors and supporters. Friends more than colleagues, Krisna Suryanata and Keith Mattson, and their sons, always helped to keep balance and perspective in life, which is no small feat.

Karen's family has also played an important role. Her father, Hank Umemoto, has been an inspiration through the writing as a fellow author who is leaving his kids his stories, the greatest gift. Karen's mother, Kay Umemoto, has always been a source of comfort and encouragement, as have Jasmine Grace, Bruce Umemoto, and Michelle and Elle Nakamura. Last but not least, a debt of gratitude goes to Brian Niiya whose patience, encouragement, and partnership in the journey of life have, along with the companionship of May Niiya, been fortunate and fulfilling beyond words.

Introduction

Angel's fights were legendary.[1] Six feet tall at sixteen, she was a formidable opponent who could smack down anyone who challenged her. Few attempted to directly confront Angel. Instead, her adversaries usually yelled derogatory remarks from across the hallways and yards at school, leading her to call back, "Oh, shut your ass up. You know I can beat your ass on the spot!" If Angel did catch up with a girl who insulted her, a fight was sure to ensue. Along with the resulting bloodied noses, torn clothing, and bruised bodies, Angel's opponents would be ridiculed for attempting, but failing, to bring her down. Only a "stupid bitch" would try to fight with Angel.

Angel felt proud of her fighting abilities, although she noted that having a reputation as a competent fighter was different for girls than it was for boys. Her male cousins, she noted, were well-respected fighters, and the fact that they had been in and out of prison for violence only added to their reputations in their community. Very few people "messed with" (disrespected) them. In comparison, Angel felt that her peers sometimes treated her as if she were "crazy" and "out of control." She recounted, "I felt so stupid about it [fighting] because everybody used to look at me like, 'Oh shit, who's it going to be next, who's next?' I'm like, what the heck are you talking about?" Angel did not want to be seen as an indiscriminant fighter who engaged in "stupid" or "crazy" physical confrontations.

Additionally, other girls targeted Angel, chastising her, avoiding her, and sometimes accusing her of being "big" and "ugly." If her foes could not bring her down physically, then they could use traditional femininity norms against her by letting her know that she was not petite, frail, or pale enough to be considered beautiful. At times, Angel resisted the narrow American definitions of beauty by saying, "Big and bold, Miss Beautiful. I'm fucking beautiful by myself!" At other times, however, she worried about her looks.

Though fighting did not elevate Angel's reputation among her female peers, Angel did not mind this social isolation. In fact, she did not particularly respect other girls. For example, one day Angel announced, "Some girls just irk me out. I'm serious." The list of things that irritated her about schoolgirls was long. How they dressed ("too slutty"), how they talked ("too fake"), and how they spent their time ("too into boys") were high on her list of complaints.

Given that Angel was one among many high school teens who was suspended frequently for fighting, she was eventually referred to a counseling-based program to help her manage her anger. This is where Katy and Karen, the authors of this book, first met her. More specifically, Angel was referred to the "lunch bunch"—a support group that met at school to provide teens with food, cold drinks, and a nonjudgmental environment in which to talk about the challenges in their lives.

The lunch bunch program began in 2007 after a collection of high school counselors spoke with us about collaborating to provide services for teens who were having trouble in school, often for fighting. The counselors organized the group sessions with students while we searched for grant funding to cover food, curriculum, activities, and field trips for the teens. It was during our attendance at the weekly lunch bunch sessions that we learned more about Angel than that she was a formidable fighter. We came to know her as an intelligent, thoughtful, and talented young woman who was facing enormous upheavals.

Probably the most salient event during Angel's teen years was her mother's death. After this, she was shuttled from family member to family member and from state to state as her aunts and uncles attempted to collectively care for her. By her junior year, Angel had been enrolled in three different high schools and was living with an aunt on Oahu. Angel did not particularly like this aunt, saying, "She is so irritating. She lifts these weights like this (flapping her arms quickly like a chicken). She's not doing anything. She eats too much. I tell her, 'You ain't got no man. You'll never get a man unless you stop eating everything out the fridge all the time!'"

At the end of her junior year of high school, Angel's aunt was preparing to send her to live with other family members on the U.S. continent, creating mixed feelings for Angel. On the one hand, when she moved, her conflicts with girls on Oahu would end; on the other hand, she would be dislodged from cherished parts of her past. She explained that once a week she visited her mother's grave. She sat, talked to her mother, cried, sometimes laughed, and complained about her auntie. What would happen, Angel worried, if she moved three thousand miles away from where her mother was buried?

· · ·

Benny, another lunch bunch teen, was also known as a competent fighter. Standing five feet, six inches tall, Benny was slim, nimble, and able to outmaneuver boys who tried to "scrap" [fight] with him. "If anybody step up to [fight] me, I can see it, react, grab, leap, something, get the hell out of the way [of a punch]." In an outcome consistent with Angel's assessment that fighting had different consequences for girls and boys, Benny was able to gain a positive reputation among his peers because of his "scrapping" abilities. He explained, "When I was younger, like sixth grade, seventh grade, stepping up, like starting fights and everything, that's what you've got to do." By fighting boys who were older, bigger, and stronger than him, Benny eventually "made his name."

There were many benefits to being male and a good fighter. For example, he was able to "step with big dogs" (that is, hang out with the older boys). Benny also noted that a boy's reputation as a fighter could raise the status of his family. He said, "This boy, he's cool, he represent his last name so well. That family is going to be known." Later, he said, "Ask anybody, any Hawaiian kid; they will tell you. You come home crying, Mom will give you a licking [beating] or your father will give you a licking. If you lose, it brings disrespect to your family."

Probably what Benny liked the most about his "rep" as a fighter was the authority it gave him among his peers. For example, Benny noted that some kids had a habit of "losing control" and going into what he called "survivor mode," meaning that they were unable to stop themselves during a fight. He described how a well-respected teen—a youth who "was known"—might be the only one who could intervene in a brutal battle: "Some kids, they up and up brawling, a big brawl. They don't stop. Unless somebody they utmost respect tells them to stop, they'll stop." Benny wanted to be that person with "utmost respect."

However, after spending years nurturing his tough reputation, Benny began to rethink his approach. The school was changing, and the other "old dogs" were "fading away." He also began to contemplate the kind of man he wanted to become. Manhood, in Benny's eyes, was equated with being a father, head of the family, and provider. He explained: "As you get older, with time you get wisdom. As you get older, you get the bigger picture of what to do. I'm trying to stay out of trouble. You cannot be doing shit all your life. I want to grow up to be the best that I can, provide the best I can. I'm going to have life lessons, a lot of life lessons to teach my kids. I will give them a childhood I never had."

What Benny wanted most for his future children was stability. Benny's mother had abandoned the family when he was nine years old, and Benny and his siblings lived with his father in a tent under a bridge for a portion of their childhoods. Eventually his father was incarcerated, leading the state to place all of the children in foster care.

Despite Benny's commitment to staying out of "trouble," his wishes for a bright future grew dim by the end of his senior year of high school. Benny had started hanging out with a crowd of young men with whom he worked on a construction team. He purchased a car (with a hefty auto loan) and stopped attending classes. During the last months of the school year, Benny started drinking heavily every weekend (and on some weekdays) with his work buddies. His goal of graduating from high school receded into the distance. One day in May, just before graduation, Benny quietly admitted to Katy that he had a drinking problem and that it was getting "out of hand." He said that he was failing some of his courses, drinking regularly, and didn't know if he was going to graduate.

. . .

This book focuses on the experiences of Angel and Benny as they faced crossroads in their teen lives. In addition, we include the stories of ninety-seven other adolescents, most of whom are of Native Hawaiian, Samoan, or other Pacific Islander ancestry, including many of mixed heritage (see table 1 in appendix 1). Based on our work with the lunch bunch and our presence in two high schools to assist with violence prevention programming, we were also able to get to know and conduct interviews with sixty-three adults (parents, high school staff, and juvenile justice and community workers) who have added depth to our understanding of the youth's experiences.

By centering this book on the experiences of teens, particularly those who have been involved in fights, we broaden our vision not only of youth violence, but also of what it means to grow up in a country that has marginalized vital segments of its population. Teens' narratives help us in at least two important ways. First, by focusing on the experiences of girls as well as boys living in the same neighborhoods and attending the same schools, we can see how violence is different for girls than it is for boys. Moreover, we can note how traditional gender ideologies and practices influence girls' and boys' lives in ways that make systems of male domination problematic for all teens.[2]

Second, by focusing on a population of teens who are often overlooked, primarily Native Hawaiian, Samoan, and other Pacific Islander youth, we can think in new ways about how racial inequalities and historic injustices throughout the United States inform the problem of youth violence. Indeed, Native Hawaiian teens (like Benny), as well as teens who trace their ancestry to other parts of the Pacific (like Angel), often struggle in communities that confront high rates of poverty, a lack of services for families, and overincarceration in ways that are disproportionate when compared with White, Asian, and most other ethnic or racial groups.[3] These teens also battle a long history of injustice stemming from U.S. colonial conquest in the Pacific, which included the imposition of a rigid racial caste system; thus, racialization in American colonial contexts is important to consider.

The youth in this study are not representative of the overall youth population in Hawai'i and we ask that readers not selectively interpret the text in any way that perpetuates negative stereotypes of Hawaiian and Pacific Islander youth as a "problem" population. One purpose of this book is to understand the patriarchal, colonial context that situates the voices of the youth that we present throughout the book. We are cognizant of the fact that scholarly narratives have historically been employed to perpetuate derogatory and demeaning depictions of "colonized subjects" with ethnic specificity that continues to burden youth. The youth whose stories are featured here have faced far more than their fair share of challenges and their voices are seldom heard in mainstream media. They have experienced the brunt of discipline by schools and courts and, partly as a result, are astute about their situation in ways that offer valuable knowledge and insight. From their grounded experiences, we hope that needed changes will become more clear to us all.

OVERVIEW OF THE BOOK

The narratives of youth can add depth to many literatures, and chapter 1 reviews some of the assumptions within the fields of youth violence, critical youth studies, and punishment in the juvenile justice system and schools. Chapter 1 also includes a brief review of the colonial history of Hawai'i.

In chapter 2, we review our research methods and explain the choices we made, given that the juveniles in this study were a vulnerable population. While we wanted to gain an intimate knowledge of teens' worldviews and experiences, we did not want to compromise their safety, and this tension determined our roles as we interacted with the teens.

We begin to lay out our empirical findings in chapters 3 and 4 by focusing on girls' narratives. Chapter 3 examines girls' early childhood experiences in families and at school, and we highlight the unique pressures that these girls experienced while growing up. We look at how the girls' family responsibilities, dress, demeanor, and their status in families and at school were constrained by gender—a set of conditions that the girls thought of as inherently unfair and "unjust." Considering these pressures, some girls spoke and struck out against those who harassed and targeted them, sometimes violently. We take up the subject of peer and school-based culture for teens in chapter 4, where we outline the femininity norms confronting female teens. In this chapter we note that notions of femininity were complicated and sometimes contradictory. In this way, girls' violence is viewed against the backdrop of multiple constraints and contradictions.

In chapter 5 we explain boys' perspectives of violence, exploring their critical consciousness of larger power arrangements. Like the girls in our study, the boys experienced gender expectations as an important backdrop. However for the boys, racial hierarchies were a primary lens through which they saw the world. In chapter 5 we look at how historic acts of injustice in colonial lands live on in the collective memories of youth. Some boys summarized these past and present injustices suc-cinctly as the "jacked-up" U.S. system. As males, the boys sensed that they had agency and strength, and they used these resources to resist or manipulate what they saw as unjust systems and stereotypes set against them.

In chapter 6 we juxtapose the work of compassionate adults against the harsh "zero-tolerance" policy environment and highlight the positive impacts of caring adults on youth at critical times in adolescence. We begin with a brief review of the rise of "zero-tolerance" policies and how they took shape nationally and in Hawai'i. We hear the stories of June and Auggie, who experienced the punitive sting of the juvenile justice system as teens under this policy environment. We contrast that with examples of school and court professionals who made a marked difference in the lives of youth and explore the meaning and importance of discre-tionary power using an "ethic of care."

Having introduced this book with Angel's and Benny's narratives, we complete the adolescent journey for these two teens and others in chapter 7. In this chapter, we examine the variety of ways that the youth prepared for young adulthood. Con-sidering that several teens in this study grew up in chaotic circumstances—facing homelessness, multiple foster home placements, and incarceration—we look at whether supportive and capable adults can intervene in teens' lives to help them as they prepare for adulthood. Just as gender shaped the childhood and teen experi-ences of both girls and boys, we find that transitions out of adolescence differed by gender according to the pressures, constraints, and opportunities facing girls and boys.

Chapter 8 showcases the theoretical interpretations of the findings outlined in chapters 3 through 7. With a focus on racial and gender inequalities, which we call the system of colonial patriarchy, we fill gaps in perspectives about youth violence and interlocking inequalities, and in the field of critical youth studies.

In chapter 9 we conclude this book with an exploration of compassionate pol-icy reforms and emancipatory practices within the rising tide of juvenile justice reform nationally and in Hawai'i specifically. We begin with a story of a family loss to highlight the failures of the existing justice system to bring resolution and restore peace in the face of violence. We press for better alternatives and describe the possibilities of ho'oponopono, a practice of healing and restoration traditional to Native Hawaiians, for work among youth and families.

1

Literature Review and Background

Several literatures have helped us build our view of violence in the lives of the girls and boys in this study. First, we explore how criminologists have traditionally explained youth violence. We also examine statements about masculinity and violent street codes (Anderson 1999), and review feminist explanations of the ways that girls' violence relates to male domination.

Because violence is only a part of the experiences of the teens, our second goal is to outline themes in the critical youth studies literature as a way to connect the experiences of these adolescents with common trends affecting youth from a variety of backgrounds. Third, we briefly outline the literature on punitive trends in juvenile justice and education institutions. Because our primary goal is to trace how youth violence is related to the histories of racialization, colonialism, and patriarchy in the United States, our fourth and last goal is to offer a thesis about colonial patriarchy.

YOUTH VIOLENCE: CRIMINOLOGISTS' EXPLANATIONS

The topic of youth violence has been a concern in seminal criminological work—including analyses of gangs and street corner boys—since the early- to mid-twentieth century (Cloward and Ohlin 1960; Cohen 1955; Merton 1957; Miller 1958; Shaw 1930; Shaw and McKay 1942; Thrasher 1936). To summarize a long history of youth violence scholarship, one might say that criminologists tend to view physical aggression as a reaction of youth to blocked structural opportunities. In other words, when teens and young adults sense that their chances of gaining conventional, middle-class success are limited, violence can be an individual and collective solution.

In addition to the focus on blocked structural opportunities, there are at least three other common trends in this literature. First, criminologists have been rather male-focused for decades, with delinquent boys and criminal young men consistently in researchers' spotlight. Second, criminologists have focused on urban areas, while suburban, small-town, and rural locales are often overlooked. Third, when discussing blocked opportunities for success, crime scholars often focus on middle-class status as a marker of success. Therefore, socioeconomic conditions and class inequalities that keep youth from entering America's middle class remain central in many statements.

Since the 1980s, researchers (especially urban ethnographers) have been especially attuned to shifts in the U.S. political economy as an explanation for youth violence. In terms of economic shifts, the outmigration of industries from U.S. borders is said to have left many neighborhoods and certain segments of the U.S. population without stable employment. From the later part of the nineteenth century to the 1950s, American industries (many of which were located in urban centers) offered stable, unskilled or semiskilled jobs for working-class men (and some women). Once these industries were gone, the urban working class became the urban underclass in just a few decades. Remembering that criminologists often explain violence (and many other types of crime) as reactions to blocked economic opportunities, one can see how the rampant poverty left by deindustrialization introduced seemingly insurmountable barriers to inner-city youth.

Researchers have also argued that neoliberalism has exacerbated the economic dislocations described above.[1] Scholars (Anderson 1999; Block et al. 1987; Katz 1989; Wacquant 2014) assert that since the 1980s, politicians have espoused neoliberal ideologies and policies that have exacerbated the economic devastation in urban areas in many ways. Specifically, a neoliberal agenda has failed to connect the unemployed to jobs and has underfunded the services and institutions that could have supported those facing the brunt of deindustrialization and unemployment in the United States. Consequently, institutions such as public schools, community-based programs, and other service-centered organizations in the poorest areas of the country have been starved for funding and political support since the 1980s. Put simply, the institutions (including schools) meant to provide opportunities for young people and families were gutted.

Race-based inequalities have also been understood to influence youth violence through residential segregation and community stigma. Because of years of racial discrimination in formal policies and informal practices, the United States has been marked by severe racial residential segregation, what some have called a system of "American apartheid" (Massey and Denton 1987, 1993). De jure segregation through Jim Crow laws (beginning roughly in the 1870s) and then de facto segregation (after de jure segregation laws were dismantled in the 1950s and 1960s) meant that Black families and recent immigrants to the United States were barred from living in White neighborhoods. Instead, those designated as "racial minorities" were often restricted to living in particular urban enclaves or ghettos (Massey and Denton 1987, 1993; Wacquant 2001). Not surprisingly, many of these racial and ethnic enclaves faced the brunt of economic restructuring.

The racial stigma cast on communities is also seen by researchers as having played a significant role in blocking legitimate opportunities for those living in the poorest urban neighborhoods. Because inner-city neighborhoods became known as crime-ridden and violent communities, these areas, and the residents within them, were consequently "marked" by the problems brought on by deindustrialization. For example, public discourse and mass media portrayals have often painted inner-city dwellers as being welfare dependent, pathologically criminal, and dangerous to society (Wacquant 2001).[2]

Masculinity, Violence, and the Code of the Streets

As noted, criminological explanations of youth violence are decidedly male centered; there are at least two reasons for this. First, because many criminologists focus on the deindustrialization of urban centers and the loss of working-class employment, men and boys are seen as central characters. It was men's industrial jobs that were lost and, therefore, it was boys and men who were seen as particularly "structurally vulnerable."[3]

The second reason for male-centric bias in violence literature is due to historic discourses, ideologies, and practices surrounding masculinity in the United States (Connell 2005). Manliness and masculinity are often associated with dominance and the potential for violence. For example, Messerschmidt (1986) has argued that in the United States, "both masculinity and power are linked with aggression/violence while femininity and powerlessness are linked with nonviolence" (59). Messerschmidt also notes that "marginalized males tend to engage in more extreme forms of violence (robbery, assault, murder) than other youth." Violence, as portrayed by scholarly narratives, becomes part of the masculine repertoire, as structurally vulnerable men and boys use interpersonal violence to gain the control and dominance that they cannot obtain through legitimate avenues.

It is important to note that men with racial, economic, and political power and privilege also use violence or the threat of violence, although not generally by means of interpersonal attacks in public. State-sponsored violence in the form of militarization and heavy-handed policing provides the link between privileged masculinity and physical violence. If one ascribes to theories of structural violence (Galtung 1969, Gilligan 1997), engineering, supporting, and justifying institutional arrangements that deny large segments of the U.S. population the material and symbolic resources that would allow them to thrive is also a form of violence. In other words, structural violence comprises those inequalities that systematically block opportunities that would allow groups of people to meet their basic needs, which include, arguably, being treated with respect and dignity.

Anderson's (1999) *Code of the Street* has become a popular explanation linking the economic, political, and social conditions that have prevailed since deindustrialization to a violent and street-based ethos governing male social relations in urban areas. More specifically, Anderson notes that inner-city men are likely to see violence as a legitimate way to gain respect, to show their "nerve" and demonstrate that they have "juice" (i.e., the potential to harm others), thus conferring high status onto men who do not have other ways of gaining legitimacy. In a similar vein, Miller (1958, 9) notes that the lower-class boys in his study were "hard, fearless, undemonstrative, skilled in physical combat." Katz (1988, 80–81) also argues that lower-class men depict "badass" personas that combine a "measure of meanness" and a message to others that "you do not know me," but "at any moment I may . . . destroy you." These and other studies document that interpersonal violence is one way that lower-class men angle for status and prestige.

Anderson, citing Black (1983, 1993), explains that violence is a form of "self help," given the neoliberal changes that have devastated institutional support systems. In inner cities, residents do not turn to the police (or other institutions) for assistance; the "law of local people and its corresponding street justice" (Anderson 1999 314) are more reliable than the law and order of the state. In this scheme, violence is more than a way to demand respect: it also allows men to gain retribution for harms, earn justice, and protect themselves.

Criminological explanations of inner-city violence are certainly plausible and help to illuminate how adolescents' life chances and choices are narrowed according to economic conditions, racial segregation, and stigma, as well as political neglect. There are, however, some significant gaps in the narratives examined above, gaps this book attempts to fill. One limitation is the emphasis, to date, on economic and political conditions after the 1950s as major factors leading to male interpersonal violence. As a result, other sources of marginalization, such as the long history of racial conflict in America, tend to be sidelined.

The roots of racism in the United States are long and deep, existing well before the outmigration of jobs from inner cities after the 1950s and influencing more than just patterns of residential segregation. Racism in the United States also comprises more than a community stigma, what Wacquant (2014, 1692) calls "territorial stigmatization." The expansive, enduring, and multifaceted effects of racism deserve more attention in our perspectives.

Girls' Violence, Patriarchy, and Multiple Oppressions

Because the youth violence literature has been male centered for decades, there are several questions about girls' and young women's place in the dislocations described above. For example, given the preceding explanations, what are we to make of structurally vulnerable girls and their violent experiences? Since many researchers have seen violence and masculinity as tightly linked, girls' place in the violent street ethos is unclear. Also, do the structural forces (i.e., economic dislocation, neoliberal politics, racial residential segregation and stigma) that deny boys and men opportunities for legitimate ways to gain status work the same way for girls?

Since at least the 1970s, feminist researchers have addressed girls' place in what was often portrayed as the masculine world of youth violence. Feminist criminologists use patriarchy (i.e., systematic male domination) as their central framework to understand girls' violence. Chesney-Lind and Morash (2013) argue that systems of male domination comprise what is called the patriarchal sex/gender system, which "exists globally and in countries, cultures, regions, communities, organizations, families, and other groups. It affects individuals by impacting their identities, imposing gendered expectations, and prohibiting and sanctioning 'gender inappropriate' behavior. Patriarchal sex/gender systems are characterized by males' exercise of power and control to oppress women (Hondagneu-Sotelo 1994)" (290).

Feminist researchers have noted that systems of and beliefs supporting male domination have particular consequences for girls. For example, scholars argue that in every institution and sphere of girls' lives, such as families, schools, communities, and work worlds, girls are exposed to ideologies and practices that maintain the subservience and dependence of girls and the dominance and autonomy of boys (Artz 1998, 2004, 2005; Campbell 1984).[4]

Girls' violence has been explained as a response to patriarchal conditions. As Brown (2003) notes, girls have many reasons to be angry, and their fights stem from their anger about "the range of injustices and indignities girls experience in their everyday lives" (17). Morash and Chesney-Lind (2009) note that girls' battles occur when gender-specific and demoralizing labels such as "slut," "bitch," or "dyke" are thrown at them by other girls (see also Campbell 1984; Batchelor, Burman, and Brown 2001; Burman, Brown, and Batchelor 2003).[5] Girls often fight other girls and not boys. Therefore, girls are seen as enacting horizontal violence (Freire [1970] 1993). The central thesis in this literature is that girls are not able to target or change the gender inequalities that place them at a disadvantage compared with boys and, as a result, they take out their anger on other girls.[6]

While the above explanations position girls' violence as a response to gender inequalities (i.e., patriarchy), others have wondered whether and how economic distress, political alienation, and racism also influence female violence and crime. For example, Miller (2001, 10) notes that gender's "significance is variable," meaning that some female crime (including violence) is motivated by gender and some "likely results from the same factors that motivate men," including racial, political, and economic alienation (see also Simpson 1989, 1991). Because scholars acknowledge that gender is not the only system of oppression faced by working and lower-class women and girls of color, critical criminologists and legal scholars (Belknap 2015; Burgess-Proctor 2006; Crenshaw 1991; Chesney-Lind and Morash 2013; Pyke and Johnson 2003; Richie 2012) have called for "multiple oppressions" explanations of female crime and violence.

Multiple oppressions theories articulate how gender operates in relation with other systematic inequalities like racism and classism. It is important to note that age, nationality, sexuality, and cognitive and physical abilities (to name a few) are also important vectors of inequalities in the lives of youth. When writing about multiple inequalities, scholars often use the terms "in relation" or "relational oppressions." Here, scholars often mean that systems of inequalities are linked, with one dimension of inequality (like gender) depending on and working in relation with other systems (like race, class, or sexuality) to distribute power, resources, advantages, and privileges (Burgess-Proctor 2006). Also, all systems are linked within structural, political, ideological, institutional, and interpersonal social systems. Making the image even more complex, these multiple oppressions operate on individual, interpersonal, community, state, and national levels (see Richie 2012, 133). One can also say that they are global, as they are forces that are not contained within national boundaries.

Girls' violence researchers have used the multiple oppressions framework in particular ways. For example, Jones (2004, 2008, 2010), Leitz (2003), and Ness (2004, 2010) advance an "alternative femininities" argument to explain girls' violence. Ness (2004, 37) argues that poor girls of color living in the inner city can "selectively appropriate" middle-class and White femininity norms (which eschew violence) and place them "alongside values that more closely fit their lives." In this view, how femininity is enacted is flexible, and violent girls can enact their own brand of tough and formidable femininity in the face of multiple forms of injustice.

Richie's (2012) work on Black women, violence, and the criminal justice system advances two important ideas that help theorize multiple oppressions and women's experiences. First, she notes that "White patriarchy imparts racial hierarchy on Black bodies" (128). For Black women, the outcome is "uniquely disparaging images of Black women's sexuality." Here, racism functions through the control of "othered" bodies and especially through the regulation of female sexuality. Richie also notes that distance from hegemonic ideals of sexuality, age, class, race, and gender translates into a set of complicated realities in everyday life. In other words, the more distant one is from the dominant hegemonic norms, the more complicated and contingent a person's life and life chances become.

Pascoe (2012) adds an important dimension of sexual control (i.e., heterosexism) to our understanding of gendered violence, arguing that heterosexist and masculinity discourses and practices rigidly divide teen girls' and boys' lives.

She views masculinity as "a sexualized process of confirmation and repudiation through which individuals demonstrate mastery over others" (14). In other words, boys are compelled to prove that they are not gender and sexual failures—meaning that they are not "fags"—by engaging in "repeated acts" and "rituals" in which they demonstrate dominance over girls and the "denial of girls' subjectivity." To prove their sexual, gendered, and moral worth, boys control, threaten, and deny girls' subjectivity through violence. Boys also violently regulate other boys' sexuality and gender.[7] Thus, the rigid gender divide among teens is policed, often with the threat or use of violence.

In terms of examining the lives of youth who are at the axis of multiple sources of marginalization, criminology might be said to be in its infancy. While there are notable interlocking oppressions arguments (reviewed above), the vast majority of work among criminologists remains male dominated and urban-centric, and cleaves to economic and political marginalization as central explanations for the problems that youth experience. Other areas of research, such as the critical youth studies field, have developed broad, multifaceted views of the youth experience in the United States. Below, we review some of the insights of the critical youth studies literature.

CRITICAL YOUTH STUDIES

Contemporary critical youth studies scholars share a concern with explaining how multiple systems of oppression, like gender, race, class, nationhood, sexuality, and age, work together to shape the opportunities for and life chances of young people.[8] Fine (2006, 83–84) summarizes the field as not only interested in understanding multiple injustices in youth's lives, but as also intending to "interrupt/dismantle oppression" and to "sustain justice in the face of ongoing political assaults."

Several common trends are underscored in critical youth studies scholarship. First, researchers examine age as an important dimension of inequality. Put simply, youth lack the power that adults have. Envisioning age as a vector of oppression marks a dramatic departure from psychological and developmental theories of adolescence. The dominant view among developmental scholars is that adolescence is a biologically and psychologically driven "natural life stage." Adolescents are said to be "in transition," via a series of stages, to adulthood (Erikson 1950; Kohlberg 1981; Piaget 1965). In the best case, developing adolescents are seen as "transforming into" adults, while in the worst case, they are seen as "lesser" and not fully socialized adults (i.e., not civilized). Because they are seen as not fully socialized, adolescents are often not trusted to make decisions about their own lives.

Critical youth studies scholars consistently point to the fact that adolescence is a historical, social invention of Western societies (Gillis 1974), meaning that adolescence has not existed in all cultures, geographic regions, and times in history.

Lesko (2001, 7) specifically points to the late 1800s and 1900s as the time when adolescence was constructed (i.e., invented) in the West, arguing that "adolescence was created and democratized (at least in Britain and the United States) when child labor laws, industrialization, and union organizing gutted apprenticeships, which had been the conventional way for youth to move from dependency to independence." Here, adolescence emerges from changing institutional arrangements rather than from one's developing physiology and psychology. Once created, the adolescent/adult divide became powerful; those who fell within in the adolescent age range were dependent on adults and lacked power on multiple fronts.

A second common trend in the critical youth studies field is a focus on resilience and collective action among young people. Here, critical scholars have specifically departed from the classic crime and deviance perspectives of youth. As some argue (Clay 2012; Jones 2010; Leadbeater 2007), crime and deviance researchers have tended to "pathologize" poor youth of color by highlighting problematic outcomes like teen pregnancy, serious violent offenses, gang membership, property crime, and general trouble among marginalized teens.[9] To counter the overly negative image supplied by criminology, some critical youth scholars have focused their attention on common strengths among teens and the processes of resilience that allow youth to overcome hardships.

Leadbeater (2007, 7) outlined the components of youth resiliency as the "many 'Cs' such as competence, confidence, connection, character, caring, control, contributions, and capacities." Other important "Cs" might include possessing a "critical consciousness" and engaging in "collective community action" (Akom, Ginwright, and Cammarota 2008; Cammarota and Fine 2008; Clay 2012; Delgado and Staples 2008; Ginwright and Cammarota 2006; Giroux 1983). In terms of critical consciousness and community action youth are "active participants facilitating neighborhood change through strong social networks" (Ginwright and Cammarota, 2006, xvii). Critical youth scholars also see involvement in social justice movements as a key to building resilience among young people who live at the axis of multiple inequalities.

A third trend in contemporary critical youth studies scholarship focuses on gendered patterns of resilience among girls (Bottrell 2009; Garcia 2012; Heath and McLaughlin 1993; Leadbeater and Way 2007; Lopez 2003; Pastor et al. 2007). Combating the male bias in research, youth scholars have chronicled the many ways that girls develop unshakable strength in the face of multiple injustices. For example, researchers have uncovered how many racialized girls growing up in poor, politically dislocated communities were bonded to strong women in their families and communities (Lasley Barajas and Pierce 2001) and had access to "home grown" versions of feminism (Lopez 2003; Hurtado 1996).[10] Researchers have also documented the ways that girls find "safe spaces"—often spaces with mothers, aunts, teachers, and other adult women—to voice themselves, be heard, and critically reflect on the forces around them (Brown 1998; Heath and McLaughlin 1993; Harris 2004; Leadbeater and Way 2007; Weis and Fine 2000). Additionally, studies have documented how girls demonstrate agency, take care of their health, speak up for themselves, and create bridges to supportive peer networks (Bottrell 2009; Garcia 2012; Pastor et al. 2007; Williams, Alvarez, and Andrade Hauck 2002).

While youth justice researchers have documented that boys (along with girls) participate in community building and collective action (Fine and Weis 1998; Clay 2012; Ginwright, Noguera, and Cammarota 2006; Cammarota and Fine 2008), boys tend to emerge in the critical youth studies field as being less resilient than girls. Findings suggest that poor boys of color must confront constructions of themselves as dangerous, potentially criminal (Cammarota 2008; Ferguson 2001), defiant, and "rambunctious" (Lopez 2003) individuals who are interested primarily in "football, fucking, and fighting" (Mac an Ghaill 1994, 56). In schools, alienated boys are likely to be seen as potential criminals (Ferguson 2001) and "bad students" (Reichert 2000), while their female counterparts are seen as "little ladies" (Lopez 2003) or as girls who have poor manners but academic potential (Morris 2007).[11] Despite these lingering negative views of marginalized boys, researchers note that many boys and young men develop a strong critical consciousness (McIntyre 2000; Rios 2011) and participate in community-based organizations (Heath and McLaughlin 1993).

There are some gaps in the literature described above. First, girls who struggle in school, "act out," fail academically, or use violence to solve problems are not given much attention in the girls' resiliency framework. The tendency to see boys as lacking the same resilience found among girls is also a problem. We know, for example, that boys (along with girls) express a critical consciousness and organize for social change (Akom, Ginwright, and Cammarota 2008; Cammarota and Fine 2008; Clay 2012; Ginwright and Cammarota 2006; Giroux 1983). Where, then, is the story about resilient boys who use their critical consciousness to empower themselves and others in the community?

PUNITIVE YOUTH-SERVING INSTITUTIONS

There is broad acknowledgement based on available evidence that youth of color receive a disproportionately higher share of disciplinary actions—from school suspensions to juvenile incarceration—shares that often exceed their proportion of actual offenses (Bowditch 1993; Boyd 2009; Giroux 2003; Gregory, Skiba, and Noguera 2010; Irwin, Davidson, and Hall-Sanchez 2013, Meiners 2010; Nicholson-Crotty, Birchmeier, and Valentine 2009; Noguera 2003; Robbins 2005; Skiba 2000; Skiba et al. 2002; Verdugo 2002; Wald and Losen 2003). There is much less agreement, however, over the reasons for the disproportionately severe impacts on youth of color of the turn toward punitive policy (see Henry and Einstadter 2006).

While some scholars have described the punitive turn in the juvenile justice system and in schools as a function of neoliberal politics, we argue that the juvenile justice system and schools—as raced, gendered, and classed institutions—have disparately impacted youth of color since long before the neoliberal rise. We build on the ideas of critical theorists who attempt to understand youth violence in the context of larger power structures. In their view, punishment is an expression of social values (such as security) that harnesses popular emotions (such as anxiety). Fear-mongering political campaigns leading to punitive policies reproduce negative stereotypes while stiffening the institutional structures that perpetuate racial inequality and buttress the overall status quo (Gotanda 1991; Tonry 2004). Garland (1990) posits a "sociology of punishment" to understand "the role played by penality in the construction of the political order, the furtherance of state control, and the constitution of individuals as social subjects" (2).

Critical theorists draw a connection between penality and race by bridging "material" changes in the economy and polity with changes in the public discourse and social imaginary. Wacquant (2009), for example, argues that the punitive turn following the apex of the Civil Rights Movement corresponded not to insecurity over actual crimes but to *social* insecurity following the ending of legalized discrimination and the fall of the ethnoracial hierarchy. He argues that the "prison symbolizes material divisions and materializes relations of symbolic power" in a way that "fuses domination and signification" (xvi). The penal system produces not only institutionalized subjects and untold collateral harm (Mauer and Chesney-Lind 2003), but also defines race, by means of the image of the unworthy prisoner.[12] "Among the manifold effects of the wedding of ghetto and prison into an extended carceral mesh, perhaps the most consequential is the practical revivification and official solidification of the centuries-old association of blackness with criminality and devious violence" (Wacquant 2001, 117).

Critical theorists extend this analysis to the punitive turn in the juvenile justice system and in school disciplinary policies (Engen, Steen, and Bridges 2002; Leiber and Mack 2003). Explanations for the rise in school discipline vary (Hirschfield 2008). Beyond functionalist perspectives that view school punishment as a means for disciplining working-class youth to prepare them for subordinate, working-class jobs (Bowles and Gintis 1976) or to train the next generation for civic and moral purposes (Durkheim 1961), Simon (2007) argues that state actors within the American polity have increasingly come to "govern through crime," manipulating fear among middle- and upper-class whites and imposing punishment on minorities and the poor. Meanwhile, other scholars have focused on more direct explanations for increased school discipline. One, for example, is the "moral panic" over the uptick in school violence and highly publicized mass shootings, which politicians fanned starting in the late 1980s in order to win elections and cinch policy changes (DeMitchell and Cobb 2003). A second is the pressure created by federal school accountability standards that encouraged the expulsion or dismissal of low-scoring students or those seen as troublemakers (Bowditch 1993). And a third is the push by school administrators and teachers for the legal authority to discipline students without due process, given concerns over risks (Arum 2005; Harcourt 2008).

We recognize the compounding historical forces behind the rush to punish and draw attention to two consequences in relation to youth violence. First, we acknowledge the indirect harms and microaggressions often registered by youth who experience punishment and, sometimes, violent responses from authorities. Critical theorists have pointed out that violence can be done to youth through routine institutional practices that may cause emotional, social, economic, or cultural distress or injury (Iadicola and Shupe 2012; Stanko 2003). This type of aggression is not always due to mean-spiritedness on the part of individuals, but is often a result of routine policies and procedures that lead to feelings of humiliation and defeat (Finley 2006), such as the rough physical handling that youth can experience when arrested and processed through the juvenile justice system.

We also assert that within a policy regime, there are actors, such as probation officers or school counselors, who, while bound by legal and administrative rules, can in their daily professional practices implement policies in ways that mitigate the punitive sting and open avenues for more restorative, therapeutic, and empowering outcomes for youth. Certainly, advocates and scholars have pointed to alternatives to harsh punishment, including restorative justice and healing (Bonnie et al. 2013; Braithwaite 1999; Cabaniss et al. 2007; Cullen 2013; Fenning and Rose 2007; McGuire 2008; Watts and Erevelles 2004), school discipline and juvenile justice policy reform (Boyd 2009; Cabaniss et al. 2007; Monroe 2005; Noguera 2003; Reynolds et. al. 2008; Stuntz 2008), and through strengthening community capacity to address issues related to violence (Sabol, Coulton, and Korbin 2004; Thornton et. al. 2000). From the view of critical theorists, political and institutional reforms that create a more egalitarian, fair, and democratic society are also in order (Delgado and Stefancic 2012; Lawrence 2007; Wacquant 2001; Watts and Erevelles 2004). These alternatives are critical in efforts to increase racial equality, democracy, and positive youth development (Alexander 2012; Giroux 2003; Roberts 2004; Stuntz 2008).

TOWARD A THEORY OF COLONIAL PATRIARCHY

As noted, there are multiple gaps the youth and youth violence literatures. Youth violence researchers tend to ignore the long history of racism in America. While the literature on patriarchy and girls' violence is vibrant, there is a need for more studies that examine how patriarchy combines with many other sources of oppression in the lives of teens. The critical youth studies field offers a hopeful vision of how youth facing many sources of structural violence can overcome injustices. Despite this, there are some girls who are left out of youth resiliency narratives. A focus on boys' resilience, critical consciousness, and community orientation is also lacking.

To fill these gaps, we offer a theory of colonial patriarchy. Moreover, we argue that a colonial patriarchy perspective offers the most appropriate lens to view histories of racism, sexism, and other oppressions among teens, for two reasons. First, the teens in our study were growing up in a colonial land, within the legacies of structural violence that linger in a colonial state. The second reason is tied to the argument that the roots of racism are long and deep in American history. Many colonial scholars trace the ways that the American brand of racism and U.S. systems of racialization are tied to Western imperial intrusion into "foreign" lands in the 1700s and 1800s. To understand racism in the United States, therefore, one would do well to understand American nation-building and imperialism.

To develop a colonial patriarchy perspective, we first look at perspectives of racial formation in the United States. We then outline the link between racial formation and colonialism. Last, we highlight how colonial conquest, nationhood, and patriarchy have been intertwined to create lasting discourses about and realities for girls and boys in America (including within the American colonies).

Racial Formation in the United States

Regarding racial formation in the United States, Omi and Winant (2015) have argued that social scientists often neglect "the institutional and ideological nature of race in America" by reducing America's history of racial oppression of African Americans, Native Americans, Latinos, and others to a mere set of "attitudes and prejudices" serving the goals of elites in their quest to gain economic advantages (6–7). Instead, Omi and Winant assert, race is a "master category—a fundamental concept that has profoundly shaped, and continues to shape, the history, polity, economic structure, and culture of the United States" (106). They argue that racial formation is a "sociohistorical process by which racial identities are created, lived out, transformed, and destroyed" (109).

Omi and Winant's thesis about racial formation in the United States does more than assert the centrality of race in American history. They also imagine how race as a master category organizes the modern world system of nationalism and nation-states (111). On this global scale, insights about racial formation and racialization connect with theories of colonialism (Blauner 1972; Fanon 1963, 1967; Staples 1975). Racialization is "the extension of racial meaning to a previously racially unclassified relationship, social practice, or group" (Omi and Winant 2015, 13). The process of identifying and classifying people (see Hacking 1999) implies, Omi and Winant argue, a simultaneous reality of "conquest and settlement of the Western hemisphere" (111) in which Europeans crossed over into non-European lands while creating "distinctions and categorizations fundamental to a racialized social structure" (113).

Racial Formation and Colonialism

Racial formation in the United States is intimately connected to the history of American colonialism and the imperial quest for land, resources, and a national identity. Western and modern concepts of race and racial categorizations began as Europeans traveled to "other" lands and then proffered notions of race based on perceived differences between themselves and others. The racial distinctions and categorizations created in modern nation-states were not benign but were lodged in "exploitation, appropriation, domination, and signification" (Omi and Winant 2015, 114). A colonial society, therefore, tends to be a racialized society, in which "institutionalized racial supremacy" organizes political, economic, and social life (Moyo and Kawewe 2002, 164). As a result of creating racial categories to distinguish groups, Western societies in general and colonial societies in particular became rigidly divided, with some groups being seen as superior and, thus, worthy of power, privilege, and resources, while racialized "others" were seen as undeserving of these advantages. Not only were racialized others excluded, but discourses and stereotypes abounded that facilitated exploitation, demoralization, and exclusion of racial "pariah" groups.

In her colonial theory, Tatum (2000a, 2000b, 2002) argues that racialization is a central force shaping economic, political, and social statuses and opportunities available to young people. To illustrate how racialization influences economic statuses, Tatum (2000b) notes that racialization includes creating and applying ideologies about which racial groups are appropriate for different types of labor. Focusing on African Americans, she argues that African Americans' economic status in U.S. history has transformed from slave laborers, to tenant farmers or servants, and then to unskilled industrial laborers.[13] Here, racialized notions of Blackness included a genealogy (or a historic progression) of constructions in which Blacks or those of "African origin" were appropriate subjects for slave labor, tenant farming, domestic servanthood, unskilled industrial labor, and the unemployable underclass.

While Tatum's work focused on African Americans (as well as Latinos) in the United States to demonstrate how racism functions to shape economic, political, and social exclusion, other groups—including Native Hawaiians—have their own racialized genealogies. As scholars using colonial theories often point out, racialization has been central to determining one's life chances throughout American history.[14]

Patriarchy and the Modern Nation-State

Lesko (2001) notes how age, nationhood, colonial conquest, and patriarchy are linked in important ways for young people in the West. Western colonial conquest was not just about establishing racial superiority and inculcating a strong, forceful national identity; it was also about establishing a national identity bound up in male domination. Lesko argues that "adolescence was a technology of whiteness that supported white boys and white men as superior but also echoed the rightness of racialized dominance at home and abroad" (46). Given that patriarchal notions of manhood and nationhood were coupled, the use of strength, domination, conquest, and violence to control threats to the national order were seen as key traits of a worthy nation. Consequently, these were also traits of a worthy boy and man. Boys, according to Lesko, were socialized into a version of manhood that paralleled notions of the ideal citizen (i.e., strong leader, morally upstanding, and willing to fight for their country), capable of buttressing a forceful nation.

In Western patriarchy, controlling images of females were engrained into the fabric of the Western nation-state, with the creation of what are often called traditional gender roles and gender scripts for how to appropriately enact one's gender (West and Fenstermaker 1995; West and Zimmerman 1987). Dominant gender ideologies supplied a counter-discourse about ideal citizenship for women. As Pyke and Johnson (2003) argue, hegemonic (or emphasized) gender scripts are thrust on and used to control women and girls. Women in these scripts were supposed to be domesticated, heterosexual, and dependent on male family patriarchs (grandfathers, fathers, and husbands). Training girls to be upstanding citizens therefore meant socializing them to be sexually restrained (i.e., sexually monogamous and dedicated to husbands), obedient, subservient, nurturing, and happy to perform family caretaking duties.

Colonialism, therefore, included the assertion of national, racial, heterosexist, and gendered domination all at once. Because American colonialism included the imposition of American ways into non-American lands, structures, discourses, institutions, and ideologies supporting Western notions of national, White, and male superiority were inserted into colonized areas like Hawai'i, Guam, the southeastern Samoan Islands (what is now American Samoa), and Puerto Rico (to name a few U.S. territories). Therein lies the formula to understand American colonialism as a racialized, patriarchal, and heterosexist system that was forced onto Hawaiian (and other) lands.

To understand how the youth in this study made sense of the system of colonial patriarchy, Alexander et al.'s (2004) vision of collective trauma is instructive. Alexander and his colleagues discuss how traumatic historical events can be woven into collective identities through mediating discourses, often through master narratives or analogies and metaphors that circulate in the present. Others write of colonialism as a producing a type of "haunting" or shadow reality in the present (Stoler 2006). The height of American colonial conquest was in the 1700s and 1800s and was punctuated with numerous injustices, forms of state-sponsored violence, and atrocities. In the present, the colonial patriarchal structure represents a mediated experience for youth, evidenced in how the youth in our study talked about and interpreted images, analogies, and metaphors of past atrocities. This book reveals the specific racist and patriarchal injustices of American colonialism in Hawaiʻi—and other parts of the Pacific—as a sort of haunting. Colonial patriarchy is a shadow reality that comes to the fore in how youth narrate, share stories, and use particular terms and constructions to make sense of colonial history and its place in their everyday lives.

THE COLONIAL CONTEXT OF HAWAIʻI

Although Tatum's model of colonialism (2000a, 2000b, 2002) was originally applied to the African American and Mexican American experience in the United States it conforms in broad strokes to the history of Western imperial expansion in Hawaiʻi and other parts of the Pacific. It is not within the scope of this book to detail the colonial history of Hawaiʻi, and others have done it well.[15] Rather, we highlight the broad historical themes that inform this study of youth and that provide a way to understand violence within the overall context of struggle for survival.

Colonial histories undergird the salience or relevance of ethnic and racial identities, especially among those whose lands were colonized. The history of U.S. colonialism in the Pacific is a living history that resides in the collective memories of those who have passed down their stories and continue to inscribe their own narratives. Collective memory shapes social identities and group affinities, especially among Native Hawaiians and Pacific Islanders, who faced the brunt of colonial domination in the Pacific. Hawaiʻi was an independent kingdom that developed in relative isolation until European arrival in 1778. Western contact and settlement brought significant transformations. For Native Hawaiians, it brought infectious diseases that decimated the population, which is estimated to have been between four hundred thousand and one million in 1778 and was reduced to forty thousand by the 1880s (see Silva 2004). Missionaries converted many to Christianity. The chieftain system was abolished and the privatization of property led to dispossession of lands, which also undermined the system of communal subsistence. The year 1893 saw the overthrow of the Hawaiian kingdom with the aid of the U.S. government, which annexed the islands in 1898 and claimed them as a territory two years later. Colonization brought new settlement, particularly the importation of laborers from China, Japan, Philippines, Korea, and Portugal during the plantation era. Hawaiʻi was declared the fiftieth state of the United States in 1959. Native Hawaiians lost further economic and political foothold with the influx of Americans from the continent and the eventual rise of mass tourism, an industry that supplanted agriculture and became dominated by multinational and Japanese corporations.[16]

A racial hierarchy emerged throughout this time, aided by policies that forced cultural assimilation. Alongside land dispossession, colonists launched campaigns designed to strip Hawaiians of their native language, indigenous knowledge systems, cultural practices such as hula, and spiritual traditions, while attempting to inculcate an American "identity and way of life" that was touted as superior (see Merry 2001; Silva 2004; Trask 1999). Racial images found in early writings by historians portray Native Hawaiians, Samoans, and other Pacific Islanders as happy and hospitable, but lazy, unintelligent, hot-tempered, or prone to violence (see Dougherty 1992; Keahiolalo-Karasuda 2010; Kame'eleihiwa 1996). These and other stereotypes have persisted over the decades, helping to reinforce inequities and injustices. Negative stereotypes are felt in schools, where Samoan youth tell of being labeled as "uneducated, troublemakers, unable to communicate, and successful only in sports" (Mayeda, Pasko, and Chesney-Lind 2006, 76). Likewise, Native Hawaiians are often implicated for the continued "ills of colonization," such as domestic violence, suicide, substance abuse, and low rates of higher education and professional employment (Blaisdell and Moku'au 1994; Cook, Tarallo-Jensen, and Withy 2005; Crabbe 1997; Kāmau'u 1998).

Colonialism has left a legacy of inequality, cultural disruption, and disenfranchisement. Native Hawaiians and Pacific Islanders fall to the bottom of nearly all socioeconomic metrics of health and well-being in Hawai'i (Fujikane 2008; Okamura 2008; Office of Hawaiian Affairs 2010). Racial stratification can also be seen in the political sphere, which has been dominated by Whites and Japanese Americans. As of 2005, in the state legislature as well as in the state Department of Education, Japanese Americans were most overrepresented and Native Hawaiians were most underrepresented relative to their overall populations (Okamura 2008). A higher proportion of Whites, Japanese Americans, and Chinese Americans held higher education degrees relative to Filipino Americans, Native Hawaiians, and Samoan Americans, who ranked lowest in average educational attainment. Similarly, Whites, Japanese Americans, and Chinese Americans were found in career fields like management, business, science and the arts at higher rates than other groups (Okamura 2008). Indicators such as representation in prisons, physical health status, and school disciplinary records show similar disparities, all of which bode poorly for Native Hawaiians and other Pacific Islanders (Office of Hawaiian Affairs 2010; U.S. Department of Education 2012).

At the same time, the Native Hawaiian sovereignty movement, which marched onto the public stage during the 1960s, has continued to grow and evolve, especially among the younger generations. It has connected with human rights struggles and the campaign for self-determination among indigenous peoples globally. "Nation building" in Hawai'i has taken a wide range of forms, from the restoration of ancient and sacred lands, forests, taro fields, and fishponds to the revival of cultural and spiritual practices in farming, fishing, ocean navigation, and healing (Finney 2003; Goodyear-Ka'ōpua 2013; McGregor 2007). Hawaiian-language preschools and Hawaiian-language and -culture charter schools have become crucial sites for the resurrection of the language (Goodyear-Ka'ōpua 2009). Moreover, movements for self-determination have won significant political campaigns, such as the return of the island of Kahoʻolawe from the U.S. military, official recognition by the U.S. government of the illegal overthrow of the monarchy, and many legal battles over the protection of native rights.

Altogether, despite its marketed image as a multicultural island paradise, Hawaiʻi remains a site of significant stratification and continuing tensions within complex racial and ethnic dynamics. It is problematic to essentialize the meaning of any single racial or ethnic category; such categories do not mean the same thing for all those who identify with a particular group or set of groups. The significance of race and ethnicity in Hawaiʻi is further complicated by the fact that Hawaiʻi has the highest percentage of residents of mixed racial ancestry in the United States. The experiences and identities of each youth in this study lie at the intersection of multiple dimensions of inequality, whether along race, ethnic, gender, class, or sexuality lines, or along other boundaries made salient in specific places and times. That said, the youth who are found to be fighting and who are punished for violent actions are disproportionately from those groups most marginalized, at the bottom of the socioeconomic ladder.

This context is important to keep in mind, for it reminds us to keep our gaze focused as much on the logic and circumstances surrounding violence as on the actions of youth themselves. Many of the youth interviewed for this study have faced extremely challenging life circumstances and can be found in the statistics that represent these hardships. They have been told their genealogical histories. They have an intimate understanding of what their families have had to overcome to survive. And they struggle themselves to survive the damaging legacies of the past as they strive for basic dignity, respect, and independence as adolescents in exciting but uncertain times. In this context, violence can be a form of tactical communication, an outburst of frustration, a defense of dignity, a way to protect one's family, a reaction to threat, a response to an offense, or a call for help. Whichever one it may be, it is the context—both the broad historical and the immediate situational—that can best shed light on the source and meaning of violence.

The Caring Adult Role and Youth Research

We don't go through life being proud of ourselves. We need support.
—BLAKE, HIGH SCHOOL SENIOR

When adults study youth, age is arguably one of the most important dimensions of difference to consider. For example, if Lesko (2001) and others (Gillis 1974; Hendrick 2011) are correct, adolescence is a social construct in Western societies that has been used to deny power, autonomy, and full citizenship rights to those under the age of eighteen. Therefore, adults who study youth must attend to several challenges, not the least of which is the possibility that adults can easily harm youth (Best 2007; Raby 2007). And when adults who have power in terms of gender, race, ethnicity, citizenship, and class study youth who lack these privileges, then the concern about harm is pressing.

Another challenge is that youth are not likely to trust and open up to adults, with the result that a child's or a teenager's view of the world often remains hidden from adults. In cases when the adults and youth are not from the same backgrounds, the likelihood that teens will not trust these adults is even greater.

Given the above concerns, we as researchers must be open about our identities, social locations, and privileges—all of which placed us in different social locations from the youth in the study. We are middle-aged women, with the age advantages afforded to most forty and fifty year olds. For example, middle-aged people are often assumed to have the best interests of young people in mind. Our age thus gives us considerable power over young people—especially in cases when our perspective of a situation may differ from that of an adolescent. Furthermore, in terms of ethnic background, economic privilege, education, and geographic location, we were distant from the teens in this study, most of whom were poor or working class and of Native Hawaiian, Samoan, Tongan, or other Pacific Islander ancestry. Many teens were also born and raised in Hawai'i, an important marker of insider status among the youth.

Katy is Caucasian and was raised in inner-city San Francisco. Karen is ethnically Japanese American from a racially diverse working-class neighborhood of Los Angeles. Both of us remained sensitive to the fact that neither of us are local (meaning from Hawai'i). In addition, both of us enjoyed school during our childhood, teen, and young adult years. In contrast, many teens in this study did not enjoy their educational experiences, and some instead felt alienated, unfairly punished, and "suspect" in school. While our status as women may have helped girls feel somewhat at ease with us, being female was not enough to overcome the other social chasms. Also, boys were not likely to trust us as much as they might have trusted a male researcher. In summary, we were distant and removed from the teens in many ways.

We are certainly not the only adults to conduct research with youth from different backgrounds than themselves. In fact, negotiating social distance between researchers and study members is a key theme in the ethnography of youth and youth crime. On the topic of overcoming key social differences, ethnographic investigations of youth tend to fall into three general categories: the "intimate familiarity tradition" (Black 2009; Jones 2010; Ness 2010; Rios 2011; Venkatesh 2008), the "least adult role" tradition (Mandell 1988), and the "critical pedagogy and participatory action research" tradition (Cammarota and Fine 2008: Weis and Fine 2001). Below, we briefly review each approach and describe our own research stance.

ETHNOGRAPHIC RESEARCH IN SUPPORTIVE SCHOOL SPACES

With the underlying belief that intimate familiarity mitigates social distance between themselves and young people, some researchers "hang out" with study members as they go about their everyday lives. Gaining intimate familiarity with youth can include attending classes, pursuing shared leisure activities, spending time in youth hangouts, and, for some ethnographers, being invited to family events (Black 2009; Chin 2001; Contreras 2012; Goffman 2014; Jones 2010; Ness 2010; Rios 2011; Venkatesh 2008).[1] Here, researchers attempt to gain emotional and physical propinquity with youthful study participants, hoping that being close and emotionally engaged will build rapport and trust. According to the logic of intimate familiarity, a trusted researcher is likely to accurately understand and represent the youth's worldview.[2]

Among researchers who access young people primarily through school settings, the option of taking the least adult role (Mandell 1988) is common. Believing that students often suspect adults at school (especially adults who are from different racial, ethnic, and class backgrounds) and that school staff tend to censor, judge, and intervene in students' lives, school-based ethnographers often try to construct themselves as being different than a "typical adult" in many ways (Adler and Adler 1998; Best 2007; Caputo 1995; Corsaro 2003; Eder 1995; Eder and Fingerson 2002; Fine and Sandstrom 1988; James, Jenks, and Prout 1998; Hey 1997; Nespor 1998; Pascoe 2012; Punch 2002).[3]

Other qualitative researchers engage in "disruptive pedagogies" (Weis and Fine 2001) that provide alternative spaces in school that encourage students to speak up and critically examine the surrounding adult and other power structures. Participatory action research (PAR) designs (Cammarota and Fine 2008; Fine et al. 2004; McIntyre 2000; Morrell 2006; O'Kane 2000; Pastor et al. 2007; Torre and Fine 2006) are those in which youth become the researchers, offering questions, designing studies, and collecting data.[4] Much PAR with students is part of the disruptive pedagogy tradition; when youth have control over the research process they are thought to be able to voice their concerns openly and to present their views without fear of adult censorship, judgment, intervention, or punishment.

Our research is informed by, but falls outside, these three traditions. In terms of intimate familiarity, we thought that it would have been problematic to hang out with teens as they went about their regular activities. The everyday lives of some of the teens included illegal behaviors, such as drinking, smoking marijuana, and fighting—behaviors that led to their referrals to counseling-based programs (the context where we first met most of the youth in this study). Directly observing the youth's illegal activity would count as acquiring "guilty knowledge" (Adler and Adler 1998), and guilty knowledge about the adolescent's crimes could have easily translated into serious consequences for the teens. Here, it is important to note that we were conducting research during an era when crimes committed by poor youth of color were taken very seriously and punished severely.

Also, we did not angle for the least adult role in the school settings. As noted in the introduction, our primary contact with the youth occurred through the voluntary counseling-based program called the lunch bunch. The lunch bunch had the stated goal of providing a supportive, safe, and nonjudgmental space for teens to share their views in a group setting. While attending the weekly lunch bunch sessions, teens were encouraged to discuss their concerns and talk about challenges in their lives, which included their relationships with adults. The lunch bunch might be best described as an alternative (rather than a disruptive) space in the school, where teens were encouraged to talk and be heard. Our research stance, therefore, might be considered that of nonjudgmental, supportive, and caring adults who listened to the teens as they expressed their views, something akin to Lopez and Lechunga's (2007) role in their research with girls.[5]

Some might argue that our choice to interact with teens primarily during the lunch bunch and to remain as distant from the youth's possible illegal behaviors compromised our in-depth understanding of how delinquency and crime play out for youth. After all, during the first half of the 2010s, many ethnographers have been praised extensively for providing rich ethnographic detail, heart-wrenching accounts, and powerful stories about what it means to be young and part of the criminal class in America. Our choice to avert our ethnographic gaze from the criminal acts of young people might also make us seem blind, naïve, or uninterested in generating thick descriptions (Geertz 1973) of the gritty underbelly of crime and criminalization of young people. Education ethnographers have noted that better data are gathered when researchers interact with students outside the watchful eyes of other adults, in times when youth are likely to be less guarded (Best 2000; Griffiths 1995; Pascoe 2012; Thorne 1999).

Whether the teens' lunch bunch conversations about violence, family conflicts, anger, sex, romantic relationships, or drug use were accurate is up for debate. For example, we assumed that the nonjudgmental and nonpunitive format of the group allowed students to be fairly candid about their thoughts, and that the regular contact with counselors and with us might have meant that valued relationships were formed over time. Students were never required to attend these sessions, which led us to assume that the students who showed up consistently did so for a reason—perhaps because of the trusting bonds formed in the group. Also, the group discussions allowed us to get to know the youth in ways that went beyond their participation in crime and deviance, and therefore permitted us to see them in less narrow terms than in many criminological studies. As Jones (2010) noted, looking at teens only through the lens of their offenses, victimization, delinquency, or crime is tantamount to forcing a "deviance/pathology" framework on them.

The youth offered many statements during this study to support the idea that they appreciated the supportive stance of some adults. In fact, most of the youth said that there was at least one adult at school whom they trusted, and when explaining what they liked about these trusted adults, teens overwhelmingly reported that the adults who cared for them, did not judge them, and encouraged them to succeed were worthy of their confidences. Blake said that the school counselors were like his "best friends," because "like, me and a couple of my other friends, we don't go through life being proud of ourselves. We need encouragement." Phillip also felt at ease with the counselors, usually because they listened to what he had to say. Describing what he enjoyed most about his counselors, he said, "For me it is that they don't call my parents every time something happens. They help me make a better decision." When we asked Darren what we specifically could do to be more supportive of teens, he said, "Nothing. What you're doing right now." Darren's sentiment was common. At the end of the year, we usually asked the teens what we could do to be more supportive. "Nothing" or "keep doing what you're doing" were usual responses.

James and her colleagues (1998) listed a number of productive research roles for adults in the field, including interviewer, friend, or coworker. The teens in our study seemed to favor adults who were "a positive force," meaning that they wanted adults to care about them, and especially about their "ability to succeed in life." Here, the role of supportive adult might be added to possible research roles for adults working with youth.

The teens' comments signaled to us that to watch passively as teens beat one another, got high, or engaged in any activity that might compromise their safety or lead to their arrest would not be appreciated by the youth. These teens' sentiments combined with our own ethics to dictate our stance. We were emotionally immersed in the field, in that we cared first and foremost about the teens' health, happiness, and well-being, while being unimmersed as possible from directly witnessing their crimes. It was enough to allow teens to describe their lives to us, choosing what they trusted us enough to know, and what they wanted to conceal from our eyes.

THE RESEARCH JOURNEY

The role of nonjudgmental and caring adult came rather easily for us, since it connected directly to our professional and personal lives as university faculty and researchers. We each had developed lifelong commitments to understanding how violence and other social problems complicate the adolescent experience. We were also committed to doing something about these problems. We knew that we were not alone in these goals and that we shared a similar orientation with numerous other adults living and/or working in communities across the state. In fact, our interest in understanding teens' viewpoints and experiences and our work with other concerned adults were the springboards that launched this study.

As University of Hawai'i (UH) professors, we were encouraged by department members and UH administrators to serve the community, and informed that if our service to local communities could come in the form of funded research projects, that was all the better. Thus, since the late 1990s (for Karen) and early 2000s (for Katy), we had worked off and on with other researchers, school personnel, and community-based program staff who were also looking for ways to support, serve, and advocate for youth. Sometimes we had grants to support this work; other times, we volunteered our time.

By 2004, our work took a dramatic turn, as we (and many others) applied for a grant from an agency at the U.S. Department of Health and Human Services (DHHS) to support the development, implementation, and evaluation of a multifaceted violence prevention initiative.[6] The grant was to cover five years of funding and included numerous community-based projects. Therefore, the research for this book began when we met with teachers, parents, community leaders, teens, and school administrators to plan and coordinate a youth violence prevention project. In essence, our working relationships with adults and teens from various communities were solidified through our coordinated efforts, first to write the grant proposal, and second, to conduct the work necessary to complete the project once the violence prevention project was funded.[7]

There were many complicated pieces to the research gathered for this book. Therefore, we need to clearly outline our research process. To simplify, our research could be said to evolve in four phases. The first phase included the selection of the two neighborhoods on which to focus the DHHS violence prevention grant. The second phase included conducting focus groups with parents and teens in these two neighborhoods. The focus group portion of the study was completed between 2006 and 2008 and was funded by the DHHS grant. The third phase was the lunch bunch program, which began in 2007 and is ongoing. The lunch bunch, while well regarded by the violence prevention grant team, was not part of the original DHHS project. The lunch bunch also turned out to be the primary way that we came to know about and spend time with most of the teens in this study. We also invited lunch bunch teens to conduct in-depth interviews with us and were able to conduct participant observation when interacting with lunch bunch teens.

The fourth and final phase of this research included conducting interviews with adults. After a few years of talking with the teens and participating in the lunch bunch, we realized that we needed to gather a fuller vision of the institutional actors who had the power to intervene in youth violence. These adults included teachers, administrators, security guards, juvenile justice workers, members of family court, and workers in youth-serving institutions. Below, we detail our data-gathering activities during each of these four phases.

PHASE ONE: SELECTING THE NEIGHBORHOODS

As noted, while pursuing the original DHHS grant, we met with school staff members, community leaders, and parents from a number of neighborhoods to discuss the youth violence prevention project. Adults from two neighborhoods, those we called Northward and Stevens Heights, expressed particular enthusiasm for projects in their neighborhoods.[8] Ms. Takada, the principal of Seaside High School in Northward, offered her unmitigated support for the project, invited us to attend regular meetings, and granted us access to school resources, including a classroom dedicated to violence prevention projects. Adults at Cleveland High School in Stevens Heights were also enthusiastic about developing violence prevention programs, and there were several teachers at Cleveland High School who expressed interest in partnering with UH.

Northward and Stevens Heights were not selected because they were particularly crime prone or blighted; instead, these communities were selected because of longstanding working relationships between community leaders and UH employees. In fact, one early concern expressed by Northward community members was that the nature of the research (i.e., that we were focused on preventing youth violence) might stigmatize the community. Similarly, the principals of Seaside and Cleveland did not want their schools to come off looking like hyperviolent and unsafe environments because of this research. This concern remained uppermost in our minds throughout our work. One promise that we made was to avoid indicating which school the youth in this study were from as much as possible. We wanted to respect school staff and community members' sentiments that youth violence can occur in any public school and community in the state.

The demographic profiles of the two communities and the respective high schools included in the study provide a background sketch for the research. Northward is a rural, predominantly Native Hawaiian, working-class community, although there are several pockets of poverty throughout the neighborhood.[9] One such pocket is a fairly large homeless camp stretching across the beach park; there are also a few smaller homeless camps dotting the bucolic landscape. These camps were, at the time of our study, fairly well integrated into the community in that several community residents spent time making sure that the homeless neighborhood members had food and as much access to health care and services for children as possible.[10] Another marker of poverty in the neighborhood was the number of small homes that housed ten or more people. Housing in Hawai'i is extremely expensive, with the median home value at the time of our study hovering around five hundred thousand dollars (U.S. Census Bureau 2014). This forced many extended family members to live together to reduce expenses.

Although Northward is not necessarily more violent than other areas of Oahu, its violent crime rate was, at the study's outset, twice as high as Honolulu's (Fuatagavi and Perrone 2008). There are many possible explanations for the relatively high violence rate in this rural setting. Northward is close to an urban center (a thirty-minute drive from downtown Honolulu), which could allow urban crime trends to diffuse to this rural context (Fischer 1980). Some researchers have argued that neighborhoods, especially in rural locales, that have few locally oriented businesses lack civic engagement in the community (Lee 2008). Neighborhoods without civic engagement are thought to lack social control, that is, to be environments in which neighbors rarely come together to solve community problems, and, thus, to be prone to crime (Lee 2008). Another explanation for the relatively high violence rate in Northward might be simply that poor rural locations are equally as crime prone as poor urban areas. Some have noted that the criminality of rural areas is not given much research attention, thus leading to a false impression that rural areas lack the crime problems found in urban centers (Osgood and Chambers 2000, 82).

One important feature of Northward, which arguably contributes to Northward's alienation from larger political influence in the state, is that the colonization of Hawai'i remains palpable for Northward residents, many of whom live on Hawaiian Homestead lands. Northward is one among a selection of areas in Hawai'i designated as Hawaiian Homesteads, plots of land leased by the state for a nominal cost to anyone with 50 percent or more Hawaiian ancestry. The stated intent of the 1920 Hawaiian Homestead Act was to "rehabilitate" the Native Hawaiian people by encouraging homesteading activities like subsistence farming that would encourage self-sufficiency and independence. Another view is that the Homestead Act relocated Native Hawaiians from cities and into remote and less valuable lands, allowing developers to buy up and control profitable real estate. Although many Native Hawaiian families qualify to live on homesteads, thousands remain on the waiting list for a lease on these government-owned lands. The "blood quantum" rule (which specifies that only those who have 50 percent or more of Native Hawaiian blood can apply to live on homestead lands) has been also denounced by many in Hawai'i as a state policy that imposes unnecessary divisions among Native Hawaiians; some see it as racist. Furthermore, many Native Hawaiian families are aware that these homestead lands, like all land in Hawai'i, were usurped (i.e., stolen) from the Kanaka Maoli, the original people of Hawai'i.

Stevens Heights, as noted, was the second neighborhood in the study and contrasted with Northward in many dimensions. Stevens Heights has long been a high-density, ethnically diverse, low-income neighborhood, and is considered a gateway community for many immigrant arrivals to the city. Resting on the edge of downtown Honolulu, it is rich with cultural diversity. At the time of the study, approximately half of Stevens Heights's residents were Asian, with most being Filipino, and less than a quarter of the residents were Pacific Islander, a group that included a mix of those from Native Hawaiian, Samoan, Chukeese, Marshallese, Tongan, and other Pacific Islander ancestry. Less than 10 percent of the residents were White, and about 15 percent reported being from two or more racial groups (U.S. Census 2010a). Stevens Heights also has one of the highest concentrations of community-based institutions in the state, including social service agencies, churches, and civic organizations.

Stevens Heights also includes several of the largest public housing complexes in the state. Some of them have suffered neglect and disrepair, prompting residents to complain to the state during the time of this study about conditions such as rodent and bedbug infestations, crumbling walls, and prolonged periods without hot water. Some of these housing projects have no recreation facilities for residents. Making matters even more difficult for neighborhood residents, Stevens Heights is intersected by major traffic thoroughfares, creating significant dangers for children as they walk to and from school and for families as they walk to visit the nearest park. It is not uncommon for makeshift shrines made of pictures, flowers, and teddy bears to be erected at street corners, memorializing pedestrians killed by drivers. Also, like the neighborhoods described by Shaw and McKay (1942) as "transition zones" between industrial and residential areas, Stevens Heights is home to many small businesses ranging from convenience stores, to liquor stores, to fish markets, to bars.

Given these economic and political realities, it is not surprising to learn that Stevens Heights's crime rate was three times higher than Honolulu's crime rate in 2007 (Fuatagavi and Perrone 2008). But the community is far from being like the "disorganized" neighborhoods described in sociological literature. Neighbors do not shrink from problems on the streets or in their homes and, instead, many adults are a visible presence in the neighborhood, standing outside their homes to supervise children and talk informally with one another. Residents of the Stevens Heights housing projects lodged complaints with the state because the Stevens Heights neighborhood association was vibrant and not likely to remain silent when problems occurred. One evening a week, a few of the older teens in the neighborhood would chaperone a group of neighborhood children across the busy intersections in the community to an indoor youth recreation facility, where they would play basketball. Also, it is common in Stevens Heights for extended families to live in the neighborhood, thus creating networks of aunties, uncles, grandparents, and adult cousins who watch over neighborhood activities. Thus, any teen who wanted to let loose, drink, and generally shirk off the watchful eye of adults, often had to leave the neighborhood boundaries, or at least retreat to the more remote corners of the community.

The public high schools serving Stevens Heights and Northward reflected these two communities in terms of ethnic diversity, poverty, and crime. Cleveland High School, located in Stevens Heights, was relatively large, with over 1,500 students, and had a mix of Filipino (approximately 50 percent) and Pacific Islander (24 percent) students (Hawai'i State Department of Education 2008). Northward's Seaside High School was a little more than half of the size of Cleveland during the 2006–7 school year, and approximately half the Seaside student body was full- or part-Native Hawaiian (Hawai'i State Department of Education 2008). Filipino and Samoan students together made up approximately 10 percent of Seaside's enrollment (Hawai'i State Department of Education 2008).[11] At both Cleveland and Seaside High Schools, approximately half the students received free or reduced-cost lunch in 2006–7 (Hawai'i State Department of Education 2008). There were, on average, ten student suspensions per week at Cleveland and seven suspensions per week at Seaside in the 2006–7 school year (Hawai'i State Department of Education 2008). The suspension rates per one hundred students enrolled were relatively equal between these two schools.[12]

Our role in these neighborhoods and schools was similar to that of many other adults who worked in but did not live in the neighborhoods. We met with other adults (residents and workers) to plan events, implement programs, talk about neighborhood and school events, and do what we could formally and informally to assist teens. By 2006, we had received grant funding to support violence prevention research and programs, and these funds allowed us the time to be active members (Adler and Adler 1987) in youth programming work, engaging in a steady routine of formal planning and program implementation meetings as well as regular socializing with community members and school staff. The activities we engaged in were numerous and included movie and dinner nights for families at school, violence prevention community consortium meetings, teacher coffee hours, assistance with mentorship programs, school assemblies, welcome events for incoming freshmen, the creation of public service announcement skits with teens, high school rally days, training sessions for school staff and students, women's empowerment group meetings, and one high school prom.

PHASE TWO: CONDUCTING FOCUS GROUPS

Our first formal data-gathering phase occurred between 2006 and 2008 and included conducting sixteen focus group interviews with Northward and Stevens Heights teens and parents. Katy was the principal investigator for this portion of the study. Understanding that social scientists have defined violence in different ways (see Brown 2003; Stanko 2003), Katy designed an initial focus group study to give adolescents and adults a chance to define and describe youth violence in their own terms. Katy specifically wanted teens and adults to identify what they felt were the primary problems facing adolescent girls and boys in their ethnic and geographic communities.[13] The focus group questions centered on participants' opinions and views about what they considered to be the most serious problems that they faced, and these groups usually ended up as conversations, rather than back-and-forth question and answer sessions.

The principal of one high school allowed youth to be excused from nonessential classes to complete the focus groups and, as mentioned, gave us the use of a classroom to complete the focus group interviews. Community-based program staff in both Northward and Stevens Heights were equally helpful in supporting the adult focus groups, contacting adults whom they thought would be interested in participating and inviting us to use the meeting rooms of their organization not only to complete the focus groups but also to report our findings back to the communities—a promise that Katy made to community members at the outset of the study.

Another way that adults in each community were particularly helpful in assisting Katy and other staff members on the violence prevention grant was by distributing consent and assent forms. We could not conduct any research with adults who did not sign the consent form or with teens who did not complete both an assent form and provide a signed consent form from one of their parents.[14] Collecting consent forms for adults was not challenging, but obtaining parental consent from a teen who wanted to join a focus group was difficult. We dropped off parent consent forms at the schools and reminded students to bring the signed consent forms to the focus group. Here, adults at schools and in the community assisted the focus group project by reminding the youth to bring forms, and providing extra parental consent forms when teens lost theirs.

We completed focus groups in community health centers, children's centers, youth recreation facilities, and neighborhood board association offices. Overall, forty-five teens and forty-one adults participated in the focus groups. Focus group members were evenly split between the two neighborhoods, with slightly more males than females participating (55 percent versus 45 percent). According to participants' self-reported ethnicity, there were fairly even numbers of Native Hawaiian and Samoan participants (44 percent and 43 percent, respectively), while the remaining 13 percent of participants self-identified as being of Filipino ancestry. The demographic profile of focus group adults and students is included in table 1 in appendix 1.

PHASE THREE: OBSERVING AND INTERVIEWING LUNCH BUNCH TEENS

Starting in 2005 our working relationships with adults expanded and were parlayed into opportunities to become involved in a range of community and school-based projects. For example, in 2007, one high school counselor, Ms. Phillips, invited us to the counseling department to talk with other staff members about working together. During this meeting the counselors explained more about the Hawai'i State Department of Education's commitment to counseling services.

Soon after an initial meeting, the counselors, Katy, and Karen began what we informally called the lunch bunch.[15] Starting in 2007, we met once a week with lunch bunch teens and counselors. Having no training as therapists, we did not counsel teens. Nor did we sit quietly at the side as counselors led group discussions. We took on the "supportive" adult role that we described earlier. This role allowed us to sit in with the groups, listen, and share our own experiences, when we felt that we could add to the discussions, although the teens and their views were always at the center of the group conversations.

How to engage with teens in education settings is a common dilemma discussed by ethnographers, as we noted earlier in the chapter (Best 2000, 2007; Ferguson 2001; Griffiths 1995; Pascoe 2012). Because ethnographers often grow uncomfortable with the rigid and punitive systems of adult authority in schools, researchers often try to interact with students away from the watchful eye of other adults. Ferguson (2001) offered one-on-one tutoring sessions with students. Best (2000) hung out with teens as they congregated in restrooms or for outdoor smoking breaks. While not researching teens, Thorne (1999) escorted students to and from classes and spent time with students during lunch and recess (see also Griffiths 1995). Corsaro (2003) used a reactive method by entering "free play" areas and waiting for children to interact with him.

In contrast, we did not see the need to catch students unsupervised, mostly because of the tone and style of lunch bunch activities and conversations. While lunch bunch counselors had an agenda, to provide safe and healthy spaces for teens, they did not rely on punishment or strict rule enforcement. Instead, they encouraged conversation and valued differences of opinions and viewpoints on a range of topics, including fighting, anger, friendships, drug use, dating, and sex. In fact, the curriculum used in the lunch groups focused on difficult-to-discuss topics, and thus conversations became fairly candid.[16] Given these parameters and the nature of the lunch bunch, within the first few weeks of school, teens usually frankly discussed their views with other teens, us, and counselors.

Although the lunch bunch groups were divided by gender, the structure of each group was similar. Both boys' and girls' group sessions usually began with a check in, in which teens would help themselves to pizza and a drink, and talk about how their week was going.[17] Then teens were given an activity that they completed together or individually, which was followed by a discussion of the activity. Counselors leading the girls' groups relied on various girls' empowerment curricula and activities, while the boys' groups used emotional intelligence activities and programming. The leaders of the groups talked with the teens in the beginning of the year to discuss the types of topics that interested the teens. Karen attended the boys' group and Katy usually attended the girls' group. Along with the counselors and teens, we ate pizza, checked in, and participated in activities. At the close, a counselor usually wrapped up the discussion, summarizing some of the ideas that had been shared.

We also periodically took the lunch bunch teens on college and university tours (approximately one trip per year), and, when grant funding was particularly abundant, with the counselors we organized and joined overnight teen camping trips. Camping trips included navigating adventure ropes courses, building campfires, canoeing, and swimming with teens. These camping trips were augmented with different curricula that included a teen violence prevention program, sex education worksheets, visits from a youth theater group, and teen leadership training. Sometimes, we used our time at the camps to film public service announcement (PSA) videos, with the teens taking control of the topics, scripts, staging, and filming of the PSAs.

The Ethics of Observing and Interviewing Teens

Because the lunch bunch allowed us to have close contact with the youth and provided a setting in which youth were quite frank, we felt that our work with the lunch bunch deserved our serious ethical consideration. As noted, adults generally have more power than youth and given that the teens in the lunch bunch program were facing numerous challenges in their lives, we felt the need to be mindful at all times about our potential to harm them. One precaution that we took, and which the University of Hawai'i institutional review board required, was to gain permission from teens' parents not only to conduct interviews, but also to write field notes about any student. This meant that we discussed our research with the teens at the beginning of the school year, so that they knew that we were researchers and not just "caring adults" who sat in with the lunch bunch. Because we interacted with teens throughout the school year, we often felt it necessary to remind teens during the spring semester that we were conducting research. We also invited teens to conduct in-depth interviews with us during the spring semester, as an additional reminder of our research role.

We created two consent forms (one for observations and one for interviews) for parents to sign, and two corresponding assent forms for the youth. This created an unwieldy, yet important dimension to our research. It meant that teens could decide to conduct interviews with us, but not allow us to take field notes about what they said and did during the lunch group activities, or the reverse. Therefore, they had control over how much or how little of our research they wanted to take part in.

Another precaution used by youth researchers is to place youth's safety and health before any research goal (Adler and Adler 1998). Research was often our last consideration during a day in the field. Listening to, finding activities for, feeding, and creating a "safe place" for teens to express themselves were often our only motivations in the field. Writing field notes occurred when we returned home and we did not write about any student who did not return both an assent form and a parent consent form, agreeing to be part of the observation part of the study.[18]

To provide the youth with a semblance of control in the research process, we also made sure that teens knew that their participation in the research was voluntary. Here, we did more than let them know that they could refuse to participate in the study. We explicitly told teens that they could say "no" to us at any time and choose not to answer any individual question for any reason. We reminded them that saying no to us was their right and we would not think any differently of them if they chose not to participate in the research. Conforming to ethical guides laid out by others (Stanley and Sieber 1992), we periodically reminded teens that they had the right to withdraw from participating in the study, regardless of whether they had signed assent forms, returned parent consent forms, or completed a face-to-face interview. We would be happy, we reminded them, to stop an interview, delete mention of them in our field notes, or erase a recorded interview. We also reminded them several times throughout the semester that the research and the lunch bunch activities were separate, meaning that they were always invited to lunch bunch activities even if they did not want to participate in the research.

Obtaining parental consent was a logistically complicated but necessary step to maximize teens' safety. As noted in the introduction, many youth's lives were chaotic and unpredictable from day to day, therefore teens often did not remember to return parent consent forms. Also, many teens had trouble distinguishing between the two consent forms (one for the observations and one for the interviews), even though we had different titles for the forms and the forms were different colors. Counselors attempted to help us as much as they could by reminding teens to return both of the consent forms, keeping extra copies to give to teens, and collecting the forms from teens. Despite these steps, teens often returned only one parental consent form, thinking that it covered both the interview and observation aspects of the study.

Approximately seven girls and seven boys participated in the lunch group program each year, and approximately a quarter of the teens attended the groups for two consecutive years. In total, approximately one hundred teens attended the lunch group program between 2007 and 2015. We interviewed only forty-two teens, meaning that over half of the lunch bunch teens were not included in our interviews. Also, only eighteen teens returned parental consent forms for the observations, meaning that approximately seventy-two teens were not included in our observation study. Again, not receiving consent forms was something that we were prepared to accept in order to conduct the most ethical research that we could.

Given that many lunch bunch teens were at risk for not graduating from school, setting times to conduct face-to-face, recorded interviews required some thought. We did not want our research to compromise their schoolwork. Also, most teens did not want to spend time after school or on the weekends to conduct an interview, which meant that we needed to interview teens during school hours. Consulting with the counselors, we decided that the best interview times were at the end of the school year, during the few days between students' last final exams and high school graduation—typically a downtime for teens and teachers.

One advantage of waiting until the end of the school year to interview teens was that the youth knew us fairly well after nine months of weekly contact with them. Also, at the end of the year, teens were likely to be self-reflective about the changes that had taken place in their lives since the start of the academic year. A few youth conducted interviews at the ends of both their junior and senior years, allowing them to reflect on their entire high school career. Interviews were conducted in a meeting room in the counseling department. We made sure to provide hearty snacks to welcome teens to the interviews.[19]

As noted, approximately half of the teens in each school qualified for free and reduced-price lunch programming. In comparison, about 75 percent of lunch bunch teens qualified for this program, although assessing the precise details of lunch bunch teens' socioeconomic status was difficult. Teens generally did not know their parents' economic standing or yearly income, but they noted that their parents "worked hard," or "busted ass." From teens' descriptions of their lives, we could glean a general picture, and estimated that 60 percent of the lunch bunch teens were living under the poverty level. Four teens talked about being homeless at some point in their childhoods, with two of the teens being homeless during their high school years. One of these teens was living on the beach in a tent with his family, and the other was sleeping on the couch at a friend's house. In terms of ethnic background, 52 percent of the teen interviewees were of Native Hawaiian ancestry, 23 percent were White, and 7 percent were Samoan. The remaining teens were of mixed-race (n=4) and Filipino (n=2) ancestry. See table 1 for a summary. Ethnic background was assessed using both teens' self-definition and school records.[20]

PHASE FOUR: INTERVIEWING ADULTS

In addition to conducting interviews with forty-two teens, we also conducted face-to-face interviews with twenty-one adults. Eleven of these adults were school staff, five were workers in the juvenile justice system, and six were staff or volunteers at community-based programs for youth. Because we had close working relationships with school staff and many juvenile justice workers, recruiting adults to participate in the research was not difficult and merely involved asking individuals if they wanted to take part in the study. We also used snowball-sampling procedures (Biernacki and Waldorf 1981) and asked adults to refer us to others whom they felt would be informative for our study.

Among those working in the juvenile justice system, we interviewed two administrators within the probation unit of the Hawai'i State Judiciary's Family Court, along with three probation officers who worked directly with youth probationers. Individuals were selected based on several criteria, including knowledge of institutional history, experience working in the communities where interviewed youth lived, and participation in one of the programs that grew out of the then-ongoing reform efforts.

In addition, six youth services professionals were interviewed. One worked in the office that oversaw youth services in the state. Two were young adults who served youth who were facing challenges similar to those who we interviewed. These two adults also had personal experiences with the juvenile justice system. And two were community volunteers who worked intimately with youth and their families in the catchment area of one of the schools where many of the interviewed youth lived. These individuals were approached for interviews because of the depth of their knowledge about the topic. Karen conducted these interviews and had contact with these interviewees through her professional and volunteer work in youth services and violence prevention.

In-depth interviews with adults and teens were similar in that these sessions lasted (on average) one hour, and ranged from fifty to ninety minutes. An interview guide was used, which included open-ended questions about the nature and

meaning of youth violence for boys and girls, ways they were addressing the problem in the work they did, and what they felt could be done to solve problems
associated with violence. For youth and school staff, we discussed what individuals
felt were the problems relating to violence in schools and the geographic communities. For juvenile justice workers, the questions pertained to violence among
youth who were in contact with the juvenile justice system. Although a guide was
used, interviews evolved in a conversational format, allowing participants to bring
up facets of violence that were not included in the guide, but that were important
to them.

3

"Us Girls Get the Second Half"

Girls' Early Socialization and Outspoken Femininity

As noted in the introduction, previous research on marginalized youth has high-lighted how racialized, poor or working-class girls and boys in the United States face a similar set of circumstances, including economic marginalization, the failure of many institutions meant to serve children, racialized stigma, and political alienation, all of which leave their communities with few resources to solve pressing problems. Given the fact that both boys and girls confront these challenges, a lingering question in the literature is whether girls respond in the same way as boys to these dislocations. In other words, do girls, like their male counterparts, embrace a tough and rugged "code of the streets" (Anderson 1999), a value system that allows them to use violence to get what they cannot get through conventional avenues, namely respect, dignity, and the chance to be somebody?[1]

After the first few years we spent observing, interacting with, and interviewing girls, we noticed that many girls who used violence to solve problems also tended to espouse beliefs about what was a respectable, upstanding, and honorable way of being in the world. If there was a code of honor among girls in Northward and Stevens Heights, we found that some major tenets were that girls should be out-spoken, brutally honest, and bold—a stance that many girls termed "being real." For example, when Angel did not like someone, she did not hide it. She said it to their face. This stance often led Angel to tell other girls, "You are dressed like a slut," or "Oh my gosh, your hair is so ugly. Yeah, I said your hair was ugly." According to Angel, this brand of truthfulness, what Ward (2000) called "truth telling," made her trustworthy because others would always know what she was thinking and that she was not faking her way through life.[2] At times, Angel did more than let people know what she thought about them. She also spoke her mind about what she would do to others, informing teens that she would "get up in your grill [face]," "Come across this room on you," or "Beat your ass" if they did not stop disrespecting or irritating her.

One instructive conversation about the importance of being real occurred during the weeks before a much-anticipated event for the teens, a visit from His Holiness the Fourteenth Dalai Lama. As part of his mission of peace, the Dalai Lama came to Hawai'i and planned a special assembly with high school teens on Oahu. His Holiness' visit was hyped for several weeks in schools throughout Oahu, and Seaside was no exception. High school teens were tasked with hanging prayer flags around campus, and teens were given lessons on the history and meaning of each color in the flags: blue for sky, white for air, red for fire, green for water, and yellow for earth. In social studies classes, teens were lectured about the turbulent relationship between Tibet and China, and parallels were made between the overthrow of the Hawaiian kingdom and the ousting of the Dalai Lama from his homeland—a move that we suspected was designed to make teens more knowledgeable about and respectful of the Dalai Lama. Youth were sometimes given a hearty dose of parental lecturing from teachers and school administrators about how to behave properly in the Dalai Lama's presence: no talking out of turn, no swearing, no fighting, and no yelling. Teens were reminded that they would be ambassadors of Hawai'i and should act accordingly.

The way that some teachers talked to the girls put Katy ill at ease. Not having conducted in-depth interviews with these girls, the teachers and administrators did not know how often the girls were mistrusted by some adults who, in many different ways, informed these girls that they were not good enough. They did not know that Annabelle's adopted mother had told Annabelle that she was "becoming overweight" or that Illeana's father had given her a strict dressing down when she made an error on the softball field. They also did not know about the constant activity in Cassey's and Trisha's houses—small single-family dwellings each housing multiple generations and approximately ten people. Cassey and Trisha were constantly fighting for positive attention amidst a gaggle of demands from brothers, cousins, aunties, and uncles. Many school staff members did not know how hard it was for Cassey and Trisha to be heard, seen, and understood in their own homes. The last thing these girls needed, in Katy's mind, was another set of lectures about how to behave and comport themselves properly.

After weeks of being cowed by a series of rules and regulations in anticipation of the Dalai Lama's visit, Miss Phillips decided to let the girls' group have fun, creative time to laugh and experience joy. Laugher and joy, after all, are essential components of the Tibetan notion of peace (at least that is what the counselors and Katy thought). For the self-expressive art project, each girl was given a choice of colored paper (blue, white, red, green, or yellow) and was encouraged to draw whatever she thought of when she thought of being happy and peaceful. Within the first few minutes, a few girls complained, "Not an art project!" "I suck at art. I just can't do it," said Illeana. "Everything I draw looks ugly," said another teen. Miss Phillips and Katy coaxed the girls just to try it. "It doesn't matter how it looks," said Miss Phillips.[3] "It's just about how you feel and having fun, guys," Katy echoed. As usual, the girls went along, albeit reluctantly, with another one of the therapeutic group activities.

Illeana tore her paper in two and set the pieces aside. "I hate this," she said. Remembering how much Illeana loathed it when her family members commented on her softball errors at the end of a game, Katy told Illeana that she thought her drawing was "beautiful, I really like it." Illeana did not say anything for a while and continued to look down as she attempted another drawing. After Katy offered a few more words of encouragement to the other girls, Illeana said, "Not everything we do is great. I don't like it when people give out too many compliments." Katy asked, "What's wrong with being encouraging?" Illeana answered, "It is not honest. I'd rather someone tell me the truth. If my work sucks, I would rather have them just say it sucks." The other girls nodded in agreement.

Initially, Katy thought that Illeana was having a hard day. It was not until months later, when Katy began to think carefully about the girls' many comments regarding the importance of being real and not fake, that an alternative interpretation emerged. Maybe Illeana was passing on an important piece of advice to Katy. As Illeana's analysis indicated, it is hard to trust people who are perpetually nice all the time: their attitude "is not honest." Quite frankly, being nice and encouraging at all times was not a version of femininity that would help Illeana, Angel, Trisha, Cassey, or any of the dozens of other girls who attended the counseling groups to become healthy young women. While criticizing and putting down these girls certainly would not have helped them to become happy adults, neither would modeling a version of womanhood that encouraged being perpetually and exclusively kind. Looking closely at the girls' many comments about "being real," a clear story emerged about how and why girls embraced a stance of "speaking up," which translated into a very loose and girl-specific ethos—or set of beliefs—about the importance of standing up for one's self. Moreover, it became clear that what we call this ethos of "being real" and "speaking up" could only be understood by looking at the girls' family backgrounds and the history of their interactions with adults who occupy institutional positions of authority.

· · ·

In this chapter we examine girls' childhood experiences as a way of explaining why girls relied on their ability to speak up, stand up, and even strike out. We note how being forthright, honest, and outspoken about their needs and engaging in forceful confrontations—even when these confrontations hurt others—worked for girls as strategies to ward off being overworked, ignored, taken advantage of, or victimized at school, in the community, or with family.

In the next sections of the chapter, we examine two key facets of girls' childhood socialization experiences. First, we look at the school and community contexts in which girls grew up, with a special focus on the organization of schools and on peer-based norms and values as they related to the gender expectations confronting girls. In school and other community contexts, girls learned an early lesson that adults often could or would not protect them from teasing and harassment. In the end, girls learned that they had to protect themselves.

Second, we focus on the girls' family lives, highlighting how many families responded to the numerous contingencies and challenges that threatened family unity. Although most families were loving, resilient, and resourceful, the multiple stresses and strains placed on families produced key challenges for girls. One challenge related to family trauma, including violence. Because girls had less freedom from home than boys, when conflicts occurred, girls were closer to family turbulence. Also, because domestic labor was feminized, girls more than boys were responsible for managing an overwhelming amount of work on behalf of families. We conclude this chapter by summarizing the girls' status in communities and families given the challenges that we highlighted.

In this chapter we also begin to answer the question posed above about whether girls, like boys, turn to a violent code of the streets to cope with severe hardships. We document that the aggressiveness of the girls in our study was not their attempt to establish themselves within a street-based and male-centered ethos. Instead, many of the girls' notions about when to speak up and strike out grew out of the gender-based realities that they confronted. Rather than street realities, the stresses, strains, and systems of dishonor that affected girls were tied to contingencies in girls' family lives and to prevailing femininity standards that dictate the attention and resources given to girls and also govern how girls are supposed to look, act, and comport themselves. In this way, this chapter offers an image of girls' violence that shifts the axis of analysis away from the streets and toward girl-centered contexts and concerns.

LEARNING TO STAND UP FOR YOURSELF: GIRLS' SCHOOL AND COMMUNITY EXPERIENCES

The girls' interpretations of what it meant to "be real" and the survival strategies that they used can only be understood by looking at the contexts in which the girls grew up. The girls in this study, like girls growing up in distressed locations throughout the United States, learned early in their lives that others would not or could not fix the problems that they faced. Moreover, there were many complicated reasons why the girls could not depend on others to overcome challenges. Jones (2010) provides insights about Philadelphia girls that also apply to girls in Hawai'i: "Social scientists often overlook the fact that today's inner-city girl comes of age in the same distressed neighborhoods as those of her male counterparts. Inner-city girls are not isolated from the social consequences of racial segregation, concentrated poverty, and inner-city violence . . . . African American inner-city girls' lives are shaped by the salience of the drug trade, a widespread distrust of social institutions and social relationships, and regular exposure to chaotic and too often violent conditions, whether at school or in the neighborhood" (20).

While the Pacific Islander girls in this study certainly faced chaos and insecurity stemming from poverty, racialization, violence, and rampant drug and alcohol addiction, there were also some key differences for girls in Hawaiʻi. One obvious difference was that many girls in this study lived in rural rather than in inner-city areas, though rural life on Oahu is not as isolated and remote as it is in the continental United States. For example, one is never more than sixty-five miles from the urban center of Honolulu. Despite this, many teens and parents in Northward noted that they were seen as "more country" and, consequently, less sophisticated, savvy, and capable than urban dwellers. This stigma, coupled with mitigated access to important services that are available in urban centers created its own type of social isolation for Northward residents.

Another key difference was that girls in Northward and Stevens Heights lived in communities that faced long histories of complicated racial, economic, and political marginalization, histories that are common in colonized lands like Hawaiʻi, Puerto Rico, Guam, and American Samoa. While, on the continent, many inner-city "girls are touched—figuratively, literally, and daily—by violence" (Jones 2010, 20) usually in the form of "street" violence with fists, knives, and sometimes guns, by contrast in Hawaiʻi, there was considerable interpersonal violence.[4] But residents also lived in the shadow of a long history of state-sponsored violence in the form of a heavily militarized state and lasting memories of how nations with imperial aspirations (e.g., the United States, Germany, and Great Brittan) had usurped indigenous lands, often at gunpoint. All residents were aware of the chilling history of lost sovereignty in Hawaiʻi and other Pacific Island nations and the idea that the state could assert itself at any time and take sacred symbolic, cultural, and material resources. For Northward and Stevens Heights residents, the lasting memory of a long history of Western takings from Pacific Islander nations flowed into a very real contemporary awareness that the state could (and often did) intervene to "take children" from parents and, consequently, break up families.

The conditions mentioned above created a particular reality in Northward and Stevens Heights, and the hard fact of everyday life for teens was that there was a marked drain on community resources, such that the girls could not rely on others to solve the problems they faced. Parents were overworked. Staff in the social services that existed (e.g., schools, health centers, and children's centers) were underpaid and bogged down in numerous strict bureaucratic mandates, while community leaders were given enormous responsibilities, but were alienated from civic centers of power. Federal- and state-funded institutions meant to serve residents in Northward and Stevens Heights, like the adults in them, were stretched thin, overburdened, and accountable to many competing demands, usually demands that overlooked the girls' needs. In such contexts, being quiet, kind, and compliant could lead to serious problems for the girls, and they learned early that they had to rely on their own personal resources, such as speaking and striking out when they faced serious dilemmas.

While adults were busy tackling monumental tasks, the girls faced their own difficult and complicated obstacles, the nature of which provides considerable evidence that the gender-specific challenges faced by the girls were generally "off the radar" for adults. One of the most common hardships that girls noted having faced during elementary and middle school was being humiliated for not having the right "looks," with the girls' body size, shape, or type being subject to constant evaluation. Boys, it should be noted, were often the instigators of this type of harassment in elementary and middle school.[5] In contrast, girls were often the ones who took up the charge of labeling other girls as ugly in high school. The condemnation of girls who failed to fit ideal beauty standards provided a couple of early life lessons. The first lesson was about the hegemonic reach of White, middle-class, American standards of beauty. It seems that even girls living in one of the most remote island chains in the world could not escape being judged according to standards insisting that female beauty is equated with being pale skinned and physically frail, which some call the thin ideal. Second, the girls learned how painful it was to fail to meet these very narrow beauty standards, and they shared with us the devastating heartbreak of being ridiculed, signaled out, and condemned for being too "dark," "fat," and "ugly."[6]

Trisha's childhood experiences conveyed not only how girls confronted hegemonic beauty standards but also how girls learned to rely on themselves when they were harassed about their physical looks. Trisha, a freshman, was shorter than her female peers (she was just under five feet tall), a fact that made her stand out and forced her to endure considerable derision from other youth. Coupled with her small stature was the fact that Trisha was told by peers and doctors that she was overweight—a message that simultaneously infuriated and depressed her. Her narratives about how she attempted to manage the stigma of being "fat" revealed many occasions when adults were less than helpful. She described her struggles against the prevailing thin ideal:

> I can often skip lunch and drink water. When my nose bleeds for some reason, I have this feeling like I am not hungry. My doctors tell me that I have to lose weight. Me and my grandma are on a diet. My sister and I go running. She's like, "You've got to work harder," but I can't keep up with her. I can't even breathe through my nose. I tell her, "You are not in my body. You don't know." The doctor says that I am overweight. When the doctor told me that, it put me into a deep depression because I have experienced

depression before. You cannot say it like that: "You are overweight." If you can, say, "You are healthy, in a way." But they said I'm fat. So focus on the positive, not the negative. Go by Hawai'i standards, not by mainland standards. It shouldn't be one standard. There are many different people. They look at the average American and apply that to everyone.

As noted, Trisha was often enraged by being called fat, and all her dieting and exercise regimes only added to her frustration. In fact, Trisha literally became sick with stress, worry, and anxiety about all the ways that she failed to conform to femininity ideals. Nosebleeds, headaches, depression, and "stress attacks" were among the many maladies plaguing Trisha. Because of this stress, Trisha was referred to counseling services, and one piece of advice for Trisha was to talk with a trusted adult about her feelings rather than "bottling them in" and making herself ill. This strategy, however, yielded mixed results. She said, "When I was in middle school, I would have stress attacks. They would have to take me out. I felt that I was suffocated. I told the A-Plus lady that [a boy] is pissing me off.[7] She said, 'Don't say that word.' Okay, 'He is frustrating me.' She is like, 'Don't say that either.' I'm like, 'Do you know how old I am?'"

Eventually, Trisha found a way to combat the irritating boys on her own. She said:

> I ended up flying scissors at a boy's eye when I was in middle school 'cause he was teasing me and I asked him to stop and he didn't. And the teacher was sitting right there and I was like, "You are not going to do anything? Are you serious?" And I am like, "Stop talking about me." And he kept going. And the teacher was doing nothing. I told him to stop three times, and he kept going. And I said, "I can handle anything as long as you don't call me fat." And he called me fat. "Stop, please." Still going. So I throw the scissors, and it hits him in the eye but not on the sharp part, on the hard part [of the scissors]. And he was like, "What did you do that for?" And I said, "I told you to stop and you didn't listen." What was I supposed to do?

In addition to launching a pair of scissors at a boy, Trisha tackled another boy to the ground when he refused to let girls play basketball with him. She said, "I asked nicely like, ten times. And if I ask nicely and he does not hear me ten times? I literally tackled him like a football player and knocked him off his feet. I felt so bad afterwards. I was crying like, 'I'm so sorry.' I cried to him, 'I'm so sorry.'" In fact, Trisha was eventually referred to anger management counseling after a few episodes of such physical attacks.

Though Trisha's family and the school staff expressed "surprise" that kindhearted Trisha was capable of physical outbursts, her narratives revealed a certain predictability to her anger. According to Trisha, when she was humiliated, bullied, or excluded from an activity, she verbally asserted herself and was often ignored. After directly telling boys to stop or asking boys for what she wanted "nicely, like ten times," Trisha turned to violence. Trisha described her violence within the family in a similar manner and said, "I used to actually go full rage on them [her brothers] .... And we throw fists and we will not stop until the other one stops. Like I keep going, he [her brother] keeps going. I tell him, 'Hit me one more time and I'll hit you back.'" Trisha's phrasing, "Hit me and I'll hit you back," is important: Trisha refused to sit still and be hit, teased, taunted, or bullied without "hitting back."

Angel had experiences similar to those of Trisha, in that Angel was perpetually teased as a child for her body size, and like Trisha, she had to rely on herself to combat this harassment. Unlike Trisha, who was shorter than her peers, Angel towered over and was stronger than most teens, boys and girls alike. Although many high school staff members thought of Angel as a boisterous and bold young woman, Angel said that she had not been that way as a child. In fact, Angel described herself as having been a very shy and sensitive young girl. She said:

Angel: Believe it or not, people used to pick on me.

Katy: About what?

Angel: About everything. This one boy, I wanted to beat his ass so bad when I was in sixth grade because he told everybody I stink. Yeah, so they all started picking on me.

Katy: Just being mean?

Angel: Yeah, just being mean. Just because I was big, people thought I would do something, but I didn't. And sometimes I used to go home crying. And after a while I was like, "What the fuck? I'm big. I don't need to take this shit." I just started fighting. And then people started to back off, and nobody called me stink, . . . Actually, my first fight with a boy that was such a dumbass, I'm going to fight a boy; he's a grade older than I was. He just didn't like me; from the first time I came to the school. He used to always crack jokes around me. Back then, I used to be very quiet. He told them that, because I'm Tongan, he thinks, I think I'm bad. I was the quietest bitch in your class, like, "What the fuck you talking about?" But I didn't talk like that. I was very quiet all the time.

A fighter was born the day that Angel realized, "What the fuck? I'm big. I don't need to take this shit." She could always fight back, and as she reported, this strategy was somewhat effective, as boys' teasing stopped when her reputation as a competent fighter became known. Unfortunately, her reputation as a fighter also meant that she would be singled out by school staff who came to believe that Angel was a "problem child" and a "dangerous girl."

Angel's experiences also revealed racialized mythologies about who was tough, strong, and, consequently, ready for a fight. The boys who targeted Angel, for example, singled her out because she was part-Tongan and she was larger than many youth. Angel explained the history that underpinned the notion that Tongans are effective fighters to Katy by saying, "Tongans, you know, have a history of fighting.

No one has ever come and taken us over. We have always fought back and won!" Here, Angel echoes a common sentiment in Hawai'i. Tonga is often celebrated in the Pacific region as a land that has never fallen under the yoke of imperialism. Put simply, Tonga has always been ruled by Tongans and has never been colonized by a foreign nation. Therefore, Tongans, as Angel highlighted, are mythologized in present-day Hawai'i as fierce and competent fighters.

Angel's conflicts with peers did more than reveal how the lasting mythologies about Tongans contributed to Angel's "tough girl" reputation. There was also considerable evidence that mechanisms of racialized gender (Pyke and Johnson 2003) were woven into teens' constructions of and attempts to degrade and denounce girls like Angel. By racialized gender, we mean the common beliefs about girls who were thought to occupy various racial and ethnic designations. For the purposes of this study, the key racial designation that came to the fore was the Pacific Islander category, and the ethnic groups most commonly mentioned in this study were Native Hawaiian, Samoan, and Tongan. More specifically, the racialized gender processes in this study were used to inform Pacific Islander girls of how they were substandard and undeserving of respect because of all the ways they violated hegemonic femininity ideals.

Angel's experiences leading up to one of her fights highlighted how the racialized gender system worked in schools on Oahu. The following field note was written after attending a lunch group meeting:

> Today in the lunch group, Angel said that there was a group of girls who were "after her." She told us that they called her a horse, they made horse noises when she walked by, and they yelled out across the campus, "We have some hay for you to eat." Angel said, "Because I am part Tongan, they say I eat and look like a horse." Angel told us that she replied to them quickly by saying, "What do a beautiful Samoan and the tooth fairy have in common? They are both fiction." Apparently, the girls who were targeting Angel were Samoan.

In addition to the historic story that Tongans are so fierce that they can ward off military invasions, another mythology circulating was that Tongans eat horses, and consequently, that they are horse-like. As noted in the introduction, part of the racialization process during colonial expansion (Austin 1983; Gabbidon 2010; Hawkins 2011; Tatum 2000a, 2000b, 2002) is to establish a rigid racial caste system, with indigenous peoples being positioned at the bottom of the colonial racial hierarchy. Mythologizing indigenous people as more animal than human buoys the racial caste system in which colonizers are seen as being from a superior, "master" racial group. Here, it is important to note that military occupation is only one way to usurp and take control of indigenous lands. The diffusion of ideologies casting Whites as a superior racial group is another way that Westerners expanded their power. For example, constructions of indigenous people as inferior, animalistic savages allow colonizers to claim that indigenous people lack the proper traits of respectable citizens, namely possessing rational minds, mastery over their passions, and the sophistication necessary to self-govern. The lasting mythology that Tongans are "horse-like" constructed Tongan girls and women as too animalistic, too large, and too strong to be considered beautiful, valuable, and dignified according to White, middle-class standards. Note also that "horse-faced" is a longstanding American euphemism for "ugly."

Angel understood how insulting it was to call a girl "ugly." Her response to her female tormentors was to throw racialized gender scripts back at these girls. In front of the whole school, Angel severely disrespected these girls when she said that a beautiful Samoan girl was a myth, just like the tooth fairy. It should be noted that very few boys in these contexts would be insulted if they were called ugly. In fact, some boys enjoyed being labeled mean and ugly because such labels only added to their tough personas.

Angel's and Trisha's narratives contain lessons about what standing up for yourself meant in these two communities. Both girls confronted significant degradation, humiliation, and taunting, usually for all the ways that they did not fit the very narrow and almost impossible-to-reach standards of Western hegemonic femininity. When Trisha was able to remain quiet, uncomplaining, and passive, the results were tragic—she was often struck down by one of a number of maladies.

Adding to these tensions, both Angel and Trisha shared the impression that adults would not and could not change these humiliating conditions. In our study, the failure of institutions and services, such as schools, to serve or protect youth was not simply due to lack of resources in cash-strapped schools and beleaguered social services (see Pastor et al. 2007). Trisha was, after all, referred to counseling, a somewhat expensive social service provided by the state. The failure of social service institutions in Trisha's case was tied to flawed ideas within institutions about what interventions are needed and who are appropriate candidates for such services. According to Angel's and Trisha's narratives, boys who teased, taunted, bullied, or excluded girls seemed to be tolerated and overlooked. Girls who threw scissors at, tackled, or fought back against boys, however, were taken seriously. They were signed up for anger management counseling, as in Trisha's case, or they were labeled as violent and repeatedly expelled from school, as in Angel's example. The takeaway point for the girls was that adults were not likely to intervene on their behalf. Moreover, if adults did get involved, they often targeted rather than protected girls.

Another lesson that girls like Angel and Trisha learned from childhood was that verbally asserting themselves might not solve problems. Trisha tried several times to set clear boundaries verbally. She said, "I asked him to stop and he didn't" and "I asked nicely like ten times." In Angel's experiences, after coming home crying, she realized that she did not have "to take shit." She was strong enough that she could overpower her tormentors.

Regardless of whether girls embraced a tough persona (like Angel) or felt ashamed of their angry outbursts (like Trisha), the fact remained that both girls learned that being accommodating was dangerous. In addition, being verbally assertive was not enough to protect them. Getting others to respect their right to live free from harassment required action. Angel's and Trisha's experiences also pointed to a no-win situation. If they remained silent, they would be continuously taunted or victimized. If they spoke up, they would be ignored, and if they acted out, they would be stigmatized, placed in treatment for their anger, or punished by adults at school.[8]

LEARNING RESILIENT FEMININITY: FAMILY SOCIALIZATION AND EXPERIENCES

While the lessons of girlhood suggest that girls learned from an early age that some adults were not likely to intervene on their behalf, this did not mean that adults in their lives were powerless and ineffective. In fact, the opposite was often true. The economic complications and strains in the two communities where the girls grew up were monumental and distracted adults with the everyday demands of keeping families united. However, while difficult and demanding, these challenges did not completely overwhelm most adults. Many parents, especially women, rose to these challenges and used several personal and community-based resources to keep their families and communities functioning during significant upheavals.

Urban ethnographers often discuss the complicated conditions confronting inner-city dwellers as a particular kind of strain. For individuals in Northward and Stevens Heights, life stress certainly threatened to overpower the best efforts of many adults. For example, many of the lunch bunch youth described their parents' and their own struggles with drug and alcohol addiction; four teens had been homeless; five teens had been placed in foster homes; two teens (one male and one female) described extensive family violence; five teens had a close family member who had recently passed away; two girls were mothers; two girls discussed experiencing dating violence; and more than half of the youth in the counseling group had a family member who had been incarcerated.

In most of the cases mentioned above, adult women were at the forefront of managing these challenges. When a family member was sick, a daughter became pregnant, or a father succumbed to alcoholism, it was mothers, grandmothers, aunts, and sisters in Northward and Stevens Heights who usually kept families united, cared for, and functioning. The high rate of incarceration among Native Hawaiian and Samoan men (Hawai'i Department of Public Safety 2008) often meant that fathers and uncles were absent and unable to assist. Women usually stepped in to fill the voids left by absent men. In fact, when a teen's father was incarcerated or suffered from addiction, the family was likely to remain intact (see Glaze and Maruschak 2008). There were two teens in this study whose mothers had been sent to prison. In both cases, the state intervened and placed these children in foster care.[9]

It is important to balance this composite image of what resilient womanhood meant to families in this study with an in-depth portrait from the girls' vantage point. Illeana's family experiences provided such a close-up view. While Illeana was growing up, her parents struggled with substance abuse, and eventually, her mother abandoned the family. In the following, she described what happened next:

> My mom and dad divorced. Actually, no. My mom left to do drugs, my dad was in the military, [and] my grandma was watching us. After my grandma died, my dad came back to watch us. He stayed around for a little while and then he left. He started to become an alcoholic and everything. All of us, all four of us [siblings], are so independent, we don't like when dad shows up. Like what are you doing here? Just go. We shut him out. Just now, he's trying to get back into our lives. It's too late. We don't want no one there. Like all I need is my older sister because she has been taking care of me. She's trying to do stuff for us . . . . I think that your parent is the one who cares for you and who buys food, provides shelter. For me, this is my sister.

Illeana's sister was like many women in the community who "do stuff" for families, who, in other words, provide the care necessary for family survival. It should be noted that Illeana's father eventually entered drug treatment, gained employment, and found stable housing. As Illeana's narrative indicates, despite her father's efforts to redeem himself in his family's eyes, Illeana's father did not become the head of family life, nor did he regain the trust of his children.

It is important to note that the community-specific version of resilient femininity that we outline above was an idealized image. In reality, this ideal model of the female pillar of the family was very difficult for women to attain. For one, there were many forces beyond women's control. No matter how resilient, resourceful, and creative women were, raising families while confronting poverty, institutional neglect, and alienation from political centers of power in the state could undercut a parent's best efforts. In the end, achieving a resilient brand of femininity was wearying.

In the next two sections of the chapter, we note that girls confronted two gender-specific challenges when family resilience was not enough to protect children from challenging circumstances. First, we examine girls' specific relationship to family trauma and especially to family violence. Second, we look at girls' role in managing the heavy demands of domestic labor for their families. In both sections, we highlight how idealized and hegemonic notions of femininity made girls' relationship to family trauma and domestic labor different and in many ways more complicated than boys' relationships to these same challenges. In fact, boys were given a special status and freedom in families that allowed them to avoid some of the more problematic aspects of family stress and strain.

Girls and Family Trauma

Given the many demands placed on adults in these two communities, stress among parents was high, and parents sometimes admitted to us that they failed to fulfill community and dominant culture models of "good" parenting. Some parents, for example, told us that they struggled with substance abuse, depression, and having "heavy hands with" (i.e., hitting) children. While both fathers and mothers sometimes violently punished children, mothers described themselves as having a "lighter touch" than fathers. In fact, every once in a while, the topic of families and violence came up during lunch group discussions, and the teens seemed to agree that boys were more likely than girls to receive "hard lick'ns," meaning harsh physical punishments.[10] Girls might not receive the same "hard lick'ns" as boys, but because of their close emotional and physical ties to the home, girls, more than boys, had a particularly intimate and constant exposure to family conflicts.

Arlene, a mother living in Stevens Heights, revealed the ways that exposure to and experiences with family violence played out differently for boys and girls. During a focus group with parents, Arlene openly discussed her husband's anger and physical violence and discussed strategies she used to manage her husband's outbursts. She explained:

> My sons, they quiet. I mean, they very close to me, all my kids are very close to me. They don't, I think they scared to talk to the father because my husband, you know, he's quiet, but when he gets mad, he will get mad. And that kind of madness I don't like 'cuz when he hit one of my kids, that kind of really Samoan feeling, that's what I call abuse. Yeah, and I see how my husband hit my oldest son, yeah? Ho, man that's the first time I seen him hitting one of my kids like that, so I just give him [her husband] the knife, "Here, kill 'em, better that way. Or stop hitting him and kill him if that's the way it is."[11]

Later, Arlene said that she had sent her three sons to Samoa to live with other family members. The girls, however, she kept with her. As many mothers explained, mothers "keep their daughters close," which included keeping girls in the family and in close proximity to their mothers, even when families were experiencing significant upheavals.

During one focus group, Justine, a mother of four and a Northward resident, offered us her story demonstrating how girls could be especially affected by family conflicts and trauma. In it, she discussed how intimate partner violence and other family problems had particularly affected her oldest daughter:

> I have four daughters, and I have a seventeen-year-old [girl] who is pretty caught up with relationships and once in a while dabbles in drugs, and it's a violent relationship . . . . My big girl had trouble, but I really think it's from some of the stuff me and her father went through. It was very violent, there was a lot of drugs, there was a lot of abandonment . . . and then another thing that they saw, or they experienced, was that their father committed suicide . . . . My big girl, she's been in fights, but as for my

youngest girl, she's totally the opposite. But by then, we [she and her second husband] came into recovery. So we got it. At that time, she [her youngest daughter] was still a baby.

Justine's story was one of redemption and, more specifically, of her own transformation from an inconsistent parent into a resilient mother. After years of struggling with alcohol and drug addiction and intimate partner battering, Justine "turned her life around." She enrolled in drug treatment, found stable employment, and became a more consistent parent. Providing further testimony to the idea that women were often strong leaders in the community, Justine had spearheaded several community-based leadership and parenting initiatives and became a revered and much treasured member of the community.

Underscoring Arlene's and Justine's narratives is the idea that girls "stay close" to their mothers in part because of the mother/daughter bond. This bond assumes a certain amount of identification between mothers and daughters, leading girls to experience and perceive family trauma differently than boys. Adding to the intimate identification with women in the family was the fact that girls had greater physical closeness with their mothers. Girls were not likely to be sent to live with extended family members in times of family turmoil. Because girls were designated as their mother's helpers in domestic tasks, girls often worked side by side with mothers, aunts, and grandmothers.[12] Therefore, if tempers flared and conflicts became physical, girls were likely to be granted a front-row seat to the unfolding family trauma. In contrast, boys were often allowed much more freedom to be away from home. This autonomy meant that boys had an outlet and an escape from family when conflicts erupted at home—with family homes in this study being anything from single-family dwellings, to apartments, to vans, to tents in public areas.

Even in families that were free from abuse and neglect, girls' relative lack of autonomy compared with boys was a serious concern for girls. The girls did not passively accept the fact that they were designated as their mothers' helpers with domestic work, while boys in the family enjoyed freedom from these chores. In fact, the unequal family obligations did not sit well with the girls, and, in particular, the girls' discomfort with unequal domestic responsibilities illustrated a different type of gendered family conflict.

"It Keeps Going and Going": Girls' Domestic Labor

Heavy domestic demands were one serious source of irritation for girls, and many girls in the study discussed the fact that boys often failed to help with family chores. In addition to not getting much help from boys in the family, the girls were often dismissed and disrespected by these same boys. The end result was that many girls felt overworked and underappreciated if not outright verbally abused in the family, with boys being the most commonly cited source of mistreatment.

As we looked at the amount of work that many girls were expected to complete, it became clear to us that the girls' labor was essential to families. In all cases when teens were living in two-parent families in Northward and Stevens Heights, both parents worked. Moreover, it was common for both parents to hold more than one job in order to make ends meet. Single-parent households with a mother, grandmother, aunt, or adult sister as the head of the home were also common in both neighborhoods. Census data indicates that, in both Northward and Stevens Heights, the average family size was four people. The smallest family size among the lunch group youth was three and the largest was twelve, with the average hovering around six family members. Census data also indicates that, in Northward, approximately 17 percent of the population lived below the poverty level in 2010, and many of the teens at Seaside were likely to come from such families. In Stevens Heights, the average household income was $56,654, although this number is skewed by the very high income of a small set of residents. Approximately 25 percent of the population in Stevens Heights lived below the poverty level, compared with 10 percent of Hawai'i's residents as a whole.

The lunch group youth were very likely to come from families surviving on less than twenty thousand dollars per year, and this income was stretched to support anywhere from three to twelve family members.[13] Given these conditions, it is clear that for many of the families studied, women's paid and unpaid work provided an important contribution to family survival. In addition, women in the study did more than provide income and unpaid domestic work for the family. They were also active members of community groups and therefore organized, spearheaded, and participated in a number of community initiatives.

With women in the workforce and completing important community-based projects, family members depended heavily on girls' work at home. The tasks necessary to keep households with anywhere from three to twelve people functioning were monumental and, as many study participants indicated, boys were not expected to complete such tasks as laundry, cooking, changing diapers, or looking after small children, although some families did require boys to clean. Cooking, shopping, laundry, and childcare were feminized labor.

During a focus group with female community leaders in Stevens Heights, Nana discussed the importance of women's work as well as the difference between men's and women's labor. She said, "There's one Samoan word, it's an old Samoan word. The lady's working, it keeps on going and going. But if [a] man's doing some work, it's maybe two or three weeks and then they cannot even finish that. But the lady is still going and going." Mia, a teenager, also expressed the idea that men and boys do not complete household tasks. At one point during the focus group, she said, "I think that some girls, they feel like ok, you [adults] always going for the boys. You pay more attention to the boys. Us girls, we get the second half. But when they [the boys] are not there, it's we [the girls] the ones that move the tables away or we take the rubbish for them. Here, the boys don't do."

Mia was deeply concerned that female labor was never-ending. Her quote highlighted the fact that, when it came time to gather the family for meals, parties, or other events, it was girls, not boys, who were the ones who "moved tables," "took out rubbish," and managed any number of other domestic tasks necessary to keep families functioning as smoothly as possible (see Mayeda and Pasko 2011). In addition, as Mia noted, boys had a special status in families, described by Mia as a stance in which adults were always "going for" or "paying attention to" the boys. In other words, Mia's descriptions suggested that girls were treated as second-class citizens in their families. They (along with mothers) did most of the labor, while boys were granted the lion's share of attention.

Considering this gendered and unequal distribution of housework in many families allows us to better understand Trisha's angry outbursts, what she referred to as her "rages." While authority figures considered them random, Trisha's episodes of violence might be partially understood as moments when Trisha was overwhelmed, at times by the unfair division of labor at home. Trisha, for example, was designated as the family cook, not only because cooking was a feminized chore in families but also because Trisha was an avid fan of cooking shows and enjoyed trying new recipes. While Trisha enjoyed the art of food preparation, being the designated cook for a family of ten and assistant chef for all family parties and get-togethers was exhausting. Trisha admitted that there were times when she felt taken for granted by the family, as well as rebuffed and verbally abused by her brothers. She described one incident:

> Regardless of whether I say that there are other people in the family who can cook, my father says, "Trisha, go in the kitchen and cook." My brother knows how to cook, but he only cooks for himself. One time I woke up, and he was the only one eating breakfast. Everyone was sitting around, and he was the only one eating. I guess everyone was sitting around waiting for me to make breakfast. He was over there eating his eggs that looked *nicely made,* his Portuguese sausage, and his side of rice. I was like, "Is there anything left?" He said, "Oh no, I only made one." I was like, "Why don't you help me!"

In addition to avoiding cooking, Trisha's brothers forged a particular deal in the family. They would perform household chores such as cleaning in exchange for privileges, such as trips to skate shops. Trisha was outraged by the inequity.[14] She said,

> Sometimes [my brother] cleans when he wants to go someplace, like when he wanted to go to a skate shop. He like complains when I get something. He complained when I got my first present in three years. It was a bracelet that I wanted my whole life. He's asking my mom, "How much did it cost?" I'm like, "You never ask a parent that!" He's like, "Oh, I just want to know." I was like, "You got to go to the skate shop. Everything you want, you get. I've never had a present in three years. You are going to ask how much it cost?"

High school boys confirmed two of the patterns that Mia and Trisha described. First, boys' narratives demonstrated that males were indeed able to avoid household chores more than girls were. Second, some high school boys demonstrated a decided lack of respect for their sisters' efforts for the family. In fact, some boys relied on patriarchal beliefs—namely beliefs that males are the heads of families—to justify why they enjoyed more freedom than girls. Chad, a high school junior and expert skateboarder, described a heated argument with his older sister:

> Every time my dad goes to Kauai for a business thing, [my sister] always thinks she is the boss. I left my plate over there one day. She told me to wash it. She was throwing my plate over there, and I said, "I'll do it later." And she said, "No, do it now. You don't even know half the things I had to do when I was your age. I did the dishes every single day." I was like, "Shut up. I don't remember you doing the dishes *every single day*. I have a life; you don't have one." She's like, "I paddled." Paddling is nothing. Anyone can get out on the water and paddle back and forth. I tried to run away, ran down the stairs. I turned around, straight punched the wall, and ran down the street. All I had was my pants, no shirt, no slippers, just my pants, 'cause I left so fast.

Chad's comments reveal many layers of the gender dynamics in families. First were his beliefs about the freedom he enjoyed. Because Chad had received a modicum of fame as a local skateboarder, winning a few local competitions, he felt enormous pride in his skateboarding ability and in the fact that he "had a life" outside the home. Second were his impressions of what freedom from the home his sister deserved. Chad's own athletic success apparently also led him to feel as though his sister's paddling experiences were nothing and that she, by extension, had "no life." In his mind, since she didn't have a life, why shouldn't she do the dishes? It should be noted that paddling is an extremely prestigious and difficult sport. Paddlers, male and female alike, are highly revered in Hawai'i.

Finally, there was Chad's reaction to family conflict. Note that when tension rose and conflict erupted, he ran out of the house wearing only his pants. It was common for boys to leave the house in times of turmoil. If a girl had run out of the house after a conflict, it was highly probable that family members would be very concerned. Calling the police to collect a daughter who fled the house was likely, as parents often feared that a girl might be hurt or "get into trouble" if she were out on the streets. Conversely, allowing boys to run outside to "blow off steam" was often considered appropriate. Sometimes boys needed a "time out" away from the home, some parents told us.

Cassey provided another example of gender tensions in families. Cassey, like Trisha, lived with a large family in a small house. At the time when Cassey was involved with the girls' group, there were many upheavals in her family. Her grandmother was very sick, her uncle had been arrested and was facing trial for assault, and her male cousins were in and out of trouble at school. In fact, we interviewed her male cousins, Joel and Julian, and neither of them talked about how Cassey was doing, although they lived with and saw her every day. Cassey, on the other hand, talked about her male cousins frequently. At one point in the lunch group meetings, she said that she was "tired of the boys always taking things from me." Cassey described much of her general frustration as stemming from her home life. The chance to talk about what was going on at home was, in fact, a rare event for Cassey. When Katy asked if she had anyone, maybe her mother, whom she could talk to, she said, "My mother worries too much and I don't like it when she worries a lot. Yeah, I don't like to tell her everything." Cassey therefore managed her emotions on her own.

There were several ways that the stress in the girls' lives manifested itself. Some girls, like Cassey, attempted to hold everything in and put on a façade of self-confidence—a countenance that often did not match how they felt. For example, after a few months of rising tensions in the family, Cassey eventually stopped going to school and preferred to be at home to help her mother. Despite attempts by her high school counselors to coax her to come back to school and finish her classes, by the end of her junior year she stopped attending school entirely.

Trisha, unlike Cassey, did not attempt to put on a tough and resilient front. Instead, Trisha discussed being overwhelmed by, yet deeply appreciating her family. Thus, Trisha faced a serious dilemma. After talking with her counselors, Trisha found a potential solution. She explained: "Our house is loud. [My sister's] baby is crying. My little sister is crying because she is hungry. She is a bottomless pit. You can feed her and she will still be hungry. That is why I want to graduate early—ten people in a small house. I can be sitting in the bathroom in the bathtub with my eyes closed. That is the only quiet place that I can go."

Although Trisha had a plan, graduating early and moving out of the family house, to solve the problems associated with family stress, and talked easily about what was bothering her, there were days when talking and planning her future did not ease her troubles. When tensions ran high and she was in conflict with her siblings, Trisha often had trouble concentrating at school. The day that we scheduled our in-depth interview was a particularly bad day for Trisha. At the beginning of the interview, she said,

> When I'm mad, I have trouble concentrating. And we had a math test today. For some reason, I kept switching the numbers in my head. I got this one wrong. Some of the instructions I couldn't read because I am so angry. And everyone kept staring at me. I was like, "You don't want people staring at you when you are crying." Sheesh. And it doesn't help that my little brother tells me that I am irritating and that he hates me. I told him to go do your chores and he was like, "I hate you." Well, thank you for bringing me down again.

In addition to being distracted and unable to concentrate at school because of family stress, Trisha, as noted previously, also frequently suffered from physical maladies, including frequent migraine headaches. Her doctors at one point advised her parents to cut twelve inches of length from Trisha's hair, which was thick and healthy and at least a yard long when Trisha joined the girls' group. Although Trisha did feel some physical relief after losing two pounds of hair, she was emotionally upset about this decision. She indicated that, with these two pounds, she had lost one of her favorite attributes—her lush, beautiful, thick hair, which used to cascade down her back. Trisha was also confused about why her parents would agree to cut her locks because, as Trisha explained, "My mom just wants me to be more feminine," and she often complained that Trisha was too much of a tomboy. When accused of not being feminine enough by her parents, Trisha retorted, "I am feminine, just not the way you want me to be." By losing her long hair, Trisha lost the battle to be feminine on her own terms—a significant loss of autonomy in her eyes.

The girls' combined narratives about early childhood experiences at school and about family socialization reveal several patterns. Growing up female was for them a complicated and difficult task. Trying to fit within community-based as well as society-wide notions of how girls are supposed to look and act was nearly impossible. While the resilient femininity modeled by adult women was demanding and difficult, there was a certain status afforded to women who achieved this brand of femininity. Grandmothers, mothers, and aunties earned respect in their communities. However girls, because of their age, did not earn the same reverence as women, so they received very little recognition and reward for their efforts, even though families depended on girls' unpaid work.

Not surprising, the girls indicated that they were bothered by the unequal division of labor in the family. What specifically piqued girls' concern was the differential treatment that they received. The failure to get the same autonomy and freedom from family labor that boys enjoyed was a serious concern. The girls also lamented the fact that they were often severely disrespected by male family members. As Trisha noted, her brother told her that he "hated her" when she reminded him to do his chores. Chad admitted that he cannot stand his sister who "thinks she is the boss," and Illeana noted that her dad is "so evil" to her older sister. While Cassey could recount every detail of her male cousins' lives, Cassey's reality remained a complete mystery to her male cousins, who were preoccupied with the trials and tribulations of the men in their home. While the efforts and labor that the girls provided for families was essential for family survival, the girls, as Mia said, "get the second half" in terms of how much respect and autonomy they were offered (Taylor, Veloria, and Verba 2007).

CONCLUSION

This chapter exposes the challenges that the girls experienced and, in particular, uncovers some of the pressures, expectations, and traumatic events that punctuated their community, school, and home lives during their pre-teen years. In neighborhoods and schools that lacked key resources and faced numerous challenges, the few resources available to assist children were often not focused on girls' specific needs. Thus, girls learned an early lesson that adults around them could not or usually did not intervene to help them solve the problems that they faced. Many of the key problems that girls faced were related to their being condemned, taunted, or tormented for not fitting within ideal gender expectations.

In terms of family struggles, we also found that girls' needs were often overlooked and that their labor was essential to family and community survival. Without girls' domestic work, families would have faltered, and, to the extent that there were vibrant and innovative community-based initiatives in these communities, there were also girls to thank for this. Without girls' assistance, women would not have been able to participate in community life to the extent that they did. While many community members recognized women for their resilience, creativity, and efforts on behalf of others, this was not the case for girls. Girls' work often went unnoticed and unappreciated.

Girls were not blind or immune to the numerous gender-based pressures, and the thesis of this chapter is that some girls' tendency to speak out and stand up for themselves (sometimes with violence) was partially shaped by the school, community, and family realities they confronted. For example, girls in the study sometimes spoke out when they felt unappreciated, overlooked, or insulted. There were also examples of times when the girls silently endured numerous aggravations, but found that the strains wore away at them, making them sick with "stress attacks," migraines, depression, and other maladies.

We admit that this chapter and the next focus on the bad news about the constraints and contingencies that girls experience, at the expense of noting how resilient and capable the girls in this study could be. It should be noted that most girls in this study were also adept problem solvers, openly discussing the challenges that they faced and designing strategies to overcome them. Girls' resilience, creativity, and their ability to rise above challenges will be outlined in chapter 7.

4

Fighting for Her Honor

High School Girls' Struggles for Respect

In chapter 3, we examined girls' childhood socialization experiences, and in the present chapter we look at the motivations underlying girls' fighting during their high school years. We also continue to answer the question of whether girls' violence is similar to that of boys, taking the high school years into particular consideration. When asked, teens, parents, and school staff frequently stated that girls were as likely as boys to fight, and when discussing why girls fought, several people—especially youth—said that girls battled to protect their reputations and for "respect." Indeed, the notion that the violence of teens (both male or female) is all about respect is a popular one. In poor inner-city areas—places that many urban ethnographers call the "ghetto" (Goffman 2014; Wacquant 2001)—individuals are said to be in a constant "search for respect" (Bourgois 2003) as they navigate the many challenges to their livelihood and status in America's poorest communities.

In this chapter, we probe beneath the surface of the notion that the attainment or maintenance of status, respect, and dignity are central goals in interpersonal youth violence by examining the meaning systems that underscore what, precisely, respect meant for the girls in the study. We also examine the situational contexts in which girls felt that they and others were being disrespected. After poring over girls' narratives about respect and violence we have identified three distinct motivations underlying girls' acts of violence. First, girls fought to protect their sexual virtue, meaning that they wanted to prove that they were sexually pure rather than "slutty." Second, girls fought to protect romance, the highly coveted romantic status of partnership. Third, girls fought as part of the overarching devaluation, denigration, and punishment of girls. In this last category, girls sometimes fought to punish the irritating behaviors or traits of other girls.

There are also important subthemes woven throughout girls' fights for sexual virtue, romance, and to denigrate and punish other girls. Sometimes when girls fought for "respect," they were fighting to prove that they adhered to the hegemonic femininity norms requiring girls to be sexually restrained as well as sexually attracted and attractive to and dependent on males. Our data also suggest that girls' fights for respect included girls' efforts to thwart and reject hegemonic femininity norms requiring girls be kind, nurturing, and compliant.

In the next sections of the chapter, we examine these three motivations for girls' violence (sexual virtue, romance, and denigration of other girls), while also highlighting the complex and sometimes contradictory sets of meaning and notions about appropriate femininity that girls experienced in their lives.

FIGHTING FOR SEXUAL VIRTUE

The cornerstone of the respectability of the adolescent girls in this study was their sexual purity. Since the girls placed a premium on sexual honor, calling a girl a "slut," "whore," or "hoochie" posed a serious threat to the girl's dignity and positive reputation. These were also "fighting words," meaning that anyone who called another girl a "skank" was likely to be confronted verbally, physically, or both.

Indeed, study participants spent quite a bit of time discussing and evaluating girls' sexual comportment. While walking across campuses, sitting in on classroom discussions, and attending assemblies, Katy often overheard conversations about girls who were "sluts," who "slept around" and "got with too many guys." This common talk emerged as what might be called *moral evaluative conversations,* in which youth judged, measured, and determined the extent of a girl's virtue (Eckert and McConnell-Ginet 1992; Eder 1995).

Among all the moral evaluative talk in schools, an unstable consensus was reached about how and if girls could earn an honorable sexual reputation; all the same, the question of how to achieve feminine sexual honor was complicated. Looking closely at the common moral evaluations directed at girls reveals that there were at least two aspects of girls' self presentations as sexually honorable that could help them gain or lose respectability. First, the girls' physical appearance and especially how they dressed were monitored and governed according to hegemonic femininity rules. The second component of girls' presentations of self as sexually respectable people had to do with girls' sexual behaviors in romantic and/or physically intimate relationships; we review girls' efforts to maintain this aspect of their sexual reputations in the section below called "Girls and Sexual Intimacy." After discussing girls' attempts to negotiate appearance and behavioral rules for girls as they pertained to sexual purity, we discuss how girls' negotiation of their physical looks and their sexual behaviors could often lead to fights between and among girls.

Hot or Hoochie? Governing Girls' Appearance at School

A girl's appearance and especially how she dressed was read as a sign of her sexual honor, with clothing being a key outward indicator of her inner moral character. Clothing that was too tight or exposed too much of one's body—one's upper thigh, butt, breasts, or stomach—was a sure sign that a girl was overly sexual and too interested in attracting the "wrong" kind of attention from boys (see Pastor et al. 2007). Such a girl was a "sleaze." When Katy told Angel that she was studying girls at school, Angel immediately advised her to focus on the "slutty" and "hoochie" clothing that girls wore. Indeed, throughout the year that Katy spent attending the weekly lunch group meetings with Angel, Angel continued to evaluate the clothing worn by female peers and concluded that many girls' shorts were too short and their tops were too small. At the age of sixteen, Angel concluded that parents were extremely permissive, allowing their daughters to dress like "whores."

While wearing clothing that exposed too much skin was a problem for girls, so too was attire that covered too much of girls' bodies. Baggy and loose-fitting clothing, like large T-shirts and long surfing shorts that end just above or below the knee was the boys' domain. At best, girls who wore boyish attire were viewed as slovenly. At worst, baggy- pants-wearing girls were "dykes." As noted, Trisha was in a battle with her parents about her appearance. Trisha told us that her parents wanted her to dress and look more like a girl, while Trisha liked wearing large T-shirts and "roomy" shorts. Donning such attire, in her parents' view, was tantamount to dressing like a "slob." A very smart girl, Trisha discerned a clear double standard in her parents' expectations. Boys, she noted, were allowed to be "slobs" in her family. They could wear long shorts and oversize shirts, while girls could not walk out of the house wearing "slovenly" apparel. Trisha chaffed at this double standard and noted, "If I had a child, I would let them wear what they wanted." Thinking a bit more carefully, Trisha revised this rule. "Well, if it is high shorts, booty shorts, no. It can be shorts below the butt cheek, thigh area, yes." Here, Trisha grappled with the prevailing femininity appearance rules. Girls, in her opinion, should be allowed to dress like boys, but she still did not think it was appropriate for girls to dress like "tramps."

The clothing rules that emerged in the teens' moral evaluative talk overlapped with the formal school dress codes. More specifically, the schools' formal dress codes prohibited girls from wearing skirts and shorts that were too short (more than halfway up a student's thigh) and tops exposing cleavage. This put most tank tops sold in popular shops catering to teens out of the question for girls. While many parents, school administrators, and teachers agreed with these dress codes because, in their view, dress codes upheld community values (Barker 2003), it is important to note that these codes do not match the realities of living in Hawai'i—a location known for its hot, tropical climate. Indeed, looking at the geographic reality of life in Hawai'i, we see yet another double standard confronting girls.

At the time when this study was conducted, there were ongoing appeals to state legislators and Hawai'i State Department of Education (DOE) administrators to do something about the soaring temperatures in public school classrooms. According to reports, only one out of every ten classrooms in the state was air-conditioned and, depending on the season, the temperatures inside some classrooms on Oahu could reach, and sometimes even exceed, ninety degrees (Vorsino 2011). In 2013, teens and teachers held a sit-in at the Hawai'i State Capital to protest the state's lack of attention to uncomfortable classroom temperatures. By the time of this writing, legislators and DOE officials had failed to offer a solution to the problem.

There were occasions when schools relaxed their dress codes to accommodate the heat. For example, just as there were rules governing girls' attire, boys also confronted dress code mandates. For example, boys were not allowed to go shirtless. Exceptions were made for boys when they were participating in sports because, as some explained, it was unreasonable to expect boys to keep covered up when physically exerting themselves in Hawai'i's piercing sun. Girls, however, were not given a parallel reprieve from the heat. Whether participating in sports or not, some girls pushed their luck and wore an inch or two less of clothing, hoping that teachers and administrators would not notice. Many girls who broke the dress codes were indeed able to avoid school sanctions, as evidenced by the fact that girls wore tank tops with spaghetti straps, tube tops, and even short shorts to school without being written up or sent home. These girls, however, were not able to avoid the punishing evaluative talk of their peers and were at risk of being "called out" in hallways or classrooms for dressing like "sleazes."

"Who You Stay With?": Girls, Romance, and Sexual Intimacy

Purity was measurable not only in terms of how girls managed their appearance, dress, and physical demeanor, including how much or how little of their bodies they revealed in public. Their sexual behaviors and romantic relationships were also up for moral evaluation. In this section, on girls and sexual intimacy, we uncover the complicated rules governing how and whether girls could claim sexually honorable statuses based on their behaviors in sexually intimate and romantic relationships. We also look at three different techniques that girls used to claim that they were behaving in sexually respectable ways, given the common codes of conduct for girls. These three techniques included the efforts of girls to claim that they were "virgins for now"; to demonstrate that they were "above it all," meaning that they were entirely unconcerned about dating and sex; and to demonstrate that their sexual activity was acceptable because they were in committed, monogamous (and heterosexual) relationships. We conclude this section by discussing the fact that boys were not held to the same sexuality rules that were applied to girls.

In the rural community of Northward, many youth grew up on Hawaiian Homestead lands within tight family networks. Even in the more urban

Stevens Heights and indeed in Honolulu itself, teens were often raised in close-knit extended families settled in urban enclaves. Therefore, both urban and rural teens were well aware of what other teens did outside school. As a result, girls' relationships—who they were "spending time with," who they "hooked up with," or, to use a common term, who they "stay with"—were common topics of moral evaluative conversation.

As noted, the boys and girls in this study placed a premium on sexual restraint and abstinence for girls. Boys often talked about admiring "clean" or "mature" girls and consequently, boys noted that these were the most desirable girls to have as girlfriends. Boys used the terms *clean* and *mature* to connote the idea that respectable girls were those who had had few, if any, sexual partners. When discussing sexual virtue, the girls, unlike the boys, did not use the terms *clean* and *mature*. Instead, the girls often said that virgins were respectable, with many of the girls using their status as virgins to project an honorable identity. Further, they felt that if a girl had sex within a committed, monogamous, heterosexual relationship, what might be called monogamous sex, she deserved respect.

For the girls, claiming a sexually honorable status was a complicated task and abstaining entirely from sex or even romance did not ensure that a girl could avoid a tarnished sexual reputation. For example, girls who were virgins could gain respect only if they displayed feminine, rather than masculine, traits. Virgins who were too "butch," dressed too much like boys, or who were too engaged in activities viewed as masculine (e.g., sports and fighting) were commonly denounced as being lesbians or "dykes." Moreover, girls who were virgins but who dressed too provocatively were decried as "trashy." The line between "butch" and "skank," "manly" and "hussy," was decidedly thin.[1]

Considering the harsh critiques launched against girls who were thought to display inappropriate sexual behaviors, the girls employed a few techniques to present themselves as sexually honorable people in their approach to boys, romance, and dating. Cassey and Angel, for example, aimed for a status that we call "virgin for now," meaning that they made a conscious decision to wait until a later date to have sex. Cassey said, "Girls will give anything to their man. But not me; I will not give anything up. I'm still a virgin. I tell boys that I am not going to give that up to you." Angel, like Cassey, also believed that her virginity was something to be proud of, and she did not hesitate to let people know that she "hadn't had sex yet."

In addition to espousing a virgin-for-now identity, Angel's story also demonstrates how girls' sexual respectability was often challenged, even when the girls had followed the rules governing female sexuality by being sexually restrained. For example, in addition to being proud of being a virgin, Angel also enjoyed her verbal assertiveness—what she called her ability to "tell it like it is." Unfortunately, Angel's straightforward proclamations did not make her popular, and, according to Angel, when girls wanted to attack, demoralize, and antagonize her, they often did so by casting doubts on her sexual honor. Angel explained the events leading up to her fight with another girl on campus:

> Like, a girl didn't like me and she heard I was from the mainland. She was like, "Oh I heard she gave birth on the mainland and she moved back to Hawai'i." So, they started making up stuff, and then, of course, I get mad because now everybody thinks, "Oh yeah she's a slut and she has a kid." If you have a kid, I won't think you're a slut. I just think, "Oh, she's a mom. That's cool." But other kids say, "She's a slut." So unreasonable. When I found out she said that, I was like, "Wow, I'm so important to her that she has to go and do research that I had a kid." Well you know, check your information again, because I haven't even had sex yet!

Angel's statement that "I haven't had sex yet," is similar to Cassey's proclamation that, "I'm not going to give that up to you." Both girls were clearly asserting a particular identity (i.e., the virgin-for-now status) within the very narrow definitions of appropriate sexuality for girls. On the one hand, virgins-for-now could claim that they were honorable for their sexual abstinence and their general restraint in being able to "wait" and not have sex "yet." On the other hand, by noting the possibility of having sex in the future, virgins-for-now could still argue that they were heterosexual. The claim of being a "virgin-for-now" was an identity maneuver and a preemptive move against anyone who might argue that a girl's sexual restraint was due to her homosexuality.

Illeana embraced a second approach to managing one's sexual honor, by being above it all. She was one among many girls in the study who abstained not only from sex, but also from dating boys, and therefore she could campaign for respectability because she was sexually restrained. She did not want to talk about sex, sexuality, or boys, and she generally felt as though she was "above it all," meaning that she saw herself as being independent from romantic attachments entirely. She said: "I don't really focus on relationships. It is like my last priority. It is not even on my list. Sports, basically, is what I do. I've just been told recently, I have a mentality like a guy. I thought I was different than all the girls, because they are all lovey-dovey and they think of one-year anniversary, six-month anniversary. I'm like 'What is that?' I was always like, 'I remember Valentine's and your marriage day, that's it.'"

Unfortunately, Illeana's positive sense of self, which was based on being "above it all," did not free her from being considered sexually inappropriate. Illeana's problem, according to her family, was that she was "too into sports" and not "into boys" enough. She explained: "Some of [my family] influence me on sports and some of them influence me to get into a relationship. They think that sports is turning me gay. They always introduce me to guys. My dad especially is like, 'When are you going to get into a relationship? Maybe you need to give the sports a break.' It is not every day you have a dad who wants you to be in a relationship."

Since girls needed to demonstrate some sexual interest in boys to ward off being labeled as gay, virgins-for-now were better able to gain respect than girls who were above it all. It should be noted, however, that even virgins-for-now could lose respect easily. Angel's conflicts with the girls who accused her of having a baby and leaving it with family on the continental United States highlight how easily virgins-for-now could be attacked and besmirched. In addition, any girl, regardless of her sexual restraint, who dressed inappropriately, by showing too much skin, was not respected.

Earlier, we noted that being a virgin was not the only route toward sexual honor for girls and that there was a third status that some girls attempted to attain in order to manage their sexual respectability. Having sex within a monogamous, heterosexual relationship was considered appropriate and acceptable by many teens. A girl who engaged in monogamous sex could maintain a positive reputation as long as her monogamous, heterosexual relationship endured. It should be noted, however, that even when a girl attained a serious, stable, and monogamous relationship, she continued to negotiate challenges to her sexual honor.

Annabelle's experiences demonstrate how tenuous the campaign for sexual respectability through heterosexual monogamy could be for girls. During her first two years of high school, Annabelle was in a "serious relationship," meaning not only that she and her boyfriend were monogamous (neither dated anyone else), but also that they spent most of their free time together—a sure sign of mutual commitment. Annabelle was not ashamed to admit that she and this boy were having sex, and she discussed, with close friends and some adults whom she trusted (including counselors and us), topics such as birth control and taking precautions to avoid sexually transmitted diseases. Annabelle had big plans and was not careless about her future. She wanted to graduate from high school and college early, earn a degree in nursing, and work as a traveling nurse, visiting new places and meeting new people. In fact, Annabelle became especially energized when discussing her career plans, and her excitement translated into her being cautious about her choices while in high school. Sex, like what courses to take, how to prepare for college, and how to manage her time in high school, was a consideration that she took seriously.

By engaging in sex in a sanctioned context (a monogamous, heterosexual relationship) and being careful about birth control and STD prevention, Annabelle felt that she was being a responsible, restrained, and sexually appropriate person. The fact that she was in a committed and long-term relationship with a boy whom she considered to be a "good guy" (meaning a kind and supportive person) only increased her sense of pride regarding her choices. There was also evidence that Annabelle's campaign for sexual honor was somewhat successful. She talked openly in the girls' group about the fact that she was using birth control, although her open discussions about sex were always couched within the context of her monogamous relationship. Other girls in the group nodded, smiled, and agreed with many of the points that Annabelle made during these frank discussions. No one contradicted Annabelle during or after these talks; in fact, we never heard anyone disparage Annabelle for the fact that she was having sex with her boy-friend. This indicates that there was tolerance for the type of sexual status to which Annabelle aspired.

Despite the fact that Annabelle's sexuality was not considered a problem in the girls' group, she had to negotiate negative stereotypes about sexually active girls. She explained:

> A lot of people thought that I was going to get pregnant. A lot of people had that in me. People thought that I devoted my time to him. I guess because my mom, she had my sister when she was sixteen, and my sister had her first kid at sixteen. So, it is going to fall into a routine like that. No one just believed me. Believe what you want to believe, but as me, how I am, if I were to ever get pregnant as a teenager, I would be very, very disappointed in myself. That is not what I want to be.

To understand Annabelle's worries about the cycle of teen pregnancy, we must look at the larger context that the Pacific Islander girls in particular confronted. Policy makers, community leaders, and school staff kept a watchful eye on teen pregnancy rates among the Pacific Islander girls as a way to assess the well-being of the youth in Hawai'i. Reacting to teen pregnancy as a community problem, these stakeholders responded to the notions that teen mothers were at risk for poor parenting, dropping out of high school, and a future of low-wage work (Males 1996). However, while they considered teen pregnancy to be a problem, the policy makers and school administrators were reluctant to provide daycare or other pro-grams to assist teen parents while they were completing school. The fear was that such programming would "send the wrong message" and encourage other adoles-cents to become parents.

The common view that teen pregnancy was a problem for Pacific Islander youth, along with the reluctance to provide programs for adolescent parents, translated into a particular reality for girls—a reality that Annabelle described. The problem of teen pregnancy was explained as a problem among, or more specifically *within*, individual girls. In Annabelle's own words, "a lot of people had that *in me*." Once again, the problem of girls' inappropriate sexuality was cast on and within the girls' bodies.

It is important to note that boys were not subjected to the same scrutiny con-cerning their sexuality. When we asked several boys in the lunch groups if they would consider it an insult to be called a slut, the boys giggled. Benny commented proudly, "I *am* a slut." In fact, in the focus groups, interviews, and observations, it was clear that boys were rarely the target of rumors, gossip, or insults questioning their sexual purity if they were "talking with" a girl or "did stuff with" a girl. In addition, boys' good names were not entirely ruined if they "got a girl" pregnant; in fact, one of the boys in the boys' lunch group was a teen father, and he never talked about his fatherhood as being stigmatizing or problematic. Moreover, this young father left the majority of the parenting to his baby's mother and her family. No one in either the girls' or boys' group discussed this boy negatively for being an absent father.

The expectation that boys would not or could not parent placed even more moral responsibility on individual girls. Pregnant girls were doubly damned, cast as "dumb sluts." First, girls were considered sluts for not taking necessary precautions to avoid pregnancy (abstaining or using birth control). Second, they were dumb for believing that their boyfriends would help them raise their children.

Sexual Double Standards and Horizontal Violence

When reviewing girls' efforts to demonstrate their sexual purity through their appearance and through their sexual behaviors, especially in romantic relationships, we have laid out two components of what are often called sexual double standards, in which girls are held to much stricter standards governing sexual comportment than are boys. How these sexual double standards contributed to girls' fights requires further explanation. In our minds, fighting for sexual honor between and among girls can be best explained by using the horizontal violence framework offered by feminist researchers (Brown 2003; Morash and Chesney-Lind 2009).

In essence, it was extremely difficult for a girl to claim a respectable status, at least as far as her sexuality was concerned. Many girls campaigned for a sexually honorable and respectable status, but found themselves besmirched, disregarded, and seriously disrespected in spite of their best efforts. Moreover, the failure to fit within narrow definitions of sexual respectability meant that girls were often fairly frustrated with their failed status maneuvers. As the horizontal violence explanation predicts, girls are not likely to direct their frustration at the pervasive sexual double standards surrounding them. Such double standards, after all, are abstract ideologies and meaning systems. There were much more tangible targets for girls who were angry. The direct targets for the girls' anger were usually other girls, rather than boys. A girl who gossiped, complained, and "talked too much" about other girls' improper sexuality was likely to be confronted by the girl who was the subject of this negative talk. These confrontations were often verbally loud, heated, and could escalate into physical violence. In addition, there were several girls at school, like Angel, who boldly denounced other girls' sexual honor within earshot. Such insults, hurled in the open, in front of other teens, could quickly turn into violence between and among girls.

FIGHTING FOR ROMANCE

The second most frequently mentioned motivation for girls' fights was to protect their romantic relationships. In addition to standing up to girls who cast doubts on their sexual virtue, some girls fought girls who flirted or "got with" (had sex with) their boyfriends—a trend that has been duly noted by many researchers (Adams 1999; Batchelor, Burman, and Brown 2001; Burman, Brown, and Batchelor 2003; Jones 2010; Miller and Mullins 2006). Looking at the culture of romance in general, researchers have noted all the ways that girls can become disadvantaged when they overemphasize intimate relationships with boys. According to the literature, girls who prioritize romance and connections to boys can become preoccupied with their appearance and attractiveness to boys (Adler and Adler 1998; Adler, Kless, and Adler 1992), take ancillary roles in boys' activities (Eder and Parker 1987), and underemphasize academic achievement (Kelly 1993). When combining insights from the literature on childhood and adolescence with the literature on girls' violence, we can see how engaging in interpersonal violence is one among many problematic outcomes for girls associated with the youthful culture of romance.[2]

As in many adolescent contexts, if a boyfriend in Northward or Stevens Heights "messed around" or flirted with another girl, his girlfriend usually blamed the other girl instead of her cheating boyfriend. Artz (1998, 2004, 2005) and Chesney-Lind (2001) and many others have noted that boys are often "let off the hook" and not held accountable for their wrongdoing, due to a "boys will be boys" ethic. Mara, Destiny, and Chevonne, three teens who participated in a focus group, discussed the fact that girls and not boys are often blamed when boys cheat:

> *Mara:* So, if there's a guy that cheated on the girl, the girl's gonna fight with the girl—the girl he cheated with—instead of, you know, just yelling at him.
>
> *Question:* So, what is that for? What does that prove, do you think, for the girls?
>
> *Mara:* Just stupid.
>
> *Destiny:* I think it makes them feel better, that they beat up the girl.
>
> *Mara:* And just to prove who's the better one.
>
> *Chevonne:* And to tell them not to mess around with my boyfriend.
>
> *Destiny:* But it's the boyfriend's fault.
>
> *Chevonne:* So, I don't know why they're taking it out on the girl.

Like Mara, Destiny, and Chevonne, many adolescents thought that it was "stupid" when girls confronted other girls instead of the cheating boyfriends. This seeming irrationality contributed to the common sentiment that violent girls were acting "dumb."

Illeana also agreed that many girls' fights were over "romance issues." Repeating a common refrain among high school youth, Illeana believed that fighting over a boyfriend was ridiculous. Earlier we noted that Illeana constructed herself as above it all, including petty concerns like sex, love, and dating. Illeana cherished her independence and did not care for anyone (girls or boys) who became obsessed with romance or who was, in her view, "clingy." She explained:

Remember how I told you about that boy: he mopes around and he thinks that I feel sorry for him, but I'm like, "Are you fucking kidding me?" I can't stand him. I'm so irritated, I want to slap him; seriously, like, "Get a life." I cannot stand clingy. When I get a reading [that] you are clingy, I run . . . . He is still moping around, acting like I should feel sorry for him, and I don't. I really don't. I pulled him out of class. I was like, "I'm sick of this. I do not like you. I honestly will never like you. I am not happy with you right now. Stay away from me. Don't come to my practices. Don't look at me in class. Just don't. You are not my boyfriend. You will never be my boyfriend." He gets jealous and starts moping around. I don't like him at all. I hate clingy guys. I hate clingy people.

In addition to being repelled by dependent and needy boys, Illeana was concerned that girls spent too much time focusing on boyfriends. The fact that some girls fought for romance was just another reason, in her mind, to avoid dating. On the topics of girls, romance, and fighting, Illeana said: "All these girls are like, 'Oh, I haven't seen my boyfriend in an hour. Oh, I miss him.' That's a bad thing. You are letting them control you. Without them [boyfriends] you can't do nothing. You can be in a relationship, but don't be so clingy. If it is not working out, break up. Don't make a big deal about it and fight with a girl."

Protecting Romance, Status, and Emotions

Despite the fact that many girls thought it was "stupid," "immature," and "ridiculous" for a girl to fight another girl because of a relationship, many girls did fight for romance. Understanding why girls fought to protect their romantic relationships requires a keen understanding of what romance meant to youth in this study and, in this section, we explore the meanings of romantic attachments. First, we note that romance (especially of the monogamous, heterosexual kind) was the only way that girls could be sexually active and still claim to be honorable girls. Second, we highlight how girls idealized romantic relationships as honored and high-status positions in the community. Third, in worlds where girls were often put down, ignored, and overworked, we argue that romance offered a chance for girls to be cherished, appreciated, and loved.

In our discussion above about why girls fought to protect their sexual honor, we also broached the topic of romance. We noted that sluts were girls who "got with" [had sex with] many boys and who were not monogamous. Beyond fighting to prove that they were not sluts, girls fought for romance for a number of reasons related to the meanings of romance in the community. Once a girl had established a monogamous, committed, and heterosexual romance, she was likely to fight to protect this coveted union.

It is important to emphasize that a girl who was not a virgin could only gain sexually respectable status if she was sexually active within a monogamous, heterosexual relationship. Inasmuch as all teens respected sexually virtuous girls, a girl who had been dumped or "thrown over" by a boyfriend would have a hard time claiming to be sexually honorable. Once she was "dumped," the source of her sexual legitimacy was gone. It is also important to keep in mind that many boys preferred to have "clean" and "mature" girlfriends, and this created a hierarchy among boys' romantic preferences. At the top were virgins and girls without a romantic past. Coming in second in boys' dating hierarchy were girls who had had, but lost, a previous monogamous and sexually active romance. Given this dating hierarchy, girls sometimes fought other girls to maintain the source of their sexual dignity.

The second reason why girls fought for romance was to demonstrate their commitment to romance as a revered type of relationship in the community. The status conferred to and the importance of the boyfriend-girlfriend union for girls can be understood by looking at the common mythologies about romance in the community, which were articulated in narratives that we call the *high school sweetheart story*. The high school sweetheart story, which could also be called the *one true love* or the *true romance* narrative, might be considered a mythology of sorts because it highlighted a type of relationship that was highly respected, often discussed, but very rare in the community. More specifically, the high school sweetheart mythology was that some high school romances could eventually lead to marriage and a happy family life.

In the following we examine the many nuances of the high school sweetheart narrative in order to highlight the importance and centrality of this idealized romantic relationship among teens in the study. Being in a high school sweetheart couple was a high status role. Girls who had a high school sweetheart not only had a chance to earn status among peers, they also had a source of intense and positive emotions. Making clear the complexity of the one true love scenario as an opportunity for a high-status role and positive emotions for girls will help us to understand why some girls would fight for their true romance.

Many teens honored legitimate examples of high school sweethearts, often citing the one or two cases of parents in the community who had fallen in love in high school. Based on these very few examples of high school sweethearts, boys and girls believed that the beginning of an enduring, happy, and successful marriage could be found in high school, although the girls, more than the boys, tended to aim for this type of relationship. Julian described his view and somewhat aloof approach to sweethearts: "High school sweetheart shit, like future wife and shit. It does happen. My mom and my dad met in high school, but they are the only ones I know. It happens and it doesn't."

In the eyes of many girls, high school sweethearts were different than couples who were "just dating" or "hanging out." Even girls who supported the idea that it was important to be "above it all" (e.g., above romance and sex) shared in the story about true romance. For example, Rae, like Illeana, vehemently warned other girls to not lose their independence "to a guy." However, she admitted that there were a few (very few) real relationships at school. She said, "The two relationships out of the high school are sweethearts. They know what they want in life and they don't hold each other back." Later in our interview, she qualified this statement and noted that some girls are not ready to be in a real "sweethearts" relationship, according to her definition. She commented, "Some girls, I really don't think that they should have a guy in high school. They are really not mature, and they think that they are going to mature with a guy. Like it is just going to rub off."

Although there were girls like Rae, Cassey, Angel, and Illeana, who avoided romantic entanglements for various reasons, there were also scores of girls who dated in high school. When pursuing romance, some girls told us that they were sure that they had found their one true love, with the sign of such a match being that they were overcome with intense loving emotions that were more passionate than anything they had felt before. These intense emotions, especially when reciprocated, were intoxicating and difficult to ignore. Surely, such a love was a sign of a real, genuine, and everlasting love. Also, if the boy continued to show the same emotional intensity over time (usually for at least two months, according to teens), the girl was sometimes convinced that she had found a legitimate high school sweetheart—her true romance.

In addition to offering intense loving and romantic emotions, the high school sweetheart narrative was compelling for girls because it offered some of them a rare opportunity to feel appreciated and special. In the last chapter, we explored how girls often felt like second-class citizens in their families and noted that they were often put down and disrespected by peers. True romance was an opportunity for girls to feel that they were loved dearly, as if they were the center of the universe, at least in the eyes of their boyfriends.

Annabelle's relatively long-term romance is a case in point. She and her boyfriend were constant companions, and both experienced an intense attachment right away. She said, "We told each other that we loved each other within the first week." There was considerable evidence leading Annabelle to believe that her union was unusual. First, the relationship was intensely emotional. Second, the relationship was enduring, lasting for many months. In contrast, typical dating relationships tended to last only two months, according to most youth. Third, Annabelle and her boyfriend spent most weekends together, watching movies, hanging out at her house, and doing any number of mundane activities together, proving that they were bonded through thick and thin, and not just during parties and fun evenings out. According to most teens, the hallmarks of a dating relationship, in contrast to a committed relationship, was that dating usually meant hanging out only on social occasions (beach parties, house parties, trips to the movies or the mall). Seeing one another regularly and spending time with one another's families was unusual and therefore a sign of a deep commitment.

Finally and most importantly, Annabelle felt that her boyfriend treated her better than her own family members did. Annabelle's mother often criticized her weight; her boyfriend made her feel beautiful. While Annabelle felt overlooked and less important than her siblings in her mother's eyes, she felt like the center of the world when she was with her boyfriend.

Unfortunately, Annabelle did not find the high school sweetheart type of relationship, and the end of her romance pointed to the problematic nature of the high school sweetheart narrative for girls. After a little more than a year of constant companionship, Annabelle's boyfriend broke off the relationship, leaving Annabelle with intense regret. She had a couple of boyfriends after her first high school sweetheart, but neither provided the warmth and companionship that she had experienced with her first love. By her last year of high school, Annabelle lamented her previous approach to romance. She said, "My boyfriend, he stopped me from a lot of things. He stopped me from going to soccer." Moreover, right before she graduated, Annabelle announced to Katy that she did not think that girls should date in high school. If she became a mother, Annabelle noted, she would advise her children to focus on school and wait to date until they reached college. High school teens, in Annabelle's mind, were too immature to manage the pitfalls of dating.

Romance and a Boy-Centered Culture

Above, we explored why some girls invested in the type of relationship called the high school sweetheart. While both girls and boys said that there were a few examples of adult couples who had met in high school and stayed together through the years, girls were much more likely than boys to invest in finding their one true love during their teen years. In this next section, we look at boys' discussions of romance. When compared with girls' tales about romance, love, and adoration, boys' discussions about girlfriends reveal a deep intimacy schism and imbalance. As many scholars note (Adler and Adler 1998; Adler, Kless, and Adler 1992; Artz 1998; Eder and Parker 1987; Eder 1985, 1995; Kelly 1993), teen culture is often boy centered, and therefore, the chasm separating girls' and boys' romantic investments has consequences for girls, lending another insight into why girls fought for romance.

In this study, some boys dated and claimed to have girlfriends, but boys often did not return girls' care and commitment, leaving the girls feeling heartbroken and isolated. Cassey described the difference between girls' and boys' approaches to love: "Girls remember everything about their relationship. They remember when they first hooked up, when they first kissed, where they went on their date. But it sucks because they [boys] don't remember. They don't remember anything, and that's what breaks our hearts."

Like Cassey, Rae noted that girls and boys had different approaches to intimacy and love. She argued that there were two types of relationships in high school: one that was characterized by "having fun," and one that was "serious." She said, "There might be a girl who wants a serious relationship and a guy who is less serious and just wants to have fun. That is just two different levels. The girl is going to want more of him and the guys is going to be like, 'I just want to have fun.'"

The gender divide in which girls "want more of him" and boys want fun had consequences for both girls' and boys' social networks. Boys with low romantic investments were able to maintain their male friendships, their activities, and other enterprises and concerns, usually concerns that had very little to do with girls. In contrast, some girls' high investment in romance mitigated their ability to maintain friendships or participate in other activities. As Annabelle said, "A person can stop you from a lot of things." During a focus group discussion, Destiny commented on friends who choose to spend time with a boyfriend instead of a friend: "You shouldn't choose between your friends or your boyfriend." Mara chimed in, "Then their friends get mad when they take their boyfriend over [them], like, 'Oh let's go out tonight,' and then she goes out with the boyfriend!"

While many girls who wanted "a serious relationship" were busy placing their romances ahead of their friendships, boys who were in search of fun, as Rae said, were busy with other plans. Instead of valuing romantic attachments to girls, many boys in this study participated in what Anderson (1999) and Bourgois (2003) describe as alternative masculinities and a code of behavior in which masculine prowess is highly valued and femininity is considered threatening. As a result, many boys in this study did not generally emphasize their connection to girls. In fact, some of the boys downplayed the fact that they had girlfriends. As the boys explained, girlfriends came and went, and sometimes acted "dumb." Instead of being identified by romantic relationships, many boys were committed to their male friends. Aaron, Junior, and Shawn, three teens in the study, described their views of girlfriends and friends as follows:

> Aaron: Some people keep it on the low, low, like they don't want anyone to know [that they have a girlfriend]. I have a girlfriend, and no one needs to know. It's between me and her 'cause your friends always come before a girlfriend or a boyfriend. Your friends come first 'cause they've always been there and stuff. If my girlfriend was acting dumb, I'd tell my friends like that. And they'd be like, "What? She's doing that?"
>
> Question: Do you guys think the same thing? Do friends come before a girlfriend?
>
> Junior: Dicks before chicks.
>
> Shawn: Joes before hoes.

Like the prevailing sexual double standards through which girls who were sexually active outside of monogamous relationships were harshly judged, but sexually experienced boys were praised for their prowess, there were also inequalities in the culture of romance that set girls up to lose respect and other important rewards. For example, the culture of romance was one in which girls, and not boys, made sacrifices including risking their sexually virtuous reputations, giving up time with their friends, and sometimes even giving up activities (like soccer). If a romance did not pan out, it was the girls, and not the boys, who lost status and their source of positive emotions, and were left with regret. Moreover, because some boys dated, but did not place much emphasis on their relationships with girls, the girls were literally "on the side" of the boys' lives. At the center were boys' friendships and activities. After all, in some boys' worlds, it was "Joes before hoes."

So far, the way that we have written about the inequality between girls' and boys' approaches to romance makes the dynamic seem particularly exploitative. The fact that some girls put up with poor treatment, such as coming second to a boyfriend's friends, giving up cherished activities like sports, and cancelling a meeting with a female friend when a boy beckoned, may make them seem exces- . sively naïve. In academic parlance, this vision makes it look as if the girls lacked any agency at all. There were, however, some key nuances in the everyday experience of heterosexual dating and romance that revealed why girls would put up with such poor treatment, at least for a while.

A few boys in this study admitted to "playing" girls (see Miller 2008). In this context, a boy played a girl by aggressively romancing her and promising, but ultimately not delivering, monogamy. Playing girls, however, must be understood carefully. It was true that there were boys who pressured girls to get sex, which many girls were reluctant to give. More often than not in this study, however, the everyday reality of "playing girls"—and the source of the girls' heartbreak—had more to do with fickle emotions than with conscious manipulation or efforts to "get over" on girls. For teens, emotions like love and passion were often intense, but also mercurial.

Benny exemplifies the male experience of intense yet shifting emotions. Benny was a particularly popular boy at school, and had a schoolwide reputation for being handsome, charming, and talented, if not a bit of a romantic wanderer. An avid poet, musician, and sketch artist, Benny possessed considerable sentimental acumen, easily talking with girls about the meanings and motivations underlying his poems, drawings, and musical riffs. Benny was also wise beyond his years and had, in Katy and Karen's opinion, the verbal skills necessary to talk his way out of many difficult situations.

During a camping trip for the lunch group teens, Benny joined Katy for a three-mile jog. Benny had competed on the high school track team and Katy was training for an upcoming race, so they made a plan to get up early one morning during the camping trip and work out. During the jog, they talked about life and what Benny was planning to do after graduation. Benny bonded easily with adults (especially women). With adults at school, for example, he often asked questions like "What makes a marriage last?" and "How do you find the right person to marry?" During the jog, Benny described the romantic dilemma he was facing at that time: "I feel bad about it, but I know what girls want to hear. I know what to tell 'em to get them to open their hearts to me." He also noted that, after a while, "I get bored. I get bored too easy." Benny seemed to feel genuinely guilty about his changing emotions.

Benny's description was typical of the rather innocent way that "playing" a girl unfolded in this study. Benny was being honest when he explained that he was searching for the right girl. For Benny and many boys in the study, pursuing a girl was an earnest effort to find love and companionship. At the same time, Benny's emotions, like those of many teens, were rash and changed quickly after the first month or two of feverish intensity. Here is where the search for a genuine high school sweetheart could end in heartbreak. Like anyone who falls deeply in love only to be "dumped" after a short duration of intense feelings, the teens, most often the girls, were devastated.[3]

If we consider girls like Cassey, we can better understand the way that capable and savvy girls could lose sexual respectability against this backdrop of unpredictable and fervid romantic attachments. For example, Cassey, by her own admission, was not likely to fall for a boy like Benny, who was known for having broken a few hearts. If, however, Cassey found a boy who had a good reputation (i.e., someone with a steadfast character), and who earnestly indicated that he was ready for love and commitment, she might be convinced to open her heart and "give up" her virginity. And if this earnest boy's emotions were fleeting, Cassey could be left feeling morally compromised. It should be noted that Cassey never found a boy worth the trouble in high school; therefore, she avoided this particular moral compromise.

Many girls in the study admitted that what they had thought was true love had been, in actuality, mere infatuation. Here, the girls were also heartbreakers. The end results of these failed romances, however, were different for boys and girls. The teens agreed that girls who were romanced and dropped multiple times were "stupid" for not figuring out the boys' games, and the teens spoke bitterly about these "dumb girls." Further illustrating how girls were disadvantaged by sexual and romantic double standards, when the boys were ready to be in a serious relationship, they avoided girls who had had multiple romances. As we noted previously, the boys were waiting for "mature," "clean" girls, so that when a girl's romance ended, she lost not only a source of positive emotions such as love, adoration, and warm affirmation, but also the chance to achieve high status as a committed and sexually virtuous girl. If a girl found that she was being "played" or if she picked an earnest boy with fickle emotions, her reputation took a notable nosedive, as she was at risk of being considered "dumb," "naïve," "too boy-centered," and "too dependent" on boys. Given this tangle of losses and negativity, it is no wonder why some girls would engage in violence if they felt that their relationship, and all the valuable assets contained within it, were slipping away.

"SOME BITCH I JUST CAN'T STAND": DENIGRATING GIRLS

The first two motivations underlying girls' fights (to protect sexual honor and romance) were relatively easy for girls to explain. Girls also alluded to a third motivation for girls' fights, but it was somewhat difficult for girls to clarify. Angel, however, tried to help us understand this third motivation by saying that she was excessively on edge one day and had fought one particular girl at school because this girl was "some bitch" who was "irritating her." Examining this phenomenon, in which some girls would beat down "some bitch" during situational contexts—times when the female attacker was feeling overwhelmingly irritated—we discovered a connection between the immediate provocative contexts in which fights between girls might erupt and an overarching, misogynistic value system in which girls were regularly denigrated, disrespected, and dismissed. In this way, these situational fights were violent outcomes of the ubiquitous denigration of girls.

To fully understand the misogyny faced by the girls in this study, we need to explore key features of girls' social worlds, especially their peer contexts. In addition to featuring several sexual double standards and being somewhat boy centered (i.e., boys enjoyed a special status and tended to be at the center of social life), the peer culture in which girls circulated was also one in which girls were commonly blamed, put down, ridiculed, and harshly judged, often for minor violations of norms. Indeed, the quotes in this chapter clearly reveal how common the denigration of girls was. Remember that Junior and Shawn referred to girls as "chicks" or "hoes"; in previous quotes, girls were described as "whores," "hoochies," "skanks," "dumb sluts," and "crazy bitches."

Boys' harsh criticisms of girls can be understood as stemming from their attempts to embrace a masculine ethic in which femininity is viewed as a threat. Here, putting down girls can be understood as a historic process of boys' socialization (Lesko 2001; Pascoe 2012). But girls also participated in the many rituals of denigrating girls specifically and femininity in general. In previous sections of this chapter we drew from the feminist literature that frames physically aggressive girls as enacting a type of horizontal violence (Brown 2003; Freire [1970] 1993; Morash and Chesney-Lind 2009), to note that when girls are frustrated, angry, and upset, they target other girls and not boys.

Girls in this study had many reasons to be frustrated, angry, stressed out, and extremely "P.O.ed" (pissed off): many of them were facing overwhelming circumstances and consequential losses. Indeed, there were times when girls were "irked out" by everything around them, and it was at these moments when some girls were likely to beat down a disliked "bitch." While this frustration was the broad situational explanation given for such violence, there were actually two more specific patterns underlying the immediate occasions when a girl lashed out at another girl who irritated her. First, girls spoke bitterly about girls who broke traditional femininity norms. Therefore, a girl who wore "hoochie" clothing instead of being sexually restrained, who "talked too much" instead of being quiet and compliant, or who was "bitchy" and "mean" instead of nice and kind might find herself the target of another girl's wrath. Second, girls were also troubled by a girl who was too "clingy," needy, and boy-centered, especially if said girl spent considerable time complaining, talking about, or crying over a lost relationship. Here, denigrating girls was a way of punishing girls not just for violating hegemonic femininity rules, but also for violating community-specific norms requiring girls to be independent, resourceful, and resilient.

Below, we draw from Angel's and other girls' experiences with peers, school staff, and adults in the lunch bunch to outline how girls attempted to manage negative feelings. We also discuss some of the lunch bunch conversations and norms, particularly in reference to anger management interventions designed to help teens negotiate negative emotions. The girls, it should be noted, were creative in applying the anger management lessons from the lunch bunch, sometimes applying these lessons directly and at other times using their own judgment and strategies about how to negotiate difficult encounters. Overall, the narrative below illustrates how girls experienced and made sense of complex negative feelings in the school context and how the schools tended to intervene when girls acted out in anger. We also directly trace how some girls' fights with other girls stemmed from girls' participation in a peer culture in which girls were condemned for violating hegemonic as well as community-specific femininity norms.

Angel was one among many girls whom the school administrators referred to the lunch group program not only for fighting but also for "acting out" in class. For example, Angel was often sent to the vice principal's office because she had verbally confronted someone in a classroom or hallway. Verbal disputes that did not end in physical violence were often categorized as "acting out" behaviors. Here, acting out served as a broad, catch-all category—something akin to the historic use of terms for wayward youth, like *incorrigible*, *disorderly*, or *ungovernable*. As in most schools in the United States, Cleveland and Seaside had informal institutional rules governing how teens were expected to verbalize their thoughts, opinions, and emotions. Critical thinking and sharing what the youth thought about class-related material was encouraged. Loud and angry talk, however, was discouraged and often labeled as disruptive. Angry talk included occasions when teens raised their voices and discussed, openly and honestly, their negative feelings after infuriated by some event, such as receiving a bad grade, a nasty look from a teacher, or an insulting remark from a fellow student.

As Schaffner (2006) recounts, there is considerable ambivalence in the United States about negative emotions like anger—especially for girls—although many of the teens in this study had, as noted, good reasons to be frustrated, upset, and enraged as well as devastated, hurt, and disappointed. Angel was grief stricken by the loss of her mother, while Annabelle and Illeana wondered how their parents could let doing drugs and getting high become more important than caring for their children. Cassey constantly worried about her mother, who was often "stressed out" after a day spent working at a fulltime job and an evening filled with heavy caretaking responsibilities for Cassey's grandmother.

Compound these significant worries and upheavals with the pressures of growing up female and we can see how angry talk might have provided girls with a chance to "blow off steam" and be heard. Hegemonic femininity norms requiring girls' to be "sugar and spice, and everything nice" can be disastrous for girls, although given how many losses, disappointments, and frustrations they confronted, the girls in this study were quite successful in finding nonviolent ways to express themselves. There were, however, bad days when someone said or did the wrong thing, at the wrong time, and a girl "just snapped."

How girls experienced and made sense of negative feelings, especially anger, came up during the face-to-face interview between Katy and Angel. Angel's dream was to go to law school. The legal profession, in her mind, was an opportunity to parlay her talent for making persuasive arguments into a career, but Angel realized that her quick temper might compromise her career plans. She described her concerns as follows:

Angel: Like this one day [in the lunch group], I asked nicely, "Can I have a drink?" and this boy just comes, he grabs my juice, and I was like, "Just don't touch my juice." I was so mad. "I'm going to put my drink down and I'm gong to fucking come across this table on you, boy." He come in here, he do whatever, because most of the boys, half of them ask me if they can have a drink, and I would refill it. But this nigger just came, grab the drink, filled it up, and then whatever.[4] I was like, "Okay, bitch! I don't know who you think you are, but that's my drink." Yeah, half of the girls asked too; if I have a drink, they are like, "Yeah, sure, I'll refill for you."

Katy: Angel, you know there will always be people who you don't like in the world. And remember, someday you will be a lawyer and you'll encounter people you don't like in that job too.

Angel: I know, but sometimes I think I can't do it, because of some bitch I just can't stand. Even when I go to class, I'm like, "Fuck this girl. She's here!"

In school, and especially during the lunch groups, Angel most often found ways other than physical violence to express her frustrations and anger. For example, sometimes just verbalizing her feelings was enough. As in the water incident she describes above, Angel could let people know when she was ready to snap. When Angel said, "I don't know who you think you are, but that's my drink," she gave clear warning to others not to step over her boundaries. Angel also did not hesitate to talk with adults and often articulately voiced her opinions and feelings to counselors, us, and some teachers. But not all of Angel's anger management strategies were what adults categorized as positive emotion management techniques. Angel admitted that on some days, the thought of getting out of bed and going to school was too much for her. On those days, she snuck alcohol from her aunt's house to numb the pain.

In the lunch group, talk about controversial matters like girls' anger was not outlawed, although counselors were likely to try to calm teens who raised their voices. Also, counselors listened to and did not verbally judge youth when teens discussed using drugs and alcohol, although they were apt to discuss how teens felt about themselves and their lives after a drinking or drug-taking episode, asking questions like, "Did your life get easier after you got high? Did the pain and frustration you were feeling before you got high really go away?" Embracing what is called a harm reduction approach (Inciardi and Harrison 1998; Nadelman 1998), counselors also asked teens if there were possible ways to manage stress and frustration other than by using drugs.

Despite all of the techniques used in the lunch bunch to help youth talk about and cope with negative feelings, Angel continued to have difficult days, and she often let someone "have it." Given this pattern, the idea that the main obstacle standing between Angel and her occupational goals was "some bitch I just can't stand" was an astute observation. At the age of sixteen, Angel could not stop fighting other girls, and this meant that she might continue to be suspended, fall behind in her classes, and fail to graduate. Without a high school diploma, completing college and law school would be difficult.

In addition to revealing that she was fairly self-aware, Angel's narrative uncovers a common trend among the girls in this study. As noted, the girls were vexed by both boys and other girls at school, but the vast majority of the fights that occurred in high school were intra-gender and not cross-gender, meaning that teenage girls fought with girls, and boys with boys.[5] As Angel described, she might become annoyed by a boy who took her drink without asking, the way a girl dressed, or how a teacher talked to her—but when bitter feelings erupted into violence, Angel (and many girls) "beat down" other girls. This pattern was relatively new for the youth: girls and boys had fought one another in elementary and middle school. One primary reason why fights were intra- and not cross-gender in high school was because teen boys who physically fought girls were usually feminized by other teens and seen as weak, unmanly, and problematic. On this topic, Junior, a Native Hawaiian student, noted, "I mean, if my best friend, like, hit his girlfriend, I'd be like, 'Brah, you know when you hit a girl, I'm on her side. I hope you get busted, you dummy.'" Here, high school boys who fought girls earned derision and condemnation, rather than respect, from their male peers.

When confronted with a girl's temper and threats in public, a high school boy would usually back down. Nonetheless, while remaining nonviolent, boys still tried to "save face." Some boys laughed at the girls who tried to engage in fights with them, often by calling an angry girl a "crazy bitch." Angel, in fact, was taller and stronger than many boys in school, and she did not hesitate to "get up in" a boy's "grill" (face) or let a boy know that she would "fucking come across this table on you" when she felt disrespected by him. In such situations, boys usually laughed at the idea of fighting with her, and Angel, in turn, would try to win these conflicts with her words rather than her fists. For example, when boys retreated from a physical conflict with Angel, she would often call them "pansies," "panties," or "queers," or hurl some other derogatory remark meant to insult a boy's heterosexual masculinity (Pascoe 2012).

In addition to verbally attacking girls, boys often spoke about and described girls in ways that revealed a general boyish disregard for girls' lives. As noted, girls did not rank high in some boys' esteem, and the overt condemnation of girls can be understood as part of a common trend among the boys in this study. As noted previously, some boys cleaved to a masculine ethic in which femininity was seen as threatening. Therefore, boys were likely to demonstrate their youthful masculine prowess by verbally undermining girls and all things associated with adolescent femininity.

Interestingly, the boys were not likely to openly insult adult women. Mothers, aunts, and grandmothers, in the boys' eyes, were important, albeit sometimes strict, matriarchs who kept children accountable to high standards. During our face-to-face interview, Phillip echoed a sentiment common among the boys in this study, who were respectful of, yet slightly irritated by, the women who were raising them. Phillip's feelings about his mother surfaced a few times during Katy's face-to-face interview with him.

[Regarding Homework]: I come home, and the first thing my mom says is, "Ho, you have any homework?" I guess it helps me get on top of my work. Some people's parents don't really care, they just bring them down a bit.

[Regarding Conflicts]: My mom is more about just sitting down and "talking it out" *[whispers]*. I don't like that. I can't handle that. Like, if I were getting mad at someone, I wouldn't just talk it out. That is how she is. She is a case manager. She has, like, a logical mind. I kinda don't like it 'cause it messes with my head. I'm more of a hands-on kinda guy.

[Regarding Discipline]: At school, I am allowed to give my own side of the story, so most of the times when I get in trouble, I think it is for stupid reasons, and I will just give my side of the story. Yeah, that's kinda how I am. My mom don't allow me to give my side of the story. She says, "This is what happens. You're in trouble."

Phillip constructed himself as being somewhat different than his mother, because he is a "hands-on kinda guy" (rather than a person who talks things out), who enjoys telling his "side of the story" (rather than being told what to do), and relaxing after school (instead of finishing his work). Despite these differences, he admitted that his mother had an important job (a case manager) and a "logical mind," and, ultimately, that she "cared" about him and helped him to "get on top of" his work.

As Phillip's narrative highlights, many boys in the study showed a reluctant respect for adult women. Therefore, boys who wanted to demonstrate their "manly" qualities by distinguishing themselves from all things feminine did not launch campaigns against mothers, aunties, and grandmothers. They reserved the full brunt of their efforts to forge an untainted masculinity for girls.

The above explains why boys disrespected girls. It does not, however, uncover why girls condemned and physically attacked other girls. As noted two important trends in aggression between girls emerged in this study. First, girls who broke with hegemonic femininity by being slutty instead of virtuous, loud instead of quiet, and pushy instead of compliant, were disrespected and considered worthy of "beat downs." Second, girls sometimes targeted girls who broke community-specific norms governing respectable feminine behavior. Being too meek, too needy, too boy-centered, and also too disrespectful of adult women in the community were seen as problems deserving a violent response, according to some girls.

Regarding targeting girls who broke traditional femininity norms, Angel's story, once again, helps explain a key trend in this study. When Katy asked what Angel felt was the biggest problem on campus, she forcefully argued, "Girls have no self-respect on this campus, for real. They wear hoochie clothing and show all their stuff to everyone. Someone has got to teach them how to respect themselves and not to go around looking like sluts." Months later, after Angel had been suspended several times for fighting, Katy asked her to describe how these fights started. Angel said, "These girls just irk me. I just don't like them. They get on my nerves. They dress like hoes, to begin with. So, I'll tell them, 'You look like a hoe.'" After Angel uttered this remark loudly in the hall, she and the girl at whom it was directed fought. Once again, Angel was suspended.

Joanna, a frequent "scrapper" (fighter), described why she picked a fight with one girl who annoyed her: "When I came to school one time, and there's this boy that I'm close with, and I didn't like his girlfriend 'cause she made him, I don't know, she made him so different. And then, like, ever since they started going out, he changed, and he went and he called out one of his own friends. I told him that if he was to do that, then I'd go after his girlfriend, and I did. Yeah, and I got suspended." Joanna, like Angel, was irritated by both boys and girls at school. The boy who "changed" and "called out one of his friends" (i.e., challenged a friend to a fight) was a case in point. Despite a general disappointment with both male and female teens, when Joanna's frustration turned into physical aggression, she challenged a girl instead of a boy. What is also interesting in her narrative is the fact that Joanna was particularly disappointed in the girl in question, who made her male friend "so different." Here, the girl in question earned Joanna's wrath because Joanna saw her as manipulative and controlling, rather than passive, kind, and supportive. Girls who were controlling and manipulative were clearly in violation of traditional femininity prescriptions, and therefore, in some girls' minds, they deserved to be physically punished.

Regarding attacking girls who broke community-specific norms, it should be noted that many girls in this study expressed a palpable disdain for feminine weakness and frailty. In fact, some, but not all, of the girls in the study who were frequently suspended for fighting, looked down on "girly girls" who made boys the center of their lives. Many of these girls were frequently bothered by, and therefore likely to fight with, girls who did not demonstrate proper resilience and independence. Angel, for example, laughed at girls who fell for the boys' many ploys to get them into bed. These girls, she said, were "stone cold stupid." Illeana sometimes spoke bitterly about other girls who prioritized relationships. During our interview, she stated, "I just don't like talking about relationships. It's like, seriously? If you don't like the guy, break up with him." Rae also mocked girls who were too focused on romance. Mimicking such girls one day, she sarcastically said, "'Oh, I'm in love. I love him so much. I like him.' I just see disappointment on my face. Honestly! I'm disappointed in you. You are fifteen, sixteen years old. Do you know how much more life you have ahead of you?"

Mona's fight with two sisters was a well-known event at school, and her explanation of the infamous physical conflict highlights how disrespect for other girls could easily end in violence between girls.[6]

There's these two girls that I never got along with because, like, it went back to last year, 'cause they messed up our whole volleyball team. And it was kind of retarded 'cause they were talking smack about everyone, and like, they were talking smack about the coaches and stuff. And so, like, ever since then, I never really had any kind of respect for them. And this past year, one of the sisters, I don't know why, but one day she just all of a sudden, like, bumped into me in the hallway, and she looked at me like I was stupid. So, I turned around and was like, "What the hell is your problem?" . . . So then the second lunch came, and I was standing by the hallway with some of my friends, and she crossed the courtyard with her friends.

So, as soon as I turned around, she, like, sidelined me. And she started drilling me, and then all the security guards came, and they held me. And so, she kept hitting me and my lip, like, busted. And so, her sister, I could hear her sister yelling, "Yeah, how's your lip taste? How's your lip taste?" And I got super pissed, so I told the security guard I was okay 'cause they were pulling the other girl into the office. And I told him I was okay and to let me go, "I'm fine." And so, he let me go, I guess 'cause he felt bad that my lip was all messed up. So, then, as soon as he let me go, I ran around everyone to get to her sister, and I started pounding her out. And, like, everybody came, and the security guard came—I felt so bad for him because I elbowed him in the face. And, like, he took me in the health room, and I was, like, hitting everything, and felt super bad after that. Yeah, that was what happened, and I got suspended for six days for that sh—crap.

Interwoven in Mona's narrative was an explanation of how girls who violated traditional and hegemonic as well as local femininity rules could be disrespected and, consequently, put in their place by other girls. Part of the reason why Mona disliked these sisters was because they had "ruined" the volleyball team the previous year, specifically by being "retarded" and "talking smack" about the coaches and "everyone" on the volleyball team. In Mona's eyes, these sisters did not deserve respect because they had been catty, mean, and gossipy. Examined in another way, Mona noted that these girls were outrageous because they failed to be kind, quiet, and cooperative—a few hallmark traits of hegemonic femininity.

These gossipy, mean, and uncooperative girls, in Mona's eyes, also threatened local femininity norms. When Mona noted that these girls were "retarded" because they were "talking smack about the coaches," she was referring to these sisters' violation of a deep-seated and community-specific femininity norm. One of the volleyball coaches was Auntie Maile, a respected matriarch in Northward. *Auntie* is a common moniker connoting reverence in Hawai'i; it indicates an adult woman who acts as an "other mother" (Collins 2000; Lopez and Lechuga 2007) and helps to guide, watch, and care for children, regardless of her actual biological relationship to these children. Auntie Maile was certainly an important female role model in Northward. She had been born and raised in Northward, and was friends with the parents of many Seaside teens; she also devoted enormous amounts of time to coaching girls in the community. There were very few free activities for teens in general, and girls in particular, in Northward; hence, Auntie Maile's and other female coaches' time was a valuable community resource that was worthy of respect. Therefore, when these sisters "talked smack" about Auntie Maile, they were denigrating a local female leader as well as "ruining" a coveted athletic opportunity for girls. All these were reasons why Mona viewed these girls as deserving a thrashing.

The girls in this study were not the only ones who commonly denigrated and targeted other girls. In fact, research on girls' violence in other settings has also suggested that physical aggression between girls occurs in places where girls are devalued or have limited opportunities for high-status positions among peers (Eder 1985; Merten 1997). In a study of gang girls, Miller (2001, 197) found that being accepted by boys "meant being willing to denigrate or accept the denigration and mistreatment of girls." Brown (2003) and Morash and Chesney-Lind (2009) framed female interpersonal attacks as horizontal violence and behavior typical of oppressed groups (Freire [1970] 1993). As we noted previously, horizontal aggression theorists suggest that because girls cannot take out their legitimate anger on boys without dire consequences, they take it out on other girls. The data from our study indicate that the girls in this Hawaiian context traversed extremely narrow, complicated, and slightly contradictory gender norms.

CONCLUSION

In this chapter we outlined the gender scripts thrust on high school girls and examined how girls negotiated them. Girls' fights were often meant to prove that girls were sexually pure rather than "slutty" (fighting for sexual virtue) and to maintain their romantic relationships (fighting for romance). In both cases (fighting for sexual honor and for romance), girls struggled to prove that they had achieved appropriate sexuality: restrained, monogamous, and heterosexual. In this way, girls fought to fit within hegemonic femininity rules, whereby good girls were expected to be sexually restrained, dependent on boys, and demure. We also demonstrated that girls fought to punish the bad behavior or traits of other girls. Girls fought not only to defend their status as sexually appropriate, but also to punish girls who violated femininity rules.

We also noted that the femininity rules governing high school girls were complicated. Girls were not just held to hegemonic femininity rules, but also to fit more community-specific rules requiring girls to be independent and outspoken and ready to become resilient women able to navigate the dislocations confronting their communities and families. In this way, any girl who was too "boy crazy," passive, and meek was also seen as a problem. The end result was that the expectations placed on girls were numerous and, at times, conflicting. Also, these complicated femininity rules meant that girls faced several no-win situations.

So far, the story about girls offers a rather pessimistic view. Girls were damned if they fit hegemonic femininity rules (i.e., they could be considered too boy-centered, needy, and dependent). They were also damned if they did not conform to hegemonic femininity ideals (i.e., they could be considered gay, too loud, or disrespectful of adult women). But as we will learn in chapter 7, girls were not passive recipients of derision and the micro-policing of their bodies, appearance, and demeanor. In chapter 7 we will reveal the ways that girls carefully evaluated their situations and crafted creative solutions to help them as they prepared for adulthood.

Boys' Fights and the Jacked-Up System

It is hard to tell time here. A persistent blanket of fog covers the city, making every hour of the day look the same. At 6 A.M., layers of mist blow through the downtown streets. Several hours later, Katy looks out of her hotel window, and things look no different. Cold. Uninviting. Obscured by white haze.

Katy is back in San Francisco, her hometown. By 2 P.M., she remains reluctant to leave her hotel room to face the fifty-degree August day. Summer in San Francisco is a depressing affair, she remembers, and she misses wearing a T-shirt, shorts, and sandals—called slippers or "slippas" in Hawai'i.

Putting on a heavy sweater, jeans, and a pair of uncomfortable shoes, she leaves her small hotel and walks a few blocks to the San Francisco Hilton—a behemoth structure in comparison to the building that she just left. The Hilton is not only big, it is also loud, as hundreds of American Sociological Association conference attendees gather in the lobby. Some chat in groups, while others stand in long lines for coffee. A few single attendees, like Katy, maneuver through the throngs of people in the lobby to attend conference sessions.

Cold and overwhelmed, Katy takes a seat in the crowded grand ballroom and waits to hear what a set of urban ethnographers have to say. Jooyoung Lee speaks first at the session titled "Young Ethnographers: The Police, Surveillance, and Violence." He discusses the phenomenon of "ghetto shootings" and how they come to the attention of emergency room workers. Next comes Alice Goffman, who talks about her research with a group of Black men from Philadelphia's Sixth Street (a fake name), whose lives and relationship to the police she described in *On the Run* (2014). Stuart Forrest presents last. He describes his research examining the survival strategies of homeless men and women, who, like Goffman's "Sixth Street boys," must "dip and dodge" the police as they go about their daily lives in the inner city.

After the speakers finish, the crowd grows silent as Elijah Anderson—respected sociologist and acclaimed author of *Streetwise* (1990) and *Code of the Streets* (1999)—takes his place at the microphone to discuss these young ethnographers' work. He offers insights with a good measure of encouragement, but in the end he puts forth a poignant critique. His words prompt another bout of reverence from the audience: he asks, "What about race?" Given that many (if not all) of the participants in Lee's, Goffman's, and Forrest's research are what sociologists call "racial minorities," where are the authors' analyses of race?

Anderson's question is prescient, resounding, and looms large in the world of professional sociology. What about race? What exact role does race play in our notions of advanced marginalization, the survival strategies of vulnerable groups, and youth violence in America?

· · ·

Back in Hawai'i with the lunch bunch teens, conditions are much hotter, so to speak. In such a location—a place where colonial control remains palpable—race, racialization, and racism have not escaped the attention of the Stevens Heights and Northward youth, especially the boys. In fact, one might say that much of the boys' activities, energy, and their campaigns for respect are "all about" race.

The boys in the present study, most of whom were of Native Hawaiian or Samoan ancestry, had the utmost concern about the race-based caste system they saw working against them. With considerable detail, they explained all the ways that they were demeaned, questioned, second-guessed, or seen as ignorant, dangerous, and troublemaking because of their membership in particular race and ethnic groups. They also explained how they fought against the injustices prevalent around them, especially derogatory racial myths. Sometimes they lashed out with harsh words, at other times with pipes and chains, but most often with their fists.

In the following chapter we outline how male violence in this study can be traced to racialization and historic race-based inequalities. The route from a history of racialization in the Pacific to present-day acts of violence between boys is a rather long and circuitous one. This chapter begins to outline the contours of that journey. In the first section of this chapter, we highlight the key features of the boys' critical consciousness of race and discuss variations and similarities in the racist stereotypes that the boys confronted. Second, we examine how interpersonal racism (e.g., racist remarks and race-based disrespect) is related to the boys' overarching understanding of how power, inequality, and corruption operate within relationships among boys, institutions, and the U.S. system.

In the third section, we closely examine those variations of racialized myths that boys felt were particularly problematic. By outlining how some boys attempted to position themselves as "fearless" and others tried to project "fearsome" personae, we note how histories of colonial racialization are connected to the boys' efforts stand up against disrespect and demoralization.

Finally, in the concluding section we examine how boys' interpretations of masculinity led them to feel that they had more power than girls and women, and therefore that they had the ability as well as the duty to fight injustice. Girls and women, in contrast were seen as vulnerable individuals who needed masculine protection.

RACIALIZED HIERARCHIES: YOUTH'S CRITICAL ASSESSMENT OF RACE

Three important subthemes emerged in the boys' critical assessment of race and racialized hierarchies. First, youth's definitions of race were highly nuanced and race, to boys, connoted different distinctions and groupings at different times. While race was varied and multilayered, teens agreed on a definition of racism, equating it with being disrespected because of their membership in particular racial and/or ethnic groups. Second, the ways that the boys experienced racist demoralization differed and seemed to map onto the history of racialization and Western colonial control in different regions of the Pacific. Because most of the adolescents in this study were of Native Hawaiian and Samoan ancestry, the distinctions between the racialization of Native Hawaiians and Samoans came to the fore. Third, attesting to the centrality of race in the boys' critical consciousness, the boys often understood other inequalities, like class, in terms of race. According to boys, having economic advantages was one among many benefits of racial privilege.

Regarding youth's definitions of race, boys certainly saw the world through a racial lens. More accurately, boys saw themselves as always and everywhere being constructed in racialized terms and as being treated according to the attributes thought to be inherent within particular racial groups. Most often, youth's discussions of race fell along ethnic lines, and many teens felt that the treatment they received was related to their status as Native Hawaiians, Samoans, or Tongans. While youth evoked ethnic groupings when discussing race and racism, their notions of race-based categories were complex. Sometimes, youth discussed themselves as being "mixed ethnic" or "mixed race," and thus they defied any effort to categorize them under a single group. There were also times when youth spoke in terms of binaries, locating themselves as "Brown" and, therefore, not White, Caucasian, or Haole (a common word for White in Hawai'i) or as "local," to differentiate themselves from those from the "mainland," meaning the continental United States. In Hawai'i, the "local" identity is a complex one that allows a person to claim participation in local culture (Fujikane 2000; Okamura 1980, 1994; Trask

2008), which includes the ability to speak Pidgin, the local language.[1] When evoking the local identity, youth traced the contours of the "mainlander" category (a word that the youth used frequently), describing mainlanders as privileged and powerful outsiders who had little respect for locals. Military families were the most frequent individuals from the continent whom youth encountered and being in the military was often synonymous with being a "mainlander."

Regardless of how youth drew the boundaries around racial groups, their constructions of race focused on a common process, namely the process of being demoralized and denigrated. That is to say, when describing racism in their lives, youth noted all the ways that they and other members of their group had been stigmatized, looked down on, demeaned, questioned, denied respect, and constructed as second-class citizens. It should also be noted that for many Pacific Islanders the moral judgments that were evoked in political debates about immigration and "noncitizens" on U.S. soil held a bitter sting. In the early twenty-first century, conservative political pundits often constructed illegal immigrants (i.e., noncitizens) as lazy, criminal, threatening, and dangerous to the moral fabric of America. What few Americans realize—but the boys were highly aware of—is that American Samoa is a U.S. territory and not a state in the union.[2] As residents of U.S. territories do not have full U.S. citizenship rights, those from American Samoa are called "U.S. nationals" rather than citizens, leaving many with a literal sense of being second class in America.

Considering that youth's definitions of race were varied, while their appraisal of the effect of racism was fairly unified, we offer a crucial insight about boys' violence that emerged from this study. Violence among these teens was often about respect—just as male violence scholars have suggested (Anderson 1999). But the boys in this study were very specific when they discussed respect: violence in their world was about fighting the myriad indignities of racialized disrespect. Masa described race-based disrespect and fighting succinctly by stating, "A lot of Hawaiians are mad at how you treat Hawaiians and stuff like that and that's how a lot of fights were started. And growing up, if you're not White, then you wouldn't get as much respect."

Discussions of racism revealed that youth were keenly attuned to particular derogatory images about themselves and their group and the youth were aware of both similarities and variations in the racist imagery they confronted. There was, for example, a common derogatory and troubling mythology about Native Hawaiians' passivity, naïveté, ignorance, and stupidity. Not surprisingly, many youth often chalked these images, which painted them as "stupid," "dumb," or "ignorant," up to racism, and they fought these racist beliefs in many ways. For example, one day, Katy asked Benny to discuss what he felt to be his greatest strengths and talents. He said: "I like poetry. Some people are judgmental because I'm dark skinned and Hawaiian. They think I'm ignorant because [of] my color, my race. But that's what they think. That's my strength, painting pictures, talking to people, people that want to learn, that want to hear me out, who want to know. I think when you hear me out, you see a different perspective of life and if you see that, and you understand that and you take it into consideration, well I did my job."

While Benny felt that talking to others and being willing to learn was one way to counteract the view that he was—because of his dark skin—"ignorant," other teens, such as Aaron, argued that he would physically fight anyone who called him "dumb." He said, "Yeah, like, it takes one to say 'Dumb Hawaiian' and all the Hawaiians get nuts!" In this quote Aaron is specifically referring to how fights are likely to start among boys.

The words "dumb" and "stupid" also came up frequently in Keith's discussions and he used these terms liberally, often to depict the traits that he considered undesirable and dishonorable. To Keith, being dumb was among the worst things that a person could be. Dumb people were lazy, unathletic, or unaware and, therefore, undeserving of his respect. His use of the terms "dumb" and "stupid" was also racialized in the sense that he tended to associate smartness with particular racial groups. As he discussed what he felt was respectable or shameful, he simultaneously evoked an underlying racial system of privilege. For example, when talking about his ex-girlfriend's mother, a woman whom he respected, he said:

> Just like my ex-girlfriend, my ex-girlfriend she is, no offence Miss [referring to Katy], but she's whiter than you. The husband [his girlfriend's father] is a realtor. He's no dummy. He is not dumb. His father [his girlfriend's grandfather] played three sports in college including water polo, football, wrestling. [My girlfriend's mother] she's a teacher, part-time teacher. She make you look stupid, that's how she is. She's full on blonde. White as light, crystal clear kind of White. She's multitasking, Miss, freaking-chronic. The most buff [muscular] fifty-five-year-old woman I've ever saw in my freaking life. Miss, you don't even know. She put me to shame. Active, paddling, community service stuff, she's active, you know how these Caucasian people are. They're always moving.

Despite the fact that Keith associated positive traits with this White family, who made Katy look "stupid" and also put him to "shame," he also understood racial privilege. Later in the interview he underscored the idea that much of the status that his ex-girlfriend and her parents enjoyed was due to their race.

> *Keith:* I'm not trying to compete with them or trying to be like them. I think life can be a lot easier.
>
> *Katy:* What do you mean by easier?
>
> *Keith:* As a Hawaiian, you know how our land and our culture and how it ends up to be. It's all jacked up. The States is jacked up, the whole United States system itself is jacked up and if you cannot see that, you're dumb and you're stupid.

Youth described confronting not only the imagery of the "ignorant" or "stupid" Native Hawaiian, but also images of Native Hawaiian passivity and ineffectiveness. Here, particular symbolic artifacts in the history of colonization in Hawai'i—such as the American suppression of the Native Hawaiian language and the dispossession of Native Hawaiians from land ownership in Hawai'i—emerged in youth's narratives and contributed to a lasting mythology about Native Hawaiians' inability to protect themselves from losses.

Some youth used imagery about Native Hawaiian losses to claim advantages in the prevailing racial hierarchies. Marcus, a Samoan boy, said, "I think we get more advantage than the Hawaiian kids. Like, we can understand—we still speak our language, but they can't. 'Cause sometimes we speak and they don't even understand what we're saying, so they don't even know if we're talking about them." Later in a group interview, Marcus, Erica, Johnna, and Travis discussed other ethnic differences that they saw.

> *Travis:* It's more like ethnic stuff. You know how, in the mainland, get like the Bloods, the Crips, yeah, all of that. But, down here, it's more like racial. Like the Hawaiians, the Samoans, the Tongans, Filipinos, Micronesians.
>
> *Marcus:* Like, all these Hawaiian kids, if one person's going to fight, and then they have one of their boys ready for jump in and attack the other person, you know, that's what they always do, always try to mob somebody. I don't know, they always causing trouble and stuff. They always want to try and fight. They always cause trouble with everybody. Like, they stir up all kind of trouble.
>
> *Erica:* I think they're just pissed 'cause—
>
> *Johnna:* Their land got taken away!
>
> *Travis:* Their land got taken away! *[group laughter]*

These teens' comments underscore the complexity of racial and ethnic hierarchies under settler colonialism. While Hawai'i is sometimes portrayed in an assimilationist fantasy as a peaceful and multiethnic paradise, these teens offered imagery about interethnic conflict and racial hierarchies. In these youths' eyes, the world is arranged along several lines of conflict, and some groups fare better than others. According to many teens, those who have lost the most, in this case, indigenous Hawaiians, who are dispossessed of land in their own homeland, rank at the bottom. Marcus, Erica, Travis, and Johnna's narrative also borders on naturalizing Native Hawaiian anger at and troublemaking because of historic losses. They assume an ingrained or innate Native Hawaiian anger about the loss of language and land, one which leads Native Hawaiian youth to "always cause trouble" and to fight everyone.

Despite their attempts to gain some symbolic advantage over others in race-based hierarchies, Samoan teens understood what it was like to bear the brunt of racist myths. For example, storied events in Samoan history have contributed to a lasting Western mythology about Samoans' ferocity, violence, and dangerousness (see Linnekin 1991), and many study participants frequently described the perception of Samoan men as being large, athletic, and powerful physical combatants. In a group interview, Jason and Cynthia, two young adults in the study, explained:

> *Jason:* We're barely ever represented as intellectual people.
>
> *Cynthia:* He's right, he's definitely right. And I guess that's why Samoans stick to that, the physical side, because we are known to be athletic people. We have a higher rate of our men getting into the football teams, you know the NFL . . . . But, my sister went out with a guy who was *palagi* [White] who was told by his other friends that Samoans are not so bright. So he perceived her to be stupid, to be like illiterate.

Interestingly, the Samoan adolescents in this study, especially the boys, acknowledged, but did not entirely lament these stereotypes. Instead, some viewed these common beliefs about members of their ethnic group as opportunities to elicit a fear-based brand of respect from others. Hence, some teens nurtured "fearsome" personas. Travis, Johnna, and Erica explained:

> *Travis:* But, I don't know what's wrong. Like, our size for our age, we're more advanced than, like, their size for their age. Like, they're all short and small, and we got freshmans all huge, all tall, sophomores, they all big.
>
> *Johnna:* All oversize.
>
> *Marcus:* I think they treat you better 'cause, like, they kind of scared. No, 'cause some people come up to me and they go, 'Oh, you guys' boys, you guys huge, yeah?'
>
> *Johnna:* Whatevers. They scared.

Palo and Jules also noted that the stereotypes about Samoans were an advantage:

> *Palo:* Stereotypes, you know, when they make assumptions about you without knowing you.
>
> *Jules:* There's a lot at my school.
>
> *Palo:* They think that Samoans are violent punks.
>
> *Question:* Is it a good stereotype if people are afraid?
>
> *Jules:* Yeah.
>
> *Palo:* It makes ourselves look good by showing their respect.

Because of these beliefs about a dominating Samoan physicality, Samoan boys in this study said that they rarely sought out fights, claiming that fights came to them. Marcus said, "'Cause its like, like every time we get into a fight, like, we don't start it 'cause other people always want to jump in, they come up to us and they want to fight. But we don't start it."

In addition to the above-mentioned variations, the overarching racial caste system presented some common challenges to all the teens in this study. For example, all teens spoke about images of the "dumb Hawaiian," the "ignorant Brown" person, or the "illiterate" Samoan, indicating that there was a universal view that being Native Hawaiian, Samoan, Brown, or local rather than White meant being treated as less intelligent. Also, many youth expressed the idea that there was a certain naturalness or biological basis for these perceived differences among racial and ethnic groups. Intelligence, Keith noted, runs in the bloodline, while Samoan participants also reported a lasting perception that Samoans are "big" and, therefore, naturally talented in athletics, as if athletic talent is a biologically determined trait of ethnic group members. And this biological difference maps onto another hierarchy whereby being big, athletic, and aggressive is juxtaposed against being smart, intelligent, and academically talented.

Teens' keen attention to race-based systems of respect did not mean that youth overlooked the importance of economic distress. As noted, many teens in the study were growing up in poverty and knew what it was like to struggle financially. Some, like Benny and Keith, had been homeless, and others were living in part-time arrangements, sleeping on floors or couches in a friend's or relative's homes. Most adolescents described their parents as "hard working" and "trying to make ends meet," although some teens admitted that their parents made money through illegal means. Given the economic profile of both schools (a little over 50 percent of the student body of each school qualified for the free and reduced-price lunch program), many were in this economic strata and, thus, did not see themselves as particularly different from their peers in terms of economic standing. Teens said that most of their neighbors struggled and "worked hard" just as their own family members did.

When boys described economic advantages and disadvantages, their discussions of class privilege tended to accompany discussions of race-based elitism. In this way, youth offered a view of racialized class, in which the privileges afforded to racial elites included, but were not limited to, economic security. The groups most likely to be considered elites in youth's eyes were Whites, mainlanders, and members of the military, whose economic advantages included getting "stuff cheaper," not having to work as hard as others, and as having everything "handed to them." Also, members of these economically advantaged groups were often believed to have racist attitudes. Chad summarized the common racialized-class view when he discussed interracial violence at school:

> Chad: There's a fight every day. Maybe it will go a month where this is not a fight, but then there will be a huge one. Last month, there was one whole week where there was straight fighting every day. In intermediate, I remember it used to be the base [military] kids and the locals. 'Cause they started calling all the locals pineapple pickers. There was a riot basically—all of the locals on one

> side of the school and all the base kids on the other side. Every single day after the school there will be four cops outside of the school. I guess the base kids they think they are better than us, guess because of their parents are doing something. I guess because they get more stuff cheaper and more things.

Katy: What does it mean to be called "pineapple picker"?

Chad: That makes it serious. It is racist. 'Cause back in the day all the locals and stuff—like, you all had to work on a farm and you had to pick things and all that. Guess that's where they are coming from on the base. They get everything handed to them. And they get things handed to them and they don't have to work as much. People see that and get all mad and there is violence.

Chad's narrative highlights a common youthful understanding of class and race in which economic differences created an underlying tension between groups, in this case between local and military families. These underlying tensions are heightened when privileged groups launch racist slurs, calling locals "pineapple pickers"—an act that, in Chad's view, started riots in school.

FIGHTING THE POWER: INJUSTICE AND YOUTH'S CRITICAL AWARENESS

At the same time that adolescents saw racism and racialized stereotypes, they also saw the world as generally divided between those who abuse power and those who struggle against the powerful. The boys were likely to use violence to "stand up" to those who egregiously abused their power. It is important to remember that the teens' sense of power was seen in racial terms. As noted, youth in this study almost universally saw Whites, mainlanders, and the military as falling into the category of the powerful. They also viewed their own history—what many might call the history of their ethnic group—as punctuated by injustice at the hands of the powerful.

So while many of the boys' fights were initiated by a racist slur, their race-based motivations for fighting also operated on a more subterranean level and pointed to the boys' critical consciousness of power relations. Violence, in this way, was often an expression of boys' efforts to fight for justice.

To date, much of the literature on street violence underscores the idea that violence can be a way of enacting justice. Violence as street justice is often viewed in terms of an act of individual self-help (Black 1983, 1993), in that perpetrators view themselves as people who cannot turn to the police or other formal legal means for assistance. In the introduction, we noted that in Anderson's (1999) thesis, the code of the street fills the gap left when social services and systems break down. As we previously quoted, the "law of local people and its corresponding street justice"—which is often violence-based—is in these circumstances more reliable that the justice of the state (Anderson 1999, 314).

But in contrast to the individualism emphasized within the street justice literature, the boys in this study focused on somewhat more altruistic facets of violent justice and noted that they sometimes used violence to maintain a balance of power and especially to punish those who were seen as abusing their power. In this way, boys were concerned about more than whether they themselves had been demoralized or were at risk for being taken advantage of. In some ways, they saw themselves as agents who were morally responsible for ensuring an overarching fairness operating among community members. Here the boys were particularly concerned that there be a system of fairness or a type of just relation among boys and men in public spheres. One variation on altruistic violence and youths' sense of justice was the boys' almost universal distaste for battles in which two or more individuals attacked one boy—a circumstance that teens called "mobbing." Jared defined mobbing: "Like a bunch of people just beating up one person. Because you should be fighting one on one, if you have a problem with that person, you shouldn't be having other people [fight]. That's like you can't fight back. Yeah, it's not a fair fight so a lot of people just look at that and that makes them mad; they really want to beat up that person."

Jared later described the problem with mobbing in more detail: "The mob thinks that they are so hard and I guess they feel like, 'Oh we're going to beat up this boy.' And then since they all have strength in numbers then they'll start feeling more power over somebody that doesn't have as much power as the others." In this way, the boys' outrage at mobbing showcased their collectivist concerns. It wasn't just the individual victims of a mobbing incident who wanted to seek retribution, but also bystanders, who balked when boys took advantage of their power in numbers to gain an unfair advantage.

Boys also felt that mobbing was unfair because it could gravely injure another person, or as Joel said, someone could be "very seriously hurt." Not only did Joel indicate that he would "jump in" during an unfair fight, but he hoped someone would intervene if he were being mobbed, pointing to what he hoped was a common courtesy in the community. He explained, "If somebody could possibly die, then I'll stand up and say, 'Hey what the fuck you're doing?' If somebody was going to kill me, I would expect somebody to stand up and do that for me. And if I would expect that, then I would do that."

The boys' concern with mobbing indicated the existence of a loose set of rules governing violence. Fights were not meant to kill or seriously injure other boys. Ideally, they were meant to be contests of physical prowess and skill, something akin to athletic competitions. If a fight was unfair—in other words, did not represent an equitable contest of strength and skill—then some teens, like Joel, believed that people should "stand up" against whoever was misusing their power. The problem, however, was that there were some gray areas, with youth disagreeing over the specific rules governing fairness in fighting. Because boys sought physical justice for an unfair brawl, one fight could easily generate subsequent battles meant to restore a balance of power.

Joel and his brother Julian described how fighting to seek justice could lead to more conflicts. Joel, Julian, and their cousins were engaged in an ongoing grievance with another neighborhood family. The trouble started with what Joel and Julian felt was an unfair fight, in which their cousin was brutally beaten and sent to the hospital with a broken jaw and nose. Joel described the fight:

> You know those metal poles they used to make those fences? He had a short one and a little boy had a bat and he brought [it] over [his cousin's] face. They bust his grill [face] up. Yeah, they broke his teeth, they piped him over his head, his elbow, yeah pretty much his face. Actually it came out of nowhere, it pretty much did. My cousin just went over there, shook everybody's hands, "What's up boys?" Came to spend time with them for New Year's and this other boy, he was a little turkey before, and then he used to get beat up. Like maybe in intermediate, he was like one hundred-something [pounds], but now he was like three hundred hundred-plus [pounds]. Yeah, he just pushes around his weight.

Joel thought that this was not a clean fight for a number of reasons. First, the fight, according to Joel and Julian's perceptions, started for no apparent reason. Their cousin had shown appropriate respect, shook these boys' hands, and sought their friendly company for New Year's day. Second, the offending boy had misused his power by "pushing around" his weight. Third, the injuries were extreme and resulted in a long stay in the hospital. Thus, the physical thrashing, in these boys' eyes, was overkill.

Julian attended school with the boy who had brutally beat his cousin, which meant that he had to endure the sight of and "mouthing off" from his enemy everyday. As the semester progressed, Julian became increasingly irritated by this boy's "shit talking" and began to anticipate getting retribution. Retribution would have to wait a bit, however, as Julian had broken his arm in a skateboarding accident and believed that fighting in that condition with the boy from the enemy family would have resulted in an unfair fight. In the following, Joel described Julian's eventual fight and the honor code governing violent justice:

> Joel: Then Julian was waiting until his cast came off and the day it came off, the boy got what he deserved because he was talking shit the whole time. Julian could have gone bust them up when he had the cast, that would be a disadvantage to the boy. That wouldn't be fair. The rule is you fight one on one. If they would respect those rules, if they were to stand by and obey by those rules, then the families wouldn't get involved, then there would be no need for retaliation.
>
> Katy: How often do people obey those rules?
>
> Joel: [Laughing] Not often.

Julian's refusal to engage in an unfair fight reveals abstract notions of justice that correspond to teens' critical evaluation of the world. Youth were keenly attuned to power between and among people and groups, and aware of power as a resource that could easily be abused. In youth's own words, people who use "power over somebody," including people who misuse their "strength in numbers," could be seen as deserving violent justice, which should play out on a "one-on-one" basis.

Corresponding with teens' understanding of abuse of power, many youth felt that corruption and manipulation among authority figures were common. The teens' discussions after a field trip to the University of Hawai'i provide an example of their cautious view of authority figures. That year, the teens' college campus tour had been hosted by members of the university outreach program, who discussed student support, scholarship, and academic opportunities at UH. While returning to the high school, the youth began to discuss how expensive college was and how their families were not likely to be able to afford school. Katy reiterated the tour guides' messages about scholarships and noted that there were scholarships that go unused because people don't apply. On that note, one teen asked, "So what do they do with the money if it doesn't get used?" Another student offered a quick answer, "They probably keep it for themselves. They probably don't want it to be used." Katy tried to explain that this would be illegal and unlikely, but the teens seemed wedded to this low opinion of the education system.

In some ways adolescents' critical lens and their perception of morally problematic behavior in the present resonated with their interpretation of oppression and injustice in the past. Youth, for example, often identified and described key historic events that highlighted injustice. The U.S. government's imprisonment of Queen Liliuokalani (Hawai'i's last monarch), the illegal overthrow of the Hawaiian kingdom in 1893, and the alienation of Native Hawaiians from land ownership were well-known events and were universally understood by the teens to be immoral acts. There was also a sense of persistence to the immorality inherent in this history, such that youth discussed these events, especially the loss of lands, as if this fact would always be present and would always organize relations between and among people. Masa, for example, discussed a common sentiment among youth that this history would "always be there," although he noted that individuals' orientation to these facts might change as they grew up: "I think when they're young they didn't really know what they meant when they're saying 'You took my land,' and stuff, but it's like, that specific person didn't take your land. There's always going to be that— 'You took my land' and all that stuff—just the way kids think. There's always going to be that type of thing with Hawaiians and others. It doesn't mean it'll be like guys are always fighting and stuff, it's just going to always be that kind of way."

Joel also believed that the problem of lost lands would always loom large in his and other young people's consciousness. He said, "Well, I always think about that [the taking of lands]. I think that it was wrong but we can't change it, what's done is done." Although Joel agreed that the taking of lands and overthrow of the Hawaiian kingdom, would "always be there," his personal orientation was decidedly resilient, uncovering a fortitude common among the adolescents. He explained his view of his life, given historic conditions: "For me, I wouldn't change my life for anything. I love my life just the way it is. But if what happened didn't happen, then I would be fine with that too."

While most youth in the study were knowledgeable about the colonial history of exploitation in Hawai'i and other Pacific Islands, youth also maintained different relationships to these facts according to their ethnic groups. For example, Mara, Chevonne, and Junior, three Native Hawaiian youth, indicated that the loss of Hawaiian lands was an important point of group identification for Native Hawaiian youth.

> *Mara:* That's another thing about Hawaiians. You have to stand up for your culture because they just took over our land, yeah? So it's like, "Oh, this is our land still. You know, still fight for it. Don't let nobody take it." And that's your place, don't let nobody take over it and stuff. That's just how Hawaiians, I guess, or Polynesian people just are. Like, "Don't let them take."

> *Junior:* As a Hawaiian, you just feel like, "Oh, they came to my land, they took over my land," you know. It just makes you feel like they're better than you are. And in actuality, they're not better than us.

> *Chevonne:* They have more power.

Some researchers might attribute the teens' discussions about put-downs and feelings of superiority and inferiority to the in-group/out-group dynamics typically at work in youth peer groups (Tajfel 1970, 1978). These teens, however, saw something deeper than interpersonal peer dynamics. They saw power imbalances between groups, especially the imbalance of power lodged in social systems that allow some groups to gain advantages over others. The interpersonal, therefore, takes on larger, more systemic significance.[3]

Adolescents' narratives returned to some common themes in their critical assessments of the world. Abuse of power, corruption, and unjust social systems haunted the teens' consciousness, both as problems from the past and as persisting dilemmas in the present. While youth could not correct these historic injustices, they could take action in the present and many boys saw violence as an effective way of righting wrongs.

BEING FEARLESS AND FEARSOME: RESPONDING TO RACIST MYTHS AND INJUSTICE

Just as there were some variations in the racist tropes circulating around the teens, there were also some differences in how the boys attempted to violently confront racial demoralization. Because most of the boys in the study were of Native Hawaiian or Samoan ancestry, the ways in which they fought race-based stereotypes mapped onto the myths circulating around these two groups. In the following section, we explain how some boys responded to racialized myths by crafting "fearless" personas, while other boys evoked a sense of "fearsomeness."

In terms of racialized myths, as noted, many youth tended to see Native Hawaiian history in terms of a history of injustice, "takings," and "loss"; stolen lands and the loss of language were key discussions that came up in the study. Also, youth noted that such losses corresponded to a sense that now, "that's how Hawaiians are. . . don't let nobody take," although no one in the study discussed literally engaging in violence to fight for land. Remember also that the imagery of lost lands, lost language, and lost culture accompanied notions of passivity, being duped or tricked, and being taken advantage of.

Some boys' discussions of violence seemed to take into account the stereotypes and imagery of historic Native Hawaiian losses. For example, some teens explained the importance of fighting against anyone who tried to dominate or manipulate them. Many youth argued that they would fight, figuratively and literally, against anyone who tried to have "power over," "mess with," "pick on," or otherwise try to take advantage of them. Phillip, for example, said, "Like me, I don't like to be told what to do. If you force me to do something, I probably won't do it. Some people that's just how they are, they like to have power over others. If someone is trying to have power over my life, I'm just like 'no.'" Kyle noted how efforts to resist domination could lead to violence. "That's what it is, domination—when others try to act up, to dominate you, that's when troubles start."

Being taken advantage of, pushed around, and passive in the face of domination was problematic in many boys' eyes. Moreover, these traits were often associated with being fearful or afraid to stand up for what is right. Being fearless, in contrast, was seen as honorable and many teens suggested that being unafraid to stand up against domination was a matter of survival. Phillip said, "You will just get picked on and all that. You have to fight to show that you are not afraid of anyone. If not, you will get taken advantage of and, if you can't handle it, then suicide." Also equating standing up with survival, Benny argued, "It's the way to survive or I would die. Yeah we had to grow up fast. Just don't take shit from anybody." Reiterating the importance of being fearless and unafraid of violence, Benny also said:

> Disrespect leads to fights. People don't back down, they usually trying to make others "awk" [act like a chicken] and back down. What really causes problems is that people come and they boss you around, do this, do that, and guys take it personally. Then they have one problem. Freshmen always try to make a name for themselves. That's what I did my freshman year, that got me into all kinds of trouble. I tried to make a name for myself and show people that I can scrap [fight] and that I'm not scared. "Oh boy, he can scrap, he's not scared!"

Male violence researchers often note that within the codes governing violence and respect in disadvantaged neighborhoods, "the most fundamental norm is 'never back down from a fight'" (Matsueda, Drakulich, and Kubrin 2006, 338). Benny's narrative reveals that the same was true in this context. Looking closer, however, Benny also points to the multidimensional meanings of respect in this context, in which toughness, "having juice" (Anderson 1999), or showing "nerve" (Katz 1988) means more than just being willing to fight. What is likely to lead to a fight, according to Benny and other boys, is being bossed around and told to "do this, do that."

It is important to note that winning a fight was desirable to many youth, but not necessary for a boy to demonstrate his fearlessness and earn respect. Benny and other boys in the study, for example, noted that they occasionally lost fights, especially against older boys, but that they were proud to come back to school ready to fight again. Boys who lost fights could still earn respect because by fighting, they showed that they were fearless and willing to confront anyone who tried to dominate them. Cornel noted, "You still get respect, even if you lose." And Benny agreed, "It doesn't matter if they win or lose, as long as they fight, they don't back down, or if they lose, some people are like, 'You lost,' but most people give you props [respect] for scrapping."

Violence was not only a way to resist negative images, it also provided some youth with a chance to manipulate common stereotypes. This was especially true for youth who discussed common beliefs that Samoans were large, powerful, and physically dominant. While adults like Jason and Cynthia (quoted above) felt that the myth of Samoan violence and ferocity was a problem, some boys capitalized on these associations and interpreted the common fears about men in their ethnic group as signs of respect. In this way, some boys used stereotypes to nurture their fearsome reputations. Travis, Erika, and Marcus, three Samoan teens attending the same high school, discussed their responses to perceptions of Samoans:

> *Erika:* Don't you guys, you hear everywhere, people are like "Oh, yeah I got beat up by a big Samoan guy" and they think they're bad, like, and they got beat up!
>
> *Marcus:* They think that we're gang people!
>
> *Question:* What do you guys feel about that?
>
> *Travis:* I feel pride! Yeah, don't mess with us! We're Samoan!

While they did not seek fights to prove that they had nerve or juice (Anderson 1999), some Samoan boys manipulated and played on others' fears of their ethnic group to gain advantages in particular situations. For example, Travis and his male friends frequently capitalized on their thuggish outward personae at school. Calling themselves the "hallway boys," they congregated in the main walkway at their school during passing periods and "stared down" other teens who walked by. Travis enjoyed this ritual and described what happened when other teens passed his section of the hallway. He said, "Yeah, they like, they'll be with their friends, they all humble. I mean, they come around, they can talk, talk, talk, walk past the aisle, [then] everybody's silent." Stopping their conversations and walking by Travis's peer group in silence was a sign of humility and respect, albeit a respect based on fear.

BEING A MAN

In the following section of the chapter we uncover the boys' sense of gender hierarchies. As we have noted, patriarchal societies often position gender in dichotomous terms: girls versus boys, women versus men, feminine versus masculine, weak versus strong, private versus public, passivity versus agency, victim versus perpetrator. Not surprisingly, a boy's attempt to "be a man" included distancing himself from femininity, weakness, passivity, and vulnerability. While the boys interpreted being a man as having agency and being strong, they also understood that "manliness" included a particular responsibility to protect individuals who were weaker and more vulnerable than themselves. Their campaigns to protect the weak (including girls and women) were waged in public arenas, and not in more intimate settings. In fact, the boys were rather silent when it came to power imbalances between males and females in families and in romantic relationships. Private, intimate domains were feminized worlds, and thus not the focus of male attention.

The boys' interpretations of weakness drew from heterosexist and patriarchal scripts (Connell 1987, 2005; Kimmel 1996), in which lacking male strength was interpreted as being feminine and homosexual, and failure to conform to dominant masculinity norms (including heteronormative expectations) held serious consequences. For example, the boys often used nuances of the masculine/feminine divide as a weapon against other boys. The boys in this study were similar to boys in other settings in showing their "supreme contempt for another boy" by calling him "a girl or liken[ing] him to female behavior" (Ferguson 2001, 173). Failure to be a strong young man or boy in this setting was almost universally seen as being "a fag," "a cry baby," or "girlish" (Pascoe 2012). Alika, a high school senior, discussed what happened after his uncle convinced him not to fight with Joe:

> My uncle told me walk away from the fight. Oh, you know, how hard is that? He tell me, "Walk away." After that, when you walk away from a fight, people going to tease, brag, all kinds, especially me—the boys that I cruise with. So I walk away. Couple of days went by, I heard rumors going around saying, "Oh, you one fag. Yeah Alika, you walk away." I was like, "Brah I had to. My uncle was right there." Nobody was believing me so I let 'em go, let them talk crap. So, I ask his friend, try to talk to Joe to see if he's still talking crap about me. Sure enough, he said I cry like a little girl. That's a rumor, I don't cry. So, right there recess came, boom.

In their efforts to construct themselves as fearless or fearsome, boys revealed a social hierarchy among peers. Individuals with masculine traits such as not backing down from physical confrontations were at the top of the social ladder. Boys who walked away from fights were seen as effeminate ("fags"), emotionally weak ("cry babies"), and childlike and feminine ("little girls").

We see that the social stratification system bestowing honor or shame was rigidly divided in terms of gender and sexuality. Though youth often noted that they hung out with a "diverse crowd," meaning that friendship groups were often multiethnic, crossing the gender division by having friends who were girls was problematic for boys. Girls were for dating and sex, not for friendship. Masa explained why he was chastised in school:

Masa: Because it was ingrained in my head that I wasn't good enough when I was young.

Katy: What's giving kids this feeling that they're at the bottom?

Masa: We just brought up knowing that we don't want to be the lowest. They kind of go by rank, like how important they are. I would be the only boy playing with the girls and then boys started calling me a girl and then I would get mad. And I had like a group of friends that I would kind of—like they were the ones that called me a girl first, and I started getting more mean with them, and the first boy I'd grabbed from behind then I just squeezed him from behind.

It wasn't just femininity that was reprehensible for some boys. Being childlike was also dishonorable. Joel, for example, argued that being a man was equal to standing up for what was right. Being a child, conversely, was seen as being passive and ineffective:

Joel: If you get into a fight, then the way I would see it is, maybe after the fight it would be all good because this guy was man enough.

Katy: Would you ever be friends with someone who stood up to you?

Joel: Yeah, I would definitely want to be friends with them. Yeah, because they stood their ground. That's when you find out who is a man and who is a child.

The association among being a child, being passive, and being defenseless was especially keen for boys with traumatic childhoods. Benny was a case in point and noted several times that he never had a real childhood because he grew up in circumstances that were "devastating." He said:

Once my mom left, it was devastating. No more mom figure and you think about it, at my age and all the shit I've been through in my life. What is there? What's to think? There's a reason why you've been through all that shit. It was devastating and shit like that. I mean what mother would leave their kid to suffer? I was put in foster care when I was in eighth grade. My real dad at least tried. At least he fucking try. You know what I mean? Like try and support us that one year before we got taken away.

That's the most effort I ever saw him put into something. I was sort of brought into the world, into this unforgiving harsh reality. When you're young and you kind of find yourself helpless.

Benny had visceral memories of being helpless, passive, and vulnerable—states of being that he never wanted to experience again. Here is a key takeaway point in this study: it was not just girls who experienced loss, trauma, and hurt. Boys' gender socialization meant that they had a different approach and response to being vulnerable and helpless.

While many youth saw the world in terms of those with power and those without, boys in particular believed that there were those who abuse and those who are abused, those who hurt others and those who are hurt. In such a scheme, it is not surprising to see that boys also saw survival in gendered terms. Being victimized, passive, taken advantage of, and conquered was to have feminine properties and to be "worthless." Being masculine and a being a man, conversely, was to have authority over your own life and the ability to confront abusers. Joel explained how he associated survival with being a man:

> For me, being a man is you're always willing to fight for what's right, whether you get physical or mental, as long as you're always willing to fight for what you stand for and believe in; then that's what makes a man I think. If I had a son, I would let him fight. I would tell him, be a man and you stand up because if this person wants to hurt you, you better hurt him or else he is going to hurt you. Just to survive, because if you can't survive, then your life is worth nothing.

The way that boys often spoke about girls and women in the community reinforced the idea that many boys naturally associated femininity with being passive and vulnerable to victimization. The mistreatment of women and girls by men, especially in public, therefore echoed larger power arrangements. And given that men were seen as possessing the authority and strength to resist domination and "right wrongs," the effort to protect women was laid at the feet of men. Luke, for example, discussed how a friend's dad had responded to one incident of sexual abuse: "I respect the military because they fight for our country. But, they make like they have a lot of power over us civilians and stuff. They think they can get anybody. My friend, we went camping and one of these military guys went up and whacked his mom, on her ass and stuff. And the dad went over there and beat the guy up like badly."

Also echoing the idea that military men misuse power, Trevor described why men fight to protect women: "Like the military guys, they act like they got the biggest dick. They go to a club and they think they can get all the chicks and stuff and they're just making troubles to themselves. They try to rub up on the wrong girls. Like the boyfriend could be standing on the side letting his girl have fun on the floor. But this guy comes up to her on the floor. That's how fights at the club start, White guys acting stupid." In this story, economic and cultural colonialism in Hawai'i and history of "takings" is told in a particular way, using gender-based metaphors of injustice. As Trevor notes, young military men are likely to assert an inappropriate masculine entitlement. They assume that unaccompanied women in Hawai'i are open for sexual contact (to be "rubbed up on"). As Trevor notes, a seemingly single woman is not free for the taking. She is likely to "belong" to a nearby man. Therefore, an inappropriate claim to a woman, like an inappropriate claim to a possession, is an act of injustice that requires an appropriate response, namely violence.

In this scheme, failure to fight against injustice is failure to be appropriately masculine. In boys' narratives, the need to fight against injustice and transgression, and to right wrongs, especially those in public realms, was a masculine enterprise. Moreover, girls and women—who were seen as passive, vulnerable, and weak— were not thought to possess the skills necessary to resist oppression, domination, and abuse. The formula for male violence, therefore, was in many ways engineered by an overarching consciousness of power that all youth shared, together with a sense of masculine agency.

CONCLUSION

Boys in this study were talented observers of the world and had developed a sophisticated consciousness of power arrangements, usually through the filter of their own personal experience with derogatory and racialized myths. Through a lens of demoralization, these boys came to understand that a rigid race-based caste system was working against them—although they also recognized that race-based hierarchies were complex and contained key variations.

While fighting was one way that boys attempted to resist these negative constructions, boys' fighting was not only about nurturing individual reputations. Because boys had a keen sense of power and corruption, they were attuned to larger injustices including key historic examples of corruption and used violence as a means to even the odds or at least to punish those who abused their power. In this vein, boys had a visceral distaste for being taken advantage of, and saw being picked on or unable to resist domination as tantamount to being unable to survive.

Boys' use of violence to punish the corrupt and resist demoralization was also tied to boys' sense of masculinity. Where several researchers have argued that boys and young men who use violence are enacting a type of "hypermasculinity," boys in this study might be said to be enacting a masculine agency, in which it is boys (and not girls) who are seen as possessing the traits necessary to correct injustices, confront those who abuse power, and fight for what is right. Girls, in contrast, are seen as vulnerable, passive, and easily abused. The boys interpreted the world in terms of conflicts, divisions, and status hierarchies. Their masculine agency gave them advantages over girls and the masculinity messages around them told them that they should avoid being vulnerable, abused, and pushed around at all costs.

6

Sea of Good Intentions

*Juvenile Protection in the Shadow
of Punishment*

There is a paradox at the heart of how the United States, as a nation, treats fighting. On one hand, the United States has a history of opting for military might over moral suasion in its international affairs while, on the other, it condemns the use of violence and harshly punishes the least powerful for aggressive behavior. America's colonial history is a model of violent conquest of land and peoples, with the right to keep and bear arms embedded in the Constitution. Over the past century, the United States has become a dominant military superpower on the world stage. Political leaders who pursue diplomacy in the face of conflict are often characterized as spineless and weak. Violence, role modeled by the state, also permeates American popular culture. Many of the most profitable pastimes involve physical battle, from football and boxing to wrestling and mixed martial arts. We are, in many essential ways, a nation-state steeped in an economy and culture that perpetuates violence.

The United States has also established a culture of discipline to control interpersonal violence. Throughout jurisdictional levels and across institutions, U.S. legal codes include a cascade of laws disciplining social behavior. Since the 1980s, a broad set of laws, passed under the mantra of "zero tolerance," have mandated punishment of students for an array of actions deemed to be harmful. Zero tolerance policies began with mandatory sentences for serious felony crimes in schools, such as those related to firearms use and illegal drug trafficking. But the reach of mandatory sanctions widened to include many less serious offenses, including, on many school campuses, tobacco use. Schools also designated a range of penalties for those who engaged in fights on campus, including out-of-school suspension and, in some cases, expulsion or transfer to another school. Rather than determining consequences for harmful behaviors primarily on a case-by-case basis, these new rules prescribed a fixed set of consequences that led to more punitive treatment of youth.

School policies often did include counseling and other interventions to prevent fighting and other acts, but supportive student services were offered after punishment had been served and were often not adequate to address the deeper issues at the source of the conflict or harm. While state policies sometimes required both punishment and supportive services, resources for the latter were often lacking, leaving punishment as the main consequence. Thus, nationwide, the balance between helping youth handle emotions and conflicts in peaceful and restorative ways versus meting out punishment was heavily weighed toward the punitive end of the scale (Hirschfield 2008), especially in communities of color (Skiba et al. 2002).

The result is that while youth are receiving messages that glorify the performance of violence in everyday life, they are also receiving some of the harshest penalties in legal history for acting with violence. We point out this irony since it is only fair to turn our gaze to the state. In this way, we take the panoramic view offered by colonial criminology and underscore the importance of historic context, highlighting the conflicting messages sent to youth about the righteousness of fighting and the harshly negative consequences they suffer for doing so.

We found stories of resilience among youth who were struggling to find their way through many institutional mazes. We also found many adults within the education and juvenile justice systems working compassionately to support youth who had been apprehended for fighting. These stories prompted us to question how compassionate interventions by a wide variety of adults has coexisted with a national environment of punitive policy.

The study findings presented in this chapter advance our scholarly understanding of punishment by building on existing critical theories. Critical theorists argue that as raced, gendered, and classed institutions, schools and juvenile justice systems help reproduce the status quo and reify the constitution of individuals as subjects in a political order (Garland 1990). While that may be the pattern in broad strokes, what we found at the local level was more ambiguous and inconsistent. Taking a close look at schools and juvenile justice institutions, we see the porous nature of institutional reach. The human element operates at the micro level, in the interface between youth and adults in positions of authority. It is at this nexus that we can see the permeability of the institutional fabric, which appears smooth and uniform at the more distant macro level but patchy and rutted up close. Despite a strict "tough on crime" policy environment, there were numerous individuals within the schools and the justice system who took a restorative approach, operating in in what we call the "grey zone of discretion," where adults had "wiggle room" to be innovative and compassionate. We found many adults who utilized their discretion to do what was in their power to help youth successfully exit the system and transition into a supportive environment.

One emerging pattern among adults in positions of authority was that some adults went to great lengths to nurture youths' ability to make healthy decisions for themselves. In contrast to paternalistic approaches towards adolescents, in which teens are perceived as lacking the capacity to make sound moral judgments, these adults took a strengths-based approach, focused on bringing out and building upon the capacities and competencies in each youth. Because they extended this support, they were able to engender an open and positive response in turn. They approached youth with respect and dignity. This respect in turn allowed them to tap and nurture youths' ability to think through problems, while aiding teens to make different decisions. They helped teens build empathy and created spaces for self-reflection.

This pattern speaks to a second, policy-relevant contribution to the ongoing debate between "harsh" versus "lenient" approaches to disciplining youth. We argue that such a dichotomy is not useful. Instead, we suggest that policymakers focus on what we call a "capabilities approach to an ethic of care," which counters the disempowering tenets of colonial patriarchy and the emphasis on authoritative punishment in shaping behavior.[1] This approach supports neither positions of harshness nor leniency. Rather, it focuses on building the capabilities that youth need to lead healthy and fulfilling lives. We urge policymakers to look more closely at the power of caring relationships and the moral education inherent in an ethic of care (Noddings 2013; Owens and Ennis 2005).

For most, caring is a natural response that arises in interpersonal encounters with loved ones. Who doesn't want to feel cared for? This feeling of caring may not exist for all people at all times, but committing to an ethic of care can be motivating in and of itself. Noddings (2013, 139), one of the early proponents of this idea, writes that "when we need to draw on ethical caring, we turn to an ethical ideal constituted from memories of caring and being cared for," which allows us to see "how to respond to loving efforts at care in a way that supports those efforts." How people treat one another may bring out the best or worse in them; when adults approach youth with an ethic of care, we see them tap youths' potential to care in return, and motivate them to build their capacity to understand themselves and others.

We begin this chapter with the stories of June and Auggie, two adults who looked back on their adolescent experiences. Both had been arrested as youth, in separate incidents, for assault. We review the rise of zero tolerance approaches over the past twenty-five years, both nationally and in Hawai'i, placing June and Auggie's experiences in a larger context. We juxtapose the harsh treatment and severe mandates of zero tolerance policies with the practices of compassionate administrators and staff in both schools and juvenile justice systems. In spite of the larger punitive policy environment, different philosophical approaches to youth violence have endured, including restorative ones. We do not use the term *restorative* as it is defined in criminal justice vernacular, nor do we dismiss punishment as part of a restorative approach (Daly 2000). Rather, we use it more broadly to mean those approaches that focus on helping youth address the problems that lie at the source of harm, on restoring individual well-being, and on mending relationships that have been broken in the course of their lives.

JUNE AND AUGGIE: PUNISHMENT AND PROTECTION

Punishment for a Punch

June was a "local boy" of Filipino ancestry born on the big island of Hawai'i. He grew up on Oahu in an urban neighborhood that had historically been home to many working-class and new immigrant families. He lived with his father and stepmother and attended the local public school. His relationship with his stepmother was highly strained, as "she just constantly trash talked" his birth mother, whom he dearly loved but who could not fully care for him at the time. He recalled that when he was fourteen years old, his stepmother once again made critical remarks about his mother. That day, it was more than he could take. No longer able control his anger, he swung a single punch and hit her in the face. His father, who was furious, jumped in to intervene. Two weeks passed and June heard his name called over the loudspeaker while in school, "June, report to the main office please." He was met by police, arrested, handcuffed, and escorted down the hallway to the police car. His stepmother had filed charges against him for assault. He described that moment:

> I was trippin' because I was a good kid and never got called to the office. So I was shocked to hear my name to go to the front office. Next thing I know I see this police officer and I go, "Oh, no, what's this for?" [The officer said,] "We got news about what you did to your stepmom," and I started bursting out into tears. And then my counselor was there to talk to me about it. Then I got handcuffed and, from the office, got escorted down the school hallway for something I didn't do in school. I was just walking in shame with my head down.

He was taken to the police station where he was patted down and was seated handcuffed to a table. He continued: "Once at the police station, that took a lot of toll on me. The police station was new for me. It was the first time I've been booked. It was traumatizing 'cause I seen a lotta shows like *Cops* and movies and all that. And I was afraid I'd be put in a cell with this huge dude who would take advantage of me or something like that. So I had a lot of fear in my mind. Like I didn't know what to expect. Honestly."

He was later transported to a detention center, where he was strip-searched and forced to shower. From the detention home, he was moved to a number of placements, starting with an emergency shelter and later to several different group homes. His father terminated parental rights, so he no longer had a home. He finally settled in with foster parents. He still saw his birth mother and sometimes his father.

Auggie went through a similar experience. Auggie, like June, had been born and raised in Hawai'i. Her parents were refugees from Southeast Asia and her father fought alongside U.S. troops during the Vietnam War. As the U.S. military exited, her parents were flown to the United States and eventually found themselves in a refugee camp. They moved to Hawai'i and Auggie grew up in the same community as June. While she was young, her father passed away and her mother developed a schizophrenic disorder. She and her three siblings and mother eventually became homeless. The children were placed in different foster homes, while their mother was sent to a shelter. Auggie had recently become a teen at that time and was very close to her siblings, whom she relied on, as the youngest of the four. She ran away from her foster home a number of times to be with her siblings. She accumulated a record of runaway charges over the next several years.

While in middle school, she fought with another girl. She was arrested and taken to the state's detention home. She was pregnant at the time and spoke of the experience in the juvenile justice system as traumatizing and demeaning. She recalled her first encounters, at the point of intake into the detention facility, having been transported there by police: "When I got there, there was intake in the front. And when they took us to the back, they had me strip down all of my clothes to see if I had tattoos or bruises and things like that. And then they had us shower. It was like a five-minute shower. It was humiliating. It was degrading. It was just unreal . . . I was given a panty that hung down to my knees. I used recycled clothes." While the detention home was designed for short-term confinement for those who could be a danger to others or to themselves, some, like Auggie, stayed for longer periods. Auggie was released to a residential shelter after her first week in detention. But she ran away from that shelter after feeling intimated and threatened by its staff. She was returned to detention, where she stayed an additional month.

Auggie's experiences in the shelter, detention home, and under probation supervision were mixed, depending on the personnel she encountered. She had a very good experience with one teacher at the detention home, where she took part in a woodworking workshop and other activities. She compared this with the treatment she received from some of the staff at the residential shelter, whom described as intimidating. She explained that it sometimes "felt threatening," when staff would "tease" her with a strong undertone of condescension. She was grateful, however, for the presence of a few "aunties" whom she felt had her best interests at heart.

Her mixed experiences with staff continued while she was under probation supervision at the family court. She had a contentious relationship with her probation officer (PO) there, who, she felt, made unnecessary threats, such as threatening to recommend to the judge that she be placed in a youth correctional facility. She recalled this threat: "That's why we got into an argument. I was sooo upset. And then she just walked away. And then she 'forgot' that I was in DH [detention home] for a long time. It was around a month, but for us that's a long time not to hear from your PO about when your next court date is or when you might be getting released."

Auggie admitted that she had not been a particularly cooperative ward. But she stated, "I thought I had to challenge her because she was constantly trying to punish me." She recalled her feelings at the time: "The things I had to go through—not knowing what was going on, being pregnant at fifteen years old—I was afraid. I was scared and I didn't know what the future was like for me or where I would live. You know, things like that." She disagreed with her probation officer's approach, especially the threats of harsh punishment. "That's not the approach I would take as a PO—to use your power as leverage. I don't think that's right." Auggie spoke reflectively, stressing that "acting out is often a cry for help."

From the point of view of probation officers, who often work hard to seek opportunities on behalf of a given youth, a probationer's repeated rebuff can lead to a level of frustration that may interfere with professional conduct. Professional self-care and continuing education for probation officers is often lacking or underfunded (Brown 1987; Whitehead and Lindquist 1985). Factors such as legal considerations and personal attitudes may also affect officers' judgments (Ward and Kupchik 2010). Moreover, youth probationers may not report unprofessional behavior on the part of their probation officers, out of fear. For all these reasons, youth can suffer as a result of embroiled relations with officials who represent the law.

June's and Auggie's stories are instructive in several ways. First, they epitomize the negative consequences that youth experience as a result of the distinction constructed between adolescence and adulthood, which undermines the ability of youth to explore their options. Both June and Auggie expressed frustration with the way they had been treated by many personnel they encountered. They often felt either "treated as criminals" or "disciplined as children," rather being acknowledged as autonomous "human beings." Both felt that if their voice had been respectfully heard, they could have gained more capabilities and developed coping mechanisms more quickly and with less heartbreak. As Auggie shared, her probation officer's threats and punitive actions only made her more resistant and rebellious. While she expressed heartfelt gratitude to those who had helped her along the way, she remained critical of those who had treated her condescendingly, as a "criminal" who needed to be "scared straight."

Second, both stories illustrate the potentially harmful consequences of punitive treatment on youth's well-being and behavior—the "collateral damage" caused by an overly harsh system of discipline (Mauer and Chesney-Lind 2003). June and Auggie felt that the trauma inflicted as they were "processed" through the system had been damaging to them and other youth, although both noted that they had the internal strength to withstand and overcome the challenges they faced. Because both had the love of parents, along with mentors from a variety of programs and networks, they endured relatively well. But they knew that this was not the case for many of their peers.

Third, for both of them the condescending attitude and punitive practices they faced in the juvenile justice system overshadowed more promising ways to resolve problems in their lives. While they both genuinely regretted throwing the punches that had led to their arrests, they also felt that the system's response occasioned unnecessary trauma and shame. In June's case, for example, the disciplinary process did not allow him to formally apologize to his stepmother and father. He regretted the fact that he could have, but was not able to mend those relationships, which was what he deeply desired.

The Caring Adult

June and Auggie were forced into early adulthood, facing adult responsibilities before they turned eighteen. But both had caring adults in their lives. As for others like them, the most effective intervention had been to have a mentor—a caring adult who guided them through life's trials and tribulations.[2] These mentoring relationships began through connections made in schools, and took the form of emotional support as well as instruction and guidance through big and small problems.

June found a close mentor in Kamaka, who taught him everything from how to drive to how to cook. June described him as the one whom "I looked up to when we had rough times . . . he helped me become an adult." June explained that "he wasn't just a case worker but an older brother and father figure . . . he really cared about me and pushed me to do my best." June eventually enrolled in a local community college, majoring in the administration of justice. He later transitioned to a four-year college where he needed "help with papers and how to study properly." Kamaka supported him at each stage. June maintained his involvement in a community-based leadership board made up of other foster care youth. June said that these activities "made me feel good about myself . . . I felt blessed and I wanted to pass on the blessing." He became an advocate for other foster care youth.

Auggie also credited her mentor, Valerie, for stepping into her life at one of the most important points during her youth. Auggie, who met Valerie at school, initially disregarded Valerie's attempts to communicate with her. Auggie confessed that she "ignored [Valerie] all the time." She explained, "I had trust and abandonment issues. I thought she was being phony. When I finally reached out, it was the best thing." She went on:

She is my earth angel. When I had to turn myself in, she would take me out to eat pho and then take me to the police station and sometimes she would wait with me until 2 o'clock in the morning until they took me. She was actually the only approved person on my list to receive phone calls and visits. She came to visit me almost every single day . . . She was the one to buy me all of my toiletries, my hygienes, my clothes, my books. That woman is amazing. I was pregnant and I was getting bigger and really uncomfortable. And she wanted me to feel good. So she bought me pink shampoo, pink conditioner, a pink toothbrush, and pink toothpaste. It really made me feel valued, that she would go out of her way to do something like that for me.

Valerie was a working professional who, along with Auggie's foster parents and mother, gave her the support she had desperately needed. At the time of this study, Auggie admitted that she was still struggling, now as a mother of two young children. But like June and other peers, Auggie remained active in advocating for foster youth.

Auggie's and June's outcomes are notable. Despite their negative experiences in the juvenile justice system, they both maintained high aspirations. Both credited a mentor for helping them turn their lives around after their arrests. These mentors were people in the community who simply cared enough to go out of their way to be there for them, and not for just a month or two. These mentors, together with unconditional love from family members as well as care from adults at school and the justice system, helped to light their way through difficult teen years. Most youth were not as fortunate as June and Auggie in finding a caring mentor. But wouldn't it be miraculous if more adults within institutions practiced an ethic of care?

JUVENILE JUSTICE IN HAWAI'I: THE CONTINUED SEARCH FOR THERAPEUTIC JUSTICE

There is a puzzling contradiction in Hawai'i. The juvenile court system has been nationally recognized as one of the more therapeutic courts in the nation. Wilma, a longtime juvenile court staff member, recalled how her office received inquiries from across the country because they had a therapeutic family court model, emphasizing the "rehabilitation and reconciliation" of families.[3] Yet, as the stories of June and Auggie reflect, youth in the system had very mixed experiences, encountering professional behavior that could be seen as empathic and empowering and other behavior that appeared harshly punitive and traumatizing.

The punishment literature portrays the ever-present reach of a punitive and retributive national policy environment toward youth as a dome with little penetrative light. Certainly, without a restorative policy framework, the scales can easily tip toward the hand of harsh retribution, especially during resource shortages. But our research revealed that the dome of punishment is much more porous and uneven than scholars have stated. In fact, there was a stronger therapeutic ethos in the Hawai'i family court than the prevailing policy environment would suggest, though paternalism also continued, both in practice and in policy.

Below we review major and recent juvenile justice policy reforms in the United States. Though mandatory sentences date back to the nation's first penal codes, the hyper-revival of this approach during the 1980s and 1990s was marked by a record-setting number of mandatory minimum penalties, the lengthiness of those penalties, and their wide application to nonserious offenses (U.S. Sentencing Commission 2011). Zero tolerance policies proliferated during Reagan's "War on Drugs," beginning in the 1980s, and expanded under the Bush administration.[4] The landmark federal Omnibus Crime Bill of 1994 along with federal- and state-level "Three Strikes" laws increased the number and scope of mandatory penalties. California's original 1994 "Three Strikes and You're Out" law carried one of the harshest penalties among states in the United States, including a prison term of twenty-five years to life for a third felony, even if was a minor as shoplifting or writing a bad check.[5] The rationale for such policies was that certain and stiff punishment would deter illegal activity. Though many remained unsure that stiff penalties did effectively deter illegal behaviors, this approach was soon applied across a wide range of problems, from environmental pollution to school violence (Skiba 2000).

Honolulu, like other midsized cities, responded to national shifts, even though violent crime rates in the state were among the lowest in the nation. These trends affected the juvenile justice system and the educational system, as well as general beliefs about the nature of violence and violence prevention. One irony is that while professionals in the justice and educational systems prided themselves in taking a supportive approach to youth, the state system was also characterized by several punitive juvenile justice policies and practices, gaps in critical services, and a lack of family-centered and culturally-grounded programs. Native Hawaiian and Pacific Islander youth were particularly affected by these problems (Umemoto et al. 2012). This is no indictment of individual professionals within the justice system. Rather the facts point to the need for critical reflection and review of systemic policy impacts, resources for supportive youth programs, philosophical orientations and attitudes of professionals, and the role of culture in restoring health and well-being among youth and their families.

The juvenile justice system in Hawai'i falls under the jurisdiction of the family court, founded in 1965 with the Family Court Act.[6] Founding reformists wanted the court to be "felt in the community as a positive force for family stability, a sympathetic friend for families in distress, and a center for research and planning in family law problems" (Corbett and King 1968, 39). In fact, according to Kuhn (1998, 68), the term "therapeutic justice" was coined by an early family court judge in Hawai'i to describe a practice that "concentrates on empowering families with skills development, assisting them in resolving their own disputes, enhancing coordination of court events within the justice system, providing direct services to families when and where they need them, and building a system of dispute resolution." Here, the definition of a therapeutic court implies that the role of the state is to establish and assist in processes through which families can "empower" themselves with skills to resolve their "own" disputes, while assisting "when and where they need them." This underlying philosophical orientation is significant, in that it suggests an assistive and facilitative role rather than the monitoring and enforcement role that is more typical of the actual operations of courts.

Despite this stated orientation and irrespective of the best intentions of professionals within the juvenile justice system, the Hawai'i family court, like most courts across the country, was not free from complaint or controversy. Hawai'i's arrest rate has been consistently higher than that of the rest of the nation and, despite an easing in the rate and number of arrests since a high point in 1996, the juvenile justice system in Hawai'i has experienced disturbing problems.[7] A 2013 study conducted by the Hawai'i Juvenile Justice Working Group found that Hawai'i was incarcerating a high proportion of youth for relatively minor offenses.[8] More youth were being sentenced to the Hawai'i Youth Correctional Facility (HYCF), the state's sole youth correctional facility, for misdemeanors (up from 47 percent in 2004 to 61 percent in 2013) than for felonies. And a greater number were confined for a nonviolent offense (72 percent) than for crimes against persons. Many of those youth could have been safely supervised in their community, but the state's "intensive supervision" programs had limited capacity. Meanwhile, incarcerating youth in HYCF was at the public expense of $199,320 per bed annually—monies that could have been used for needed supportive services (Hawai'i Juvenile Justice Working Group 2013). And while admissions to HYCF had decreased by 41 percent from 2004 to 2013, the average length of stay had increased 188 percent during that period, from 2.5 months to 7.2 months. Another problem was the increasing length of probation supervision, which increased 155 percent between 2005 and 2013, from 8.1 months to 20.6 months. Incarceration was often used as a "stick" for those on probation. Between 2010 and 2013, probation violations and revocations accounted for more than four of every ten admissions to HYCF (Hawai'i Juvenile Justice Working Group 2013).

Being imprisoned was a stepping-stone to further entanglement with law enforcement. While arrest rates as a whole across the country were on the decline (Snyder 2012), the rearrest rate remained high among youth who had been incarcerated. A Hawai'i study published in 2010 found that among their sample, 86.5 percent of those who had been incarcerated were rearrested as juveniles or adults and 75.5 percent were rearrested as adults within the first three years after their initial arrest.[9]

HYCF had a history of problems that added to the negative effects of incarceration on the well-being of youth. The American Civil Liberties Union brought the problem of officers' abuse of wards to public legal attention in 2003.[10] White (2003) pointed out overcrowding, poor living conditions, brutality and use of excessive force, sexual assault and harassment, lack of privacy at the girls' facility, inadequate programming, inadequate training and supervision of staff, a defunct grievance process, among other problems. The situation was found to be so serious that the U.S. Department of Justice Civil Rights Division conducted an investigation and concluded that "certain deficiencies violate the constitutional and federal statutory rights of the youth confined at HYCF" (Schlozman 2005, 2). That organization's memo to then-governor Linda Lingle stated, "The absence of rules or regulations has permitted a culture to develop where abuse of youth often goes unreported and uninvestigated" (Schlozman 2005, 4).[11]

One of the persistent impacts of colonialism is the overrepresentation of Native Hawaiian and other Pacific Islander groups in the criminal justice system (Office of Hawaiian Affairs 2010). A 2012 study commissioned by Hawai'i's Juvenile Justice State Advisory Council found an almost two-fold rate of juvenile arrest for Native Hawaiians when compared to Whites (Umemoto et al. 2012). Once arrested, these youth experienced disproportionately negative outcomes at nearly every point of contact within the juvenile justice system, from being referred to court to being placed on probation or protective supervision. Filipino and other Pacific Islander youth, along with those of mixed racial ancestry, also experienced disproportionally negative consequences at multiple points in the system. And Native Hawai'i and Pacific Islander youth comprised the vast majority of those held in the youth correctional facility.[12]

Scholars who have studied this problem nationally have identified some of the factors accounting for racial disparities, such as indirect bias in decision-making by court personnel, familial or community context that are characterized by racial inequality, and process variables such as the unavailability of services in communities (Bishop and Frazier 1996; Bridges and Steen 1998; Daly 1989; Engen, Steen, and Bridges 2002; Feld 1999; Leiber and Mack 2003; Leiber et. al. 2007; Pope, Lovell, and Hsia 2002; Skiba et al. 2002). For Native Hawaiian and Pacific Islander youth in Hawai'i, one can arguably add the effects of colonialism as they relate to poverty, land and political disenfranchisement, and problems such as disproportionate adult incarceration. These factors, combined with the caring but paternalistic stance of court personnel who desire adult supervision and services for youth, congeal into a rather "sticky hold" on youth once they have entered the justice system.

Evidence suggests that youth who encounter the law are in need of care and support. A random sample of adjudicated youth in Honolulu who had been arrested in 2009 found high incidence of depression (32 percent), psychological or physical abuse (30 percent), low school achievement (77 percent), substance abuse (72 percent), lack of positive relationships with maternal (35 percent) and paternal

(62 percent) guardians, and behavioral challenges such as impulsivity (82 percent) and lack of anger control (66 percent).[13]

There are many programs for youth in Hawai'i, but services such as mental health and substance abuse treatment are sorely lacking on the "high end" of the spectrum of need. Even when services are available, strict eligibility criteria, insurance restrictions, or jurisdictional restrictions often close the doors to programs for some who are in dire need of those services. And for those in need of secured residential mental health care, aside from short-term hospital confinement, only one such facility existed in the entire state (Umemoto et al. 2012).

The irony is that the only place where the full suite of mental health, substance abuse, and social and educational services is available is at the Hawai'i Youth Correctional Facility. For many years, prison became what some call the "provider of last resort." Thus, incarceration was ordered for many youth who should not have been sent to HYCF simply due to lack of other alternatives.[14] Probation officers struggled with the decision to incarcerate under these circumstances. One probation officer shared the angst they felt when contemplating placing a youth in HYCF in order to ensure that they received needed services, stating, "But, the ultimate decision is they are going to get services when they are in there. And that's really sad, but at a same time it's, like, that's their best chance. It's so awful to say that."[15] The fact that youth were unnecessarily incarcerated due to a lack of secured residential therapeutic beds for juveniles with mental health and substance abuse problems speaks to the persistent public neglect of the least powerful in U.S. society.

SCHOOL POLICIES ON FIGHTING

The nationwide trend toward harsh punishment spread to schools across the country (Simon 2007) and Hawai'i's public school system was no exception. A watershed piece of federal legislation was President Bill Clinton's 1994 Gun-Free Schools Act (GFSA), which institutionalized zero tolerance policies in schools nationwide. The GFSA required states receiving federal funds under the Elementary and Secondary Education Act of 1965 to pass legislation requiring local school districts to expel for at least one year any student found bringing a firearm to campus and to report these cases to the U.S. Secretary of Education. This requirement was later expanded to any instrument that may be used as a weapon. States soon amended their statutes to conform to federal law.[16]

Many school districts further expanded the scope of predetermined consequences and stricter punishment beyond weapons to include drugs, alcohol, fighting, and verbal threats. By as early as 1997, over 90 percent of public schools in the U.S. reported having enacted some type of zero tolerance policy (Heaviside et al. 1998). In regards to fighting and physical attacks, the National Center on

Education Statistics found, in their national survey of schools taken in 1997, that 79 percent of schools had predetermined consequences or punishments for violence that took place on campus (Heaviside et al. 1998), with some schools expanding the geographic scope beyond their physical school boundaries (Skiba 2000). A wave of school shootings in the late 1990s and early 2000s spurred moral panics and a new round of punitive reforms. The federal government increased funding for security officers, tripling the number of full-time law enforcement and security personnel in schools between 1996–97 and 2007–08, amidst a fear-stricken public (Kang-Brown et al. 2013).

Following the passage of the 1994 Gun-Free Schools Act, Hawai'i incorporated the language of mandatory punishment into what is locally referred to as "Chapter 19" of the Hawai'i Administrative Rules (State of Hawai'i, Board of Education, n.d.), which are administered by the Hawai'i State Board of Education, the unitary school board that governs all public schools in the state of Hawai'i.[17] The stated philosophy of Chapter 19 is to provide students a collaborative system of support. It cites the 1996 implementation of the Comprehensive Student Support System, "which provides a continuum of academic, social, emotional, and physical environmental supports and services to all students to facilitate their learning and their meeting of high educational standards." It states that "it is the responsibility of every student to demonstrate respectful, responsible, safe, and ethical behaviors." However, it adds, "when a student's behavior violates established policies, rules, or regulations of the department, state or local laws, the department may take appropriate disciplinary action in accordance with this chapter."

The state administrative rules define "fighting" in rather broad terms. In Chapter 19, fighting is defined as "instigating or provoking physical contact involving anger or hostility." The scope includes: "(1) Engaging in mutual physical contact involving anger or hostility; (2) Teasing, harassing, threatening, or intimidating others resulting in physical contact involving anger or hostility; (3) Retaliating physically for teasing, harassing, threatening, or intimidating behavior; verbally inciting; or (4) Physically supporting a fight by one's presence and encouragement" (State of Hawai'i, Board of Education, n.d.).[18] Fighting falls under the most serious class of offenses and is subject to an array of consequences, ranging from parent conferences and time in the office to detention, suspension, transfer, or dismissal from school. In determining disciplinary action, the rules give authority to the principal or their designee to consider "the intention of the offender, the nature and severity of the offense, the impact of the offense on others including whether the action was committed by an individual or a group of individuals such as a gang, the age of the offender, and if the offender was a repeat offender" (State of Hawai'i, Board of Education, n.d.).

These school disciplinary codes were followed by sweeping changes in national school accountability policies, designed to raise academic standards for performance, most notably under the 2001 No Child Left Behind Act (NCLB). While schools were assuming greater authority in disciplining students for a broad range of behaviors codified as disruptive or dangerous, schools were also under federal pressure to increase academic performance. This focused the attention of teachers and administrators on "teaching to the test" and limited the range of subjects that schools invested in.

This was particularly devastating for Native Hawaiian and Pacific Islander youth, whose cultural traditions were steeped in unique pedagogical approaches and epistemologies. Education scholars, for example, have shared the pedagogical approaches best suited to Native Hawaiian students, highlighting the importance of a culture-based educational philosophy, the relational nature of knowledge in Hawaiian culture, and the centrality of Hawaiian epistemology or worldview to a holistic understanding the natural, social, and spiritual world (Ah Nee-Benham and Cooper 2000; Goodyear-Kaʻōpua 2013; Meyer 1998; Sing, Hunter, and Meyer 1999). As Meyer stated, "What we know matters, who we are matters, *how* we know makes a difference in the who we become" (Meyer 1997, quoted in Meyer 1998, 27). The shift to narrowly defined accountability standards under NCLB took place to the detriment of a more inclusive educational philosophy and a broader spectrum of metrics for evaluation (Darling-Hammond 2007) across overlapping realms—the emotional, physical, cultural, moral, spiritual, social, behavioral, and intellectual.

The results of stricter rules on student conduct showed in the overrepresentation of Native Hawaiians and Pacific Islanders among students receiving disciplinary action. While the rate of disciplinary action in Hawaiʻi public schools was less than the national average (suspension rate of 4 percent versus 11 percent in 2009–10, for example), the ethnic differences were disturbingly high.[19] As in the juvenile justice system, Native Hawaiian students faced the greatest degree of overrepresentation, comprising about 26 percent of the public school population but over 42 percent of total suspensions in 2013–14. Samoans, Micronesians, Tongans, American Indians, African Americans, and Portuguese, though smaller in number, were also overrepresented (Terrell 2015).

EXTENDING AN ETHIC OF CARE IN SCHOOLS

Lipsky (1980) revealed the many ways that "frontline" workers in many professions from probation to social work exercise a remarkably high degree of informal discretion within a set of formal rules and processes. Lipsky illustrated how these professionals weigh a host of considerations in meting out consequences for those whom they are charged to serve or supervise. He revealed how public servants are steered by legal and administrative rules as well as workload and resource constraints, yet continue to make a wide range of decisions that are influenced by their individual ideologies, philosophies, pool of experiences, and ideas about their mission and purpose.

In the following two sections, we describe the efforts of frontline workers—from teachers and counselors to probation officers and judges—who worked within the legal constraints of their jobs to provide support despite the ideological dominance of a zero tolerance policy environment. And we highlight some of the ways in which these "street-level bureaucrats," as Lipsky called them, intervened to prevent or address conflicts and fights without relying on punishment. We note the ways in which an ethic of care is manifested in practice and what its hallmark features are.

Opening Lines of Communication Based on Respect

Certainly, school administrators would rather prevent fights than deal with their aftermath. Adults who had open lines of communication with students and who were trusted by them were often the most effective in deterring violence. Most adults in schools echoed the fact that it was important to have a good rapport with and trust of students in order to know when trouble was brewing.

But what does it take to develop this type of rapport and trust? Unfortunately, there are many barriers to healthy rapport between adults in positions of authority and youth who may need a responsible adult to talk to. One student, Jay-Jay, described her hesitancy about confiding in school staff. What made her reluctant was being "put off" more than once when she tried to approach adults on campus. She explained: "I don't know, like you kind of really want to talk to them but then sometimes they're busy and then they're just like, 'I'll just talk to you later,' you know, the whole putting you off for a while. I'm kind of like 'Whatever,' like, 'I knew it,' kind of like that. Yeah I've had it where like, I need help and they're like, 'I'll be there in a minute.' That happens to me kind of all the time." The experience of being ignored reinforced her feeling that they "don't know what I'm going through."

In contrast, Anita, a teacher's aide, was someone who many students trusted. They called her "Auntie" instead of "Miss," the usual term that students used to address female teachers and staff. Anita was from the Seaside community and had been very active in church and community organizations, including a vibrant youth organization. Some of the students knew her first through community activities, while others came to know her through her classroom work. She was an informal mentor for many students who were going through difficult times. Anita explained, "I'm all about mentoring . . . giving them solid people that they could feel comfortable with and a safe place they can come to."

School staff like Anita, who informally developed mentoring relationships in the course of everyday work, exemplified how adults can play a helpful role for youth. She often extended her hand to students who, she felt, needed more positive role models in their lives, and made efforts to get to know what they were experiencing on and off campus. Anita shared with us a moment she had had with a student who had been arrested after getting into a scuffle. Anita knew that this particular student had been moved from one foster home to another. Abuse had taught this student how to defend herself physically when threatened. Anita described how her relationship with the student opened opportunities to provide guidance at a critical moment in time:

> Actually she got into a little tiff and she actually was held in court like a few weeks ago. [Her friend] brought her to me and I'm like, "What are you doing? What happened?" . . . And she was just kind of sitting there. So I just started to stroke her hair like this and you could just see her, just like this. And I'm like, "Ok, we've got to make better choices," I said, "because you're here to get an education so you've got to make better choices," from that place of caring. She's like, "Yeah I know, auntie." . . . I feel for her because I know what her lifestyle has been. I know she was getting lickings [beatings] at this one home and she didn't say a word [about it]. And you could see it on her face when she'd come and I knew it. It was pulling at my heart.

Anita often reached out to family members as well, drawing from her local knowledge to work tactfully with other parents. She believed that her background as a Native Hawaiian woman in some cases allowed her to read the meaning of words and actions in ways that would have been more difficult for someone who did not share the same interpretive lens. Anita shared one example in which she believed her cultural understanding of shame from a Hawaiian perspective helped her to work with a parent whose child had been into a fight. She understood that being reprimanded by the school could prompt a feeling of public shame on the part of the family—a feeling that could result in quite harsh physical punishment of a child by a parent. As she explained:

> Okay well, if this father is going to flip off his chair when you tell him [about what his child did], then how can you tell them in a way that he'll receive it and not be mad and beat his kid up to a pulp when you leave? Well, you need to tell him all the kid's strengths. You need to build this kid up . . . Yeah and then you need to say "Okay, we're still struggling in this area. How can we help you and how can you help us?" So just really assessing each situation because each family has a different dynamic. So if you don't know how to relate, then your words are as good as nothing.

Anita approached the parent from the angle of working in partnership based on respect for the parent as well as the child. With loving care, Anita was able to work effectively with many youth as well as members of their families.

Empathy, understanding, and respect were important in establishing trust. Student told us that respect meant not being talked "down to" and being seen for their positive traits and actions as well as their shortcomings and mistakes. Respect also meant listening with full attention, maintaining confidentiality, and showing concern through helping actions. As Angel put it about respectful adults, "When you talk they listen. They don't tell other people what you said to them." She added, "They don't try to speak up while you're talking to them. They give you comfort. And even like when you tell them something, they'll try to help you."

Keith resented paternalistic teachers. He saw respect as something that was earned, not something that automatically came with a position of authority. He described one counselor whom he respected, and how the counselor motivated him to stay out of trouble: "He know us. He don't look at us as different people, like students. He put us on the same level. Not 'I'm the counselor. I look down to you.' He put us higher than himself. I look up to you, like when I talk to you. He's a good counselor. So it's like he's straight up with us, we're straight up with him. There's nothing to apologize, it's all good. So, that's how we respect [him]." Keith continued to praise this counselor: "If you get this kind of [exchange], you can relate to students, you get that trust, you get that caring, that wanting to learn." He wished that more adults at school would take this counselor's lead and "try not to disrespect the kid or try not to put the kid down or try not to challenge the kid." Keith also made it clear that respect was not in contradiction with being strict. He said, "You will be like, 'This teacher's strict.' But she's strict for a reason. She's strict because she wants you to succeed in life and every kid will give you the utmost respect, no matter who you are."

Providing Guidance and Support

Jay-Jay described how fellow students bullied her and her sister after they arrived from the Philippines. She recalled a teacher who continued to give her advice even after the semester ended. "He asks me like those really good questions and it gets me thinking about it." Guiding her to think about the consequences of her actions filled a role she was missing in her life in the absence of her father. "My dad isn't here. He's in the Philippines and we're in the middle of the whole separation thing with my mom and my dad and it's been really hard. And so I told him that too, because it was bothering me . . . . He was so like a father figure in school. So that's been really good."

Suspension was the most common form of punishment for fighting. Suspensions may once have been effective, in the days when a responsible parent was home to supervise the child and give them guidance. But many students described suspension as a "vacation." For some, it was time to get into more trouble. Angel was suspended after getting into a minor tussle with another girl. She explained her reaction to being harshly punished for what she saw as a minor conflict. "I don't think we should suspend kids. Sometimes I think it just gives them a reason to be more pissed. Like when I got suspended and I didn't even get the girl. It made me want to hit the girl so I can get my suspension worth it, you know?"

Suspension without adequate counseling and conflict mediation could turn up the heat of hostility. Certainly, there were instances when suspension was appropriate, especially when there was risk of physical retaliation or escalation of violence among students. In these instances, suspension kept students from confronting one another on campus and allowed emotions to "cool down." But even in these situations, suspension alone was not enough to diminish the chances of retaliation or further harm.

Another problem with suspension was the instructional time that students lost, especially when the suspended students were struggling academically. In fact, studies have shown poor academic performance to be a risk factor for violence. Out-of-school suspension often exacerbates those challenges. Darren shared the pressure he felt returning to school after suspension, explaining that "You want to catch up but it's like, you don't know what to do, you have all this feeling, you're all confused and everything." Angel explained her feelings after serving suspension, "It was hard, especially because I had problems this semester and I just got suspended." She continued, "He's [my teacher's] telling me I need to do this worksheet, I need to do that worksheet, and I don't even have the notes for those worksheets."

In contrast, some students spoke thankfully about teachers who took time to help them catch up with missed coursework. "They will write all the things I missed and they can help me do some of it," explained Travis. Darren explained how positive attention helped him: "Well, my teachers tell me that I'm doing a good job and I'm very smart and all that. When a teacher tell me that it actually gives me more confidence to come to school and learn more."

EXTENDING AN ETHIC OF CARE IN THE COURTS

Some of the probation officers and judges with whom we spoke revealed a variety of ways that they supported youth. Probation staff connected youth with community-based mentors, provided professional training, and tried to provide social services and youth programs to those under their supervision. Most importantly, some court personnel helped teens build their capacity to gain the knowledge, skills, and resources that would allow them to make healthier decisions for their own and their families' futures.

Reshaping the Institutional Culture

The family court personnel whom we interviewed acknowledged that an ethic of care was unevenly practiced within the profession. They had different explanations for this. Some cited the fact that new hires sometimes did not fully understand the unique history of the family court in Hawai'i and its stated commitment to therapeutic justice. New hires, they theorized, might not fully understand what therapeutic justice meant or how to operationalize its philosophical underpinnings in their day-to-day practice. A shortage of training in therapeutic methods also tended to undermine what opportunities there were to engage with youth in creating optimal scaffolds of support. Therapeutic skillsets often varied, with those trained in social work more likely to have them than those trained in criminal justice. Some family court personnel cited the lack of consistent leadership, messaging, and incentive structures to reinforce a therapeutic, healing approach. Others expressed concern over an institutional culture that created a monitoring-oriented, "office-bound" environment rather than a family-centered, field-intensive one.

Despite these constraints and conditions, there were many individuals who maintained a commitment to strengthening a therapeutic justice model. One worker shared her commitment to ongoing training from a systems perspective, saying, "I think because if I see social injustice I get really upset about it, because I care. I'm lucky if I can do stuff to make some changes, especially to save somebody's life and prevent harm."

Changing institutional culture, however, is always challenging. Wilma was a longtime administrative staffer in the family court who coordinated training opportunities for judges, probation officers, and court administrators. She noted that the types of cases that enter the family court have changed over time, and that youth today enter the system with more complicated problems, from multiple mental health diagnoses to trauma in the family. She explained, "One of my key things I like to do is provide training for people, give them the opportunity to acquire new knowledge and skills. And the rest is their choice how they want to use it. I'm a systems person, so I want the whole system to work together." Regardless of the training provided, she emphasized that it came down to having people who genuinely cared: "You need to have the right people—the people that have the right philosophy, the right understanding and value system to go with the issues, and of course the passion to go along."

Developing Culturally Grounded Interventions

In the 2010s there were some new initiatives under the family court that were grounded in Native Hawaiian cultural knowledge and practices and were designed to help adjudicated youth complete their court-ordered community service requirements. Papa Hoʻile Kuleana was one such initiative. Faith, the program developer, sought programs that engaged Native Hawaiian, Pacific Islander, and local youth and families in ʻāina or land-based agricultural and conservation activities.[20] She enlisted a half-dozen or so nonprofit organizations doing this work that were willing to involve the youth, as they fulfilled their court-ordered community service obligations. Organization staff and volunteers mentored youth, alongside probation officers and family members. Faith recognized the value of helping youth create "natural support systems" within their own communities, relationships that can extend long beyond the youths' involvement with the family court. She allowed Papa Hoʻile Kuleana probation officers to use flex-time, so that they could take youth on service outings and excursions after office hours and on weekends, when youth and their families were available to engage in such activities.

Rather than calling themselves probation officers, the Papa Hoʻile Kuleana staff decided to call themselves "WIN mentors." WIN stood for "What's Important Now." Brandon, a WIN mentor, commented on the name: "That's really what this program is about—trying to be for them what's important now." One ʻāina-based partner organization, Hoʻoulu ʻĀina, is located on conservation land at the mountainous edge of downtown Honolulu, and carries a name that means "to grow land as well as to grow because of the land." Their motto is ʻO ka ha o ka ʻāina ke ola o ka poʻe—the breath of the land is the life of the people. Through partnerships like these, the WIN mentors opened opportunities for learning that were symbiotically restorative and rejuvenating for both youth and the land. Their hope was that youth who were exposed to the richness of these community organizations and to their broader mission of restoring and stewarding land and community would be able to see possibilities for themselves and their place, far beyond what they might earlier have imagined.

CONCLUSION

We opened this chapter by pointing out the double-sided nature of violence in the United States—a nation that advocates for military might and threats of violence while imposing increasingly strict punishments for interpersonal violence amongst its citizenry. We caught a glimpse of some of the harmful results of living under a zero tolerance policy environment, through the eyes of June and Auggie, while also appreciating the critical role that caring adults played in their triumphs. As local schools and courts have been pressed to follow the lead of federal policy in its punitive swing over the past several decades, we also saw that the system was not a homogenous whole and that an ethic of care in the schools and an ethos of therapeutic justice in the courts managed to live on, through the exceptional acts of committed individuals.

These stories can offer insights to critical youth studies. First, they suggest a critique of the persistent assumptions that youth lack competency and capacity due to their age and lack of development. Instead, we focus on youths' agency and suggest a "capabilities approach" to an ethics of care. This is based on accounts and our observations of the kinds of interactions between youth and caring adults that raised youths' capacity to apply critical knowledge, weigh moral considerations, and reflect on their life and situations. Youths' chance of success was greatly increased when they had the love and support of adults who helped them build on their knowledge, skills, and problem-solving abilities. In our interviews and observations, we found that youth responded best to those who showed them respect, took time to understand what they were experiencing, and offered their knowledge and guidance. We found that caring adults made a practice of speaking *with* and not *at,* empathizing *with* rather than sympathizing *towards,* and problem-solving *alongside* rather than *for* youth, all hallmarks of a "capabilities approach."

The insights on zero tolerance policies also advance understandings in colonial theory. Some institutional practices in schools and juvenile justice systems perpetuate the racial and ethnic inequalities embedded in settler colonialism. The disproportionate rates of discipline for Native Hawaiians and other Pacific Islanders in the schools as well as in the juvenile justice system remain disgracefully high. The findings gathered here illustrate how, even without conscious intent or malice, existing disparities can be reproduced and magnified through the use of blunt and punitive disciplinary instruments. These one-size-fits-all punishments are not designed to address the deep causes of violence and the many inequalities that stem from a colonial past. However, we caution that though "rehabilitative" and "therapeutic" approaches may be more humane than "corrective" and "punitive" ones, they are still laden with a degree of missionary-style paternalism. The paternalistic narrative, as some teens noted, tends to be seen as condescending; for actors within institutions who advocate for caring and empowering solutions, paternalistic approaches remain a stubborn obstacle.

Youth Prepare for Adulthood

On the horizon, therefore, are tens of thousands of severely morally impover-
ished juvenile super-predators. They are perfectly capable of committing the
most heinous acts of physical violence for the most trivial reasons (for exam-
ple, a perception of slight disrespect or the accident of being in their path).
They fear neither the stigma of arrest nor the pain of imprisonment. They live
by the meanest code of the meanest streets, a code that reinforces rather than
restrains their violent, hair-trigger mentality.

—JOHN J. DILULIO (1995, 23)

The above quote is taken from Dilulio's 1995 article in *The Weekly Standard*, "The Coming of the Super-Predators," and it aptly captures the tenor of Dilulio's entire thesis. He claims that there are uncontrollable juveniles in the world who fear nothing, not arrest, not incarceration, and not even death. He goes on to argue that the remorseless offenders of the 1990s are only the beginning of a coming wave of teen predators. In the mid-1990s there were, according to him, "tens of thousands" of children growing up in moral impoverishment who would soon enter their teen years. Americans, according to Dilulio, needed to brace themselves.

Dilulio's super-predators thesis may have been one of the most influential juvenile justice statements of the time. It was followed by two decades of dramatic increases in the number of teens who were waived to adult courts and given harsh sentences like life in prison or the death penalty.[1] A super-predator, after all, is viewed as so "morally impoverished" and so lacking in basic human traits (e.g., remorse, empathy, and self-restraint) that the only reasonable solution seemed to be to lock up these deranged teens for as long as possible.

There is an important subtheme running through the super-predator thesis, namely that once "morally impoverished" children have reached their teen years, they are permanently marked, that is to say that they will forever lack moral decency. The core idea is that by the adolescent years, a teen's moral character is intractable, unchangeable, and set "in stone." Many political pundits, legislators, and Americans in general continue to cling to the notion that deeply troubled and horribly violent teens can never change.

One of the most important findings of our study is that violence is not a fixed trait. If there is an affliction that corresponds to Dilulio's "moral impoverishment," it is certainly not unchangeable. All of the teens in this study (even the most violent among them) changed their thinking, motivations, and behaviors. Most importantly, every teen became less violent and aggressive over the course of this study, and some of teens ceased lashing out violently altogether. Not one of the teens in this study was remorseless.

In this chapter we examine some of the core processes that influenced the changes in teens' lives, including their decreased reliance on violence to solve problems. We highlight the two dominant ways that change unfolded for the adolescents. The first process of change occurred with the help of what we call "the second line of defense." When a youth's family members would not or could not help a youth make important changes, it was often a set of adults outside of the teen's family who became "the second line of defense" by stepping in to offer long-term support and advocacy.

The second process of change was one that we call "going it alone," meaning that many youth relied on their own wits, talents, and assets to help themselves. Teens who were "going it alone" believed that adults would not or could not help them solve problems or support them as they prepared for adulthood.

In the following sections of this chapter we examine the process of change for the adolescents. We first examine the key components that made up the "second line of defense" for some, and we explore Alika's, Cornel's, and Masa's stories. Next, we turn to the process of "going it alone" and note the circuitous and complicated ways that youth used their self-reliance and independence to negotiate the safest journey possible toward adulthood.

We conclude this chapter with a summary of what happened to many of the youth who graduated from the lunch bunch program. Because Hawai'i is a rather small state, characterized by tightly knit social networks, we "bumped into" and were able to stay in touch with some of the teens after they left high school. The final section of this chapter provides a sort of epilogue to a few of the teens' stories.

THE SECOND LINE OF DEFENSE

The common phrase "choose your parents wisely" indicates that forces outside of a person's control often structure one's life chances. If a teen comes from what we call a chaotic childhood—or what Schaffner (2006, 80) calls an "empty family"— her or his chances of becoming a happy, stable, and healthy adult are thought to be diminished. Chaotic family lives in our study included families in which there were severe upheavals due to any combination of factors including severe financial strain, homelessness, substance abuse, and sexual and physical violence.

But what if there is a second line of defense? Can caring teachers, foster parents, counselors, coaches, neighbors, and family friends provide enough support for a youth to overcome family trauma and chaos? Our findings indicated that there was a collection of teens, including Alika, Cornel, and Masa, who benefited from relationships with caring, capable adults; their stories illustrate how the second line of defense can unfold.

We learned at least three lessons from youth's experiences with their second lines of defense. First, we found that some state-funded therapists, psychiatrists, counselors, and foster parents were steadfast and talented when working with teens, and thus made a difference in youths' lives. Our second lesson was that the state was not a necessary ingredient in providing a supportive safety net for troubled teens. There were also what might be called "organic" adult networks. We found that there were numerous capable adults in the community (program champions, leaders of community organizations, and other well-respected adults) who stepped in to help adolescents in need of support.

The third lesson was that regardless of whether the second line of defense came in the form of state-funded therapeutic services or organic community support systems, the most effective and supportive adults were trained in and/or had vast experiential knowledge in what are often called therapeutic approaches to working with traumatized youth (see Rios 2011). It is important to note that many of the teens in this study displayed defiant, aggressive, or otherwise difficult behaviors. It was unlikely that an adult without considerable savvy or formal training in working with traumatized youth would be able remain patient with teens who were easily labeled as "troublemakers," "deranged," and "morally impoverished." As a result of their skills, these adults were steadfast, caring, and consistent in their approach when adolescents acted out. When they made a commitment to a teen, they did not give up on or abandon a troubled youth.

Alika's Story

Those who subscribe to Dilulio's (1995, 23) "super-predator" thesis, could easily have been classified Alika as a morally impoverished juvenile "growing up surrounded by deviant, delinquent, and criminal adults in abusive" settings. Alika told us that by the age of five, he was "raising himself." His parents were distracted by "partying," drinking, and drug taking. While Alika's father was unassuming and quiet when he was intoxicated, Alika's uncles were not. Alika would watch with excitement to see fights erupt between his uncles after a night of heavy drinking. He said: "I was raised on the streets, from five years old, running the streets, no curfew. I would come home at two, three o'clock. Sleep at whoever's house. My family would fight at every party. I would bet money with my friends and say like, 'My uncle is gonna fight at this party.' And I would win bets. That's how I used to hustle. When I was young, I used to love seeing that. I used to like these fights."

While Alika enjoyed the nights when "anything can happen," there were other aspects of his family life that unsettled him. Sleeping soundly, for example, was not common for him, and he worried that someone would "come after" his family members. Of particular concern for Alika was the possibility that someone would come to the house with a gun seeking retribution for a past insult or a drug deal "gone bad." Another constant worry was the police. Because of their drug involvement and violence, the adults in his family lived under the looming threat of arrest and incarceration, a threat that turned into reality for his uncles, who were in and out of jail and prison throughout Alika's childhood.[2]

Alika's childhood experiences could be seen as the stuff of moral impoverishment. If there was any moral compass in Alika's young life, it pointed in the direction of fighting and drug use rather than toward school, employment, and a stable adult life. After all, since the age of five, Alika had been allowed to "run the streets," and when he was at home with his family, his uncles in particular, exposed him to a healthy dose of the "meanest code of the meanest streets" (Dilulio 1995, 23) in their dealings with one another. Indeed, Alika's childhood seemed to be a lesson in hustling, getting high, and responding with vengeance to any insult. It was no wonder that by the age of sixteen, Alika had been incarcerated for assault.

But despite his troubled beginnings, Alika did not become a remorseless criminal. Instead, by the age of seventeen, Alika became a thoughtful young man who felt that the drug abuse and violence he witnessed in his family was "not a good thing." He told us that he had always wanted to become "a better man."

When we asked Alika what helped him change his life, he said that being on probation and living under the threat of reincarceration was part of the reason:

> If I get into a fight, boom I'm in the boy's home [juvenile correction facility] until I'm nineteen. But say if I do good? If I change my life around, and not fight, I picked a better option. I get to be with my girlfriend. I get to play sports, go to college, get a good job, learn more things in life and in school, and not get in more trouble in school. I would get into more trouble in [juvenile correction facility]. There's chaos in there. There's only murderers and all kine [kinds of] people you no wanna meet.[3] I would rather pick the good choices. Do I want to lose all of that? That's why I don't fight no more. I get straight As.

Despite the predictions of the moral poverty thesis, which suggest that a person with chaotic beginnings would fail to feel the stigma of arrest or the pain of imprisonment, Alika suffered while he was incarcerated and felt the heartbreak of being separated from what he loved most in life: sports, his girlfriend, and his bright future.

In some ways, Alika's question, "Do I want to keep those good things?" makes his transformation seem like a simple matter of making up his mind and thinking rationally, given the looming threat of reincarceration. His story, however, reveals that his choice to refrain from violence and "keep those good things" came after a particular process that had multiple elements. It was not one event, like a stint in juvenile lockup, or one person who made a difference in Alika's life, but rather a collection of people who supported Alika, talked with him, and encouraged him until he was ready to pick "a better option."

The second line of defense was forced on Alika. When the state learned about the violence and substance abuse in his family, he was placed with a foster family. It should be noted that many of the youth in this study were being raised in the foster system and few of these teens found foster families to be safe and stable environments. Many foster-raised youth had experienced two or more foster family placements, a fact which suggests that the system exposed youth to some degree of upheaval and instability. Alika was an exception. His foster family was reliable and attentive. Moreover, Alika's foster parents, Ramie and Marshal Billings, were tightly networked with a number of community-based organizations in Northward. As noted in chapters 3, 4, and 6, many community adults were dynamic leaders who were involved in countless neighborhood-based programs and initiatives, and the Billingses were two among many Northward adults who played the role of steadfast youth advocates.

Alika's case was one in which the state welfare system paralleled more organic and community-based support networks. Through the Billings' work with teen advocacy groups in the neighborhood, Ramie and Marshal learned about Alika's case and invited Alika into their family. Instantly, Alika joined his foster parents and siblings as they attended youth council meetings, outreach efforts, and church gatherings. As longtime members of the local evangelical church, Ramie and Marshal were also proponents of unconditional love. They consistently communicated their behavioral expectations to their children, but they also offered understanding, forgiveness, and second chances when their children violated the family's rules. Ramie and Marshal expected their children to take responsibility for their actions and to "make it right" when they hurt others. In the Billings family, there was no mistake so large that it would challenge Ramie and Marshal's commitment to love others, even those outside the family.

Alika described his foster parents' orientation: "They are into Christ. And in Christ there is—forgive everyone who sinned against you, who did bad to you. Forgive someone who killed your son. I don't know if I could do that." After three years of living with the Billingses, Alika remained unsure of whether he could live up to his foster family's example. In fact, he noted that he sometimes slipped into his old ways. He said: "I made a lot of wrong choices. I get busted all the time. I told my parents already, 'If I'm gonna die, just remember me as one hard-head boy.' I still get those days, those days when I think, pride. I used to be the guy who fight. I see one big guy acting all tough and I'll be the small little boy that knock him out. You know pride. I still get that thinking."

Although Alika did not fully subscribe to all of his foster parents' religious principles, he admitted to benefiting from living with Ramie and Marshal. When asked what helped him change his life, he said: "I felt like how a family feels like—to have a family. Love, I felt love. I felt cared for. I felt a lot of things that I never felt with my dad. I felt safe. You can go to one house and sleep and not worry about someone coming in and calling you out [challenging you to a fight], calling your family out. You can sleep peaceful. Two years, three years. I no need worry now. I no more of that thinking, 'Oh, is he gonna come after me tonight?'"

It wasn't just a lucky foster placement that assisted Alika. He also profited from progressive state policies allocating funds for counseling services. Alika had been assigned to a therapist as well as a school counselor. In addition, Alika's athletic achievements and straight-A average in his senior year of school were due in part to the assistance of his coach and teachers. Combined with his foster parents, these adults formed a type of adult team on Alika's side. Therefore, Alika's decision to "make a change" in his life was the result of several years of building trust, developing relationships, and experiencing patience from every member of his team. Indeed, when Katy asked what adults can do to help teens who are struggling, Alika alluded to the need for forbearance:

> If you gonna work with him, don't give up. Just keep working, keep working, keep working. Things will change. You just got to give 'em time. Like with me, say you were working with someone like me, bad boy all the way. I stressed out so many workers who tried to help me. They give up already. They gave up. The only one who did not give up is the school counselor—my therapist. Oh, I gave him hell. He went through hell with me. But, I find out he loved me. He stayed strong with me. He stay strong with me, saying, "Don't fight, don't fight." He was irritating, like a preacher. But, you look at it, it is something good he say to you. He just keep working and don't give up, no matter how hard.

Cornel's Story

Like Alika, Cornel made enormous leaps in his life, also thanks to policies allocating funds for counseling services. Cornel's early life was chaotic, and at the time our interview with him, his father was serving time in prison for assault and his mother was supporting the family through prostitution. Unlike in Alika's case, the state did not place Cornel with a foster family, most likely because Cornel's mother kept her illegal activities hidden from the state. When Cornel's father was incarcerated, the state did intervene in Cornel's childhood by referring him to therapeutic services including psychiatry, talk therapy, and school counseling. Cornel described the array of resources that helped him: "I see three psychologists and one psychiatrist. The psychiatrist, I started seeing one year ago and others since I was little. When people have issues and have no one to talk to, they are people who you can talk with. That is their job, to listen to your problems. If I didn't have so much help, I guess that I would be very violent."

His older brother, who lived with other family members on the Big Island, did not have access to counseling services, and as a result, his brother's life progressed differently than Cornel's. Cornel said, "My brother inherited the thing with my dad. My dad hurt a lot of people. He was a hit man. He was in a gang. I don't want to be seen that way. People fear my dad badly. I'm not like my dad. I don't like hurting people."

Through years of therapy, Cornel had developed finely honed verbal skills and insights about his life. Instead of intimidating and hurting others, Cornel said that he enjoyed talking with and helping people. Also, thanks to his school counselor, whom he referred to as his fourth psychologist, he made plans to attend college and study psychology, and maybe become a counselor himself one day. The influence of extensive counseling services became evident when Cornel explained his efforts to help others:

> A lot of kids are hooked up on drugs and stuff. They call me and I go over to their house and stuff and I keep them occupied and stuff. Their parents are all into drugs. You can see that it is bothering them and it hurts to see that. I'm there to support them. If their parents are not there to support them, then I will be there. I grew up with a mom that was [into] drugs and stuff and [my] dad did drugs—all that. I never really had a childhood because I was introduced to all this at a young age.

As Cornel suggested, without extensive therapeutic support, his life might have turned out differently. He might not have developed his verbal skills, counseling aspirations, or plans for college, and like his brother and many of his friends, he might come to think that fighting was the best way to resolve conflicts. He said, "All my friends like to fight. I think there is better way to resolve something. I would rather talk things out."

Masa's Story

Masa was another youth in the study who benefited from a team of committed, capable adults. At a young age, Masa had difficulty managing anger, a problem he discovered after being teased by peers. Masa said:

> Yeah, I used to get teased a lot that's why I became violent. In sixth grade I just got fed up with it, with other people. So, I just turned around and one day I just punched a kid back, and it felt good. And he never bothered me again. So, I was like, "It works." It got to a point [when] I was fighting all the time. Like I don't take anything, like I was crazy and stuff. I was just doing whatever I wanted. And I'd go into blackouts where I [didn't] remember.

After a few fights during which Masa would "black out," he earned a reputation as someone not to be "messed with." As a consequence some avoided Masa and his "crazy" violence. Others, however, physically engaged with Masa as a way to earn an equally menacing reputation. The end result was that Masa was arrested and incarcerated for assault two years before our interview with him. After serving time in a youth correctional facility, Masa was referred to counseling services and a boy's group focused on anger management. Through these counseling-based services, Masa learned to control his temper. He said:

> Just like the school actually, like counseling, like [my counselor], she taught me through my first year. Like she was there when I need her. My family, I know they don't want me to fight. And just knowing that I don't want to get locked up and stuck in [correctional facility] and stuff like that. When I was in the program, they would let us know that there were more important things in life, like your family is more important, how you feel about yourself is more important. Is fighting with that person really worth you getting locked away? Like there's another crime against you. So it made us think, when I was in the programs, that the boys I talk to would help calm me down.

Even with steadfast assistance from others, teens like Alika, Cornel, and Masa were sometimes tempted to return to old habits. Some youth, like Cornel, continued to interact with family members, and all youth attended school and hung out with other teens. When in these settings, youth thought about solving problems using old methods from their past—by fighting or using drugs. Alika, for example, told us that even after three years of living with his foster family, he still got "that thinking in the back of me." Masa said:

> I have a problem with someone right now actually. The boy is eying me out [staring at him, indicating he wants to fight] and I eye them out and then think about it and I don't want to go back to my old ways. When he's with his boys he always acts all big and when I have my back to them and walking down the hall, then they'll say something and I'd turn around and he'd just stand there. So he always does that. I notice and one day I was leaving outside the back gate and he came walking down with his friend and they were looking at me, like eying me out like they want to fight and stuff.

Walking away from a fight required a different approach to and definition of situations, one that could allow the youth to retain positive senses of self or, in Alika's words, maintain their "pride." One solution was to see these invitations to fight as a part of a larger game. Physical "beat downs" were one way to win the game. Another winning method was to outsmart one's antagonist. Alika described:

> Me, right now I can go out and fight somebody and boom, right in [youth correctional facility]. It's just like that where you can take the harder route and go to the good side. Be good. Somebody call you out [challenge to fight], walk away. If I continue to do all this good rounds and the boy calls me out and I walk away, I am going to bet on myself, not on him. Everybody's going to be like, "Yeah, you just walk away." But that's right. If I was to fight with him, boom, I get locked up and he's out. He walks away and he's free. He's going to be like, "Look where I got him now."

As Anderson (1999, 71) found, boys and men can often avoid violence by "outwitting their adversaries." In Alika's case, outwitting others meant defining adversaries as boys who were trying to fool him. They were, in other words, people who would trick him into losing his freedom. Alika was a smart and savvy teen who, above all else, refused to be physically or intellectually outmaneuvered.

Just as teens' decisions "to make a change" occurred after multiple interactions with adults, teens' abilities to reframe these violent invitations, to "save face," and maintain a positive sense of self also took place within a context of adult support, mostly through conversations with foster parents, teachers, or counselors. The youth had emotional bonds with these individuals, an indication that the process of making a change was a long one that usually occurred when there were lasting, trusting relationships with adults. Alika alluded to the time and effort involved in these supportive relationships when noting that he "stressed out so many workers who tried to help" him. Alika knew, however, that an adult loved him when that adult "stayed strong" and did not "give up."

"GOING IT ALONE": RESPONSES TO INSTITUTIONAL FAILURE

Most youth in this study did not have a second line of defense on their side. Some foster families were poor fits for troubled youth. Teachers were often too overwhelmed to pay attention to every student, and, in some youth's eyes, school counselors were not to be trusted. The result, for many teens, was a feeling that adults could not help them. Indeed, a number of teens became masters of their own destinies and rejected the idea that they needed anyone, especially adults, to help them prepare for their future. In essence, these teens decided to "go it alone," meaning that they relied on themselves for support. Importantly, girls and boys had different experiences with "going it alone."

The decision to go it alone is best understood by looking closely at institutional failure, political neglect, and racialization in these neighborhoods. Urban ethnographers often tell of how social service institutions have failed in impoverished neighborhoods. Anderson (1999, 34) notes that a violence-based street code is "actually an adaptation to a profound lack of faith in the police and the judicial system," while Jones (2010, 5) writes that interpersonal violence "thrives in social settings where formal institutions, like the schools or the police, have abdicated responsibility for protecting inner-city residents."

Teens in this study certainly understood what it meant to grow up with meager social services, and the youth were never surprised to hear that a local politician or police department was under investigation for corruption, or that a much-loved program was being canceled. For example, in one housing development within Stevens Heights—a location without any parks or recreation facilities for the nearly one thousand residents—children played in a parking lot or in the neigh-borhood library, which contained only a few books. In Northward, teens (usually boys) walked to the beach and congregated on any bench or tree stump that had not become absorbed into the homeless camps that spread out along the beach-front. Keith probably described this reality best when he talked about growing up in a "broke-ass boring neighborhood and a broke-ass boring school. No music lessons, no dance programs, nowhere to go, and nothing to do."

Teens' narratives reveal another facet of institutional failure. Living without mean-ingful activities, institutional support, or opportunities was certainly palpable to teens, but what truly devastated the youth were the failures of the adults in their lives. Teens' decisions to forgo looking for help from others can be seen through a lens of human failure rather than institutional neglect. Teachers who didn't care or were rac-ist, vice principals who yelled at students, and police who abused their authority were memorable characters to adolescents, all proving that adults could not be trusted.

As noted, going it alone was different for girls and boys. Girls learned lessons of self-reliance earlier in life than boys did. As we saw in chapters 3 and 4, girls were taunted, teased, and tormented in school (often by boys) throughout their childhood, and adults often did not intervene to help them. Even worse, some girls found themselves blamed and targeted when they did turn to adults. In childhood, girls learned that they were on their own, at the same time that they understood that they were expected to accomplish many tasks for their families.[4]

Boys, on the other hand, tended to be older than girls when they came to the conclusion that adults could not help them, and thus the sting was fairly new for boys. Also, boys were not subject to as much regulation and monitoring as girls were, so that, when going it alone, the boys embraced a sense of independence rather than of self-reliance, associating independence with ideals of freedom and autonomy, especially in civic life. In contrast, self-reliance, for the girls, connoted a sense of their competence in accomplishing tasks in domestic worlds and in school without assistance from others.

Girls' Self-Reliance

During the period of our study, only one of the girls, Auggie, had found safe refuge through a second line of defense. As noted previously, very few teens in foster care found stability with their foster parents and this reduced the chances that any youth—male or female—would find sanctuary through the child welfare system. When exemplary foster families did emerge, they were likely to be assigned to the most difficult cases, indicating a gendered pattern. Because boys were often viewed as the most challenging children, boys were considered to be worthy of the best foster families.

Even when some girls were placed in stable foster homes or with other family members, there was another gender pattern that worked against the girls. Foster families, like many other families in America, often operated within patriarchal ideologies about how girls are supposed to look, act, and generally comport themselves. Like the girls discussed in chapters 3 and 4, the girls in foster placements therefore "got the second half" and faced enormous domestic responsibilities, often while boys were allowed extensive autonomy and freedom. Girls were also looked down on, teased, and shunned by boys in their foster families. Thus, even when some girls were placed with capable adults, the gender inequalities common to family life in the United States often made girls feel like second-class citizens, a reality that added a bitter edge even to otherwise stable foster experiences for girls.

Annabelle's experiences illustrate how a stable foster placement was not necessarily a safe refuge for girls. Like many youth in the lunch group, Annabelle had had an early life punctuated by extensive chaos and trauma. Both her parents were addicted to drugs and her father was eventually imprisoned. There was also sexual abuse from uncles, leading social service workers to look outside Annabelle's family for solutions. The goal for Annabelle was a foster placement that would lead to adoption, and on this score, the social service workers found an ideal context. Annabelle was adopted by a foster parent who was a single mother raising daughters close to Annabelle's age. In the eyes of these workers, Annabelle's case seemed like a welfare system success story.

But from Annabelle's vantage point, this foster context was imperfect and led to conflicting emotions. She was appreciative of having a home free from violence, sexual abuse, and drug addiction. She was also appreciative of having a "strong female role model," but Annabelle occasionally felt unappreciated, overlooked, and unloved. Her adopted mother was often overworked, tired, and critical of Annabelle, and Annabelle noted that her adopted mother was a perfectionist who had high expectations for her daughters. The result was that Annabelle felt blamed for not helping her adopted mother enough around the house. When Annabelle did finish her chores, she felt inadequate for not accomplishing them as well as her mother. In addition, her adopted mother criticized Annabelle for gaining too much weight. Having a perfect house, family, and body were emphasized in her foster family. Fat, lazy, and inadequate was how Annabelle sometimes felt in this context, and these emotions drove a wedge between her and her adopted mother.

Girls who remained with their biological families had complaints similar to Annabelle's, usually because patriarchal values and differential attention to and treatment of boys and girls were common features of many families. As a result, parental interventions were often seen by girls as forces to survive and overcome, rather than a source of support and guidance. Remember that Illeana received constant criticism from her father, who told her that she should spend more time thinking about dating and less time thinking about sports. Angel described receiving similar messages within her family and said, "My family criticize me all the time, 'Oh Angel you need to lose weight. Oh Angel you've got to do this.' And I'm like, 'I'll do it when I feel like it.'" In fact, Angel despised it when girls and women monitored what they ate, how they looked, or what they said in order to please men. As Angel argued, some girls and women "need a guy in their life to feel beautiful. I used to think that and after I was like, No I don't, I'm fucking beautiful by myself!"

Girls were not only let down by adults, but they also did not trust their friends. As noted in chapters 3 and 4, in settings where girls are devalued or have limited opportunities for high-status positions among peers (Eder 1985; Merten 1997), girls often mistrust and avoid other girls. The problem for girls was that boys were not particularly safe havens for them either. Therefore, girls were left adrift without any sources of support.

For example, Angel did not have many female friends and generally felt that girls were "too into boys." In contrast, she claimed that boys, especially her brothers and male cousins, were easy to trust. She said, "I could find a guy who is loyal on the spot." A loyal female friend, on the other hand, was rare, in Angel's view. Though Angel trusted her brothers, she admitted that they sometimes irritated her, and she argued, "My cousins and brothers they tell me when they fuck. It's so weird. I'd be talking to them on the phone, talking about school and stuff and next thing you know, 'Oh you know this girl, yeah, yeah, yeah, we had sex. Yes, she was easy.' I'm like, 'Ouch, really bro?'" Angel also noted that male friends were great, but that they often teased her, offering comments to remind her that she was not one of the guys. She said, "Like he's going to ask me do you have a pad or do you have a tampon, do you know what I mean?"

As noted in chapter 4, some girls who felt let down by family members and other adults looked for stability and support through romance. But as Annabelle's story in chapter 4 indicated, most girls found boyfriends to be disappointing. Even the most promising and passionate romances eventually cooled and some of the most loving boys experienced fickle emotions, making boyfriends poor prospects for long-term support.

Many girls, including Trisha, Illeana, and, eventually, Annabelle, became self-reliant, meaning that these girls looked to themselves for support and dedicated themselves to a series of tasks to accomplish as they prepared for adulthood. The mantra for self-reliant girls was to get through high school and get out into the world "on their own." Girls imagined that once they reached adulthood they would finally be able to obtain the type of independence, freedom, and autonomy that adolescent boys enjoyed. In other words, they knew that during their teen years they would not be able to escape scrutiny, surveillance, and gendered double standards. They would have to wait until they were out of high school to gain independence.

Importantly, self-reliant girls imagined independent womanhood to contain particular features. They wanted employment that would provide them with interesting work and financial independence. Self-reliant girls also imagined that they would need a college education or technical training to obtain such employment.[5] And getting into college or technical school required that other tasks be accomplished, including earning educational scholarships, getting good grades, selecting the right college or technical school, and preparing applications. The road to independent womanhood was paved with a series of tasks, and these girls were accustomed to accomplishing tasks without help from others.

For example, Annabelle's plan was to earn straight As in high school, graduate from high school a year early, go to community college for two years, transfer to a four-year university, and, eventually, become a nurse. Angel's plan was not as detailed as Annabelle's, but she promised herself to keep up her grades despite her frequent suspensions. Trisha also planned to graduate from high school early and enroll in a community college with a strong culinary arts program. Illeana used her sports successes to guide her, and she aimed for an athletic scholarship to attend college.

Boys' Masculine Independence, Autonomy, and Honor

The failure of adults and institutions translated into a reality in which the girls focused on their ability to set goals and accomplish tasks (i.e., their competence and self-reliance) without the help of adults or peers. Boys had a different response to institutional and adult failures, one that we describe as boys' independence.

There were at least three patterns within the boys' sense of independence. First, the meaning of independence for boys echoed historic themes of American individualism, citizenship, and masculinity. Second, compared with the girls, the boys expressed a stronger emotional response to adult failures around them, indicating that male independence was, in part, an emotional response to the lack of adult support. Third, the boys clung to an honor code to guide them in the absence of institutional and adult support.

To understand how the boys' sense of independence relates to the history of individualism and citizenship in America, it is important to detail the features of the boys' sense of independence. Boys who embraced independence emphasized their individual will to "make it on their own." Keith explained this common sentiment when he argued that: "If nobody is there for you, then say to yourself, 'I'm going to be better.' Say to yourself, 'I will succeed. I can't lose.' Mentally wise, if you're mentally wise, you're strong." Here, Keith is discussing moral, not physical strength. He also pointed out that moral strength can help people cope when "nobody is there for you."

Independence for many boys meant having strong, steadfast moral characters. Independent boys wanted to be respectable young men with the moral traits necessary to "be better," to "succeed," and to not "lose," as Keith articulated. Here, the boys' image of independence and strong moral character echoed the twin notions of American individualism and civic responsibility. As Lesko has argued (2001, 41), since the late 1800s, ideologies regarding good citizenship in Western nation-states were particularly masculine: citizenship emphasized "duty, courage, loyalty, and patriotism" among boys and young men. Lesko notes that within the historic project of raising boys to become men, there was also an overarching notion that a Western nation-state needed "both strongly willful and team-oriented citizens" who were "tough" and "courageous," and, therefore, potential leaders in civic life.

The boys in this study who felt let down by adults embraced the strongly willful and courageous aspects of American citizenship that Lesko discussed. These boys, however, were not "team oriented," nor were they patriotic; they did not trust institutions, organizations, and programs. And, as noted in chapter 5, they had many critiques of the rampant injustices and inherent racism of the "jacked-up" American system.

The type of independence embraced by the boys who were "going it alone" emphasized the power of a boy's individual will and the development of an internal moral compass determining what was a morally correct and respectable way of being in the world. Viewing themselves as autonomous agents who did not need the support of organizations, institutions, and (in some cases) parents, the boys cobbled together a sense of honor by themselves. They took cues from the world around them, but in the end each individual boy was the one who decided what was morally right and wrong. In addition, their sense of honor was particularly masculine in that they were not focused on domestic spheres or concerns.

As noted, the boys' sense of masculine independence had an emotional component. Boys' disappointment with human failures and, by extension, institutional neglect, was particularly acute, suggesting that adolescent boys, more than teenage girls, were upset by adult and institutional failures. Indeed, it was the boys, more than the girls, who offered particularly harsh critiques of school staff and other adults. For example, according to many boys, teachers were people who just picked up a paycheck or who demanded, but did not give, respect. Social workers, similarly, were heartless bureaucrats with little to offer, and even parents were portrayed as ineffective.

Keith criticized teachers who felt that they were superior to students because they have a "stupid little piece of paper." Chad, who is Native Hawaiian, believed that many teachers were racist. Comparing his experiences with those of Filipino students, he said:

> She is racist against students who are not Filipino. I proved it. Last year I had her for geometry. We had a group. This one student is like 100 percent Filipino. I said, "I'm going to ask for her help on this problem, you ask her for help on this other problem." He asks her for help, and she comes right over. She takes her time and helps him. I raise my hand like, "I need help." She's all, "Ask people in your group. Take out your notes." Some people say that's not racist. I'm like how is that *not* racist?

Joel described his frustration with teachers:

> Every teacher has a troubled child. That should be the kid that they would *have* to pay attention to. They see, "Oh this kid is just a pain in my ass." They shouldn't think of it like that. They should try to figure out what is going on for this kid. Don't look at it as a job. Look at it as something bigger than, "Oh that is my paycheck. I'm just here for the money. This is not just some kid who is irritating me." This [kid] could be the next president.

Some boys felt that their parents were failures and focused on parents' inability to provide financially for their children. Keith noted, "My parents are lousy parents." As noted in Benny's story from our introduction, Benny and Keith's mother abandoned the family, and their father was not able to hold down a job, forcing the family into homelessness. Joel and Julian preferred their dad to stay out of their business, claiming that his temper usually exacerbated any conflict or problem that Joel and Julian faced. Extracting a general moral lesson from his father's example, Joel explained, "I think when adults get involved, they just make it worse." The best course of action for parents, according to Joel, was to leave their children alone.

With their deep sense of disappointment with the adults around them and their keen desire to succeed even when, as Keith said, "nobody is there for you," independent boys developed and rather zealously clung to their personal value systems. Here, independent boys imagined that having "strong moral values" would provide them with the foundation they needed to live a dignified adult life. In fact, the independent boys in this study held on relentlessly to their morals, often seeing the world in strict good and bad, and right and wrong terms, and leading many of the boys to argue forcefully for what they felt was the "right" thing to do and a "good" way to think.

Although some might argue that these independent teens were drawing from a "code of the streets" (Anderson 1999), or, as Jones (2010, 5) said, a "system of accountability that governs" interpersonal relations, for their moral compass, we found that the boys' sense of a common moral code governing respectable male behaviors was probably more illusory than real. There are at least four reasons why we argue that there was no agreed-upon, coherent "code of the streets" in these neighborhoods. First, many youth lived in rural locales, making it unlikely that they would live by an urban, street-based value system.

Second, when we asked boys to describe the details of their values, we found many points of disagreement among boys living in the same neighborhood. Some believed that it was acceptable to use pipes, chains, or other heavy objects during a fight, while others felt that fights should be "old fashioned" with fists only. A few boys thought that winning a fight meant injuring another teen, perhaps even sending the boy to the hospital (i.e., causing morbid injuries). In contrast, there were other boys who felt that sending a boy to the hospital was unacceptable. Hospital visits were expensive, and some boys thought that it was unfair to inflict serious economic strain on another person's family.

In fact, many of the fights between and among boys were based on boys' disagreements about what were "right" and "wrong" ways to act and to treat one another. Violence was used as a tool to correct another boy who was acting "incorrectly." In this way, the boys' steadfast dedication to their own moral codes set them up for conflicts when others saw the world differently or lived by a different set of rules. And it was common for the boys to encounter other boys who had different perceptions of right and wrong.

The third reason why we believe that there was not one coherent moral code governing male behavior was that male friendship networks in these neighborhoods were not stable. Boys' peer groups shifted and changed, and it was common for friends to get into physical frays, often because, like male acquaintances, male friends also disagreed about what was morally right and wrong. When a boy felt that he was being "disrespected" by a friend, he was likely to retaliate with violence. Male violence in this study, therefore, grew out of differences in values and beliefs regarding respectability between and among boys rather than from their common adherence to an agreed-upon set of rules.

Teens' moral disagreements, we argue, also led male friendship groups to be unstable. During their first couple years in high school, many boys touted the virtues of their male friends, who some boys called "their boys." Many boys even explained that they were dedicated to a male ethic of "Joes before hoes," and that real friends "have your back," meaning that boys would physically protect one another from threats.

Despite their verbal pronouncements about being dedicated to their male friends, by their last two years in high school, many of the boys had found themselves betrayed, insulted, and let down by their peers. Blake was one teen who initially loved the company of his friends, who were in the "fast crowd." His friends were fun, partied on the weekends, skipped school, and got high while also promising camaraderie and devotion, which Blake appreciated. Blake, who joined the lunch bunch group during his junior year of high school, explained how these relationships ended: "My first couple years, I was trying to be with the popular crowd. I always dreamed and idolized that clique. The popular kids caused fights, these kids ended up getting suspended and kicked out of school, stupid stuff. I joke around all the time and teased one of my friends, so he decided to get up into my face [challenged Blake to a fight]. That just opened my eyes. These kids take things too seriously. That is the only way they know how to solve problems, is with their fists."

Many boys were like Blake and eventually fell out with friends. At some point, it was inevitable for friends to irritate and intentionally or unintentionally disrespect one another. Jared discussed how these irritations could lead to fights among friends, "They could all be just joking around and somebody just takes it the wrong way and then they just start arguing and then they start fighting. I guess they can't hold their temper. I guess they just get mad at every little thing and want to fight."

Beyond Good or Ghetto: Youth Imagine Adulthood

The fourth reason why we believe that the moral codes underlying youths' fights did not represent a coherent "code of the streets" was because the boys (as well as girls) in this study expressed many traditional and conventional values, rather than street-based and countercultural beliefs. While self-reliant girls and independent boys looked to themselves rather than to adults as they navigated their way toward adulthood, this did not mean that these youth were unconventional or completely rebellious. In fact, when these youth discussed their futures and adulthood, they revealed how deeply committed to conventional, American notions of success they were.[6]

In the introduction of the book, we met Angel and Benny, who faced significant crossroads in their young lives as they entered their senior years of high school. Interestingly, while both youth had been suspended multiple times and were seen as troublemakers by some teachers, these teens were conventional when they imagined their futures. Angel wanted to be a lawyer and was particularly proud of the fact that she was able to make good grades. Angel understood that she was smart and that, when circumstances demanded, she could focus and make academics her priority. Angel also knew that she would have to fight others with her words rather than her fists in the future, and there were moments when she looked forward to that task.

Unlike Angel, Benny did not have a specific career in mind when he thought about his future. Nevertheless, Benny wanted to be a successful adult, and when Benny discussed success, his traditional desires came to the fore: "I don't want to be like my parents and my parents before them and all that stuff. I mean, my parents living paycheck by paycheck. I mean they didn't have no success—they had success by having children they love and all that stuff, but like no success to make their name known in a positive way. I want to just have a good job and have a decent car, a truck. I want a decent house. Something to say like, I work so hard. I need to accomplish all this."

As noted in the introduction, in his senior year of high school, Benny had started to work with a team of construction workers, imagining that a life of manual labor would give him the financial wherewithal needed to have a "decent" house and a secure family. His job also allowed him to qualify for a loan for his first truck. The problem was that Benny started drinking with his coworkers after work. He was skipping school and his grades were suffering. By April of his senior year, Benny learned that he did not have the grades to graduate—a fact that made his dream of a stable conventional life hang in the balance.

Julian was similar to Benny in terms of having a long history of suspensions as well as hopes for a stable adult life. Because of his propensity for fighting, Julian had been transferred out of Seaside and into Hill School, an alternative high school, in his sophomore year. The move to Hill School marked a shift for Julian, as it uprooted him from his friendship group at Seaside. At this same time, Julian's father was facing a long prison sentence for assault, and this family turmoil proved extremely perplexing for Julian, leading him to become particularly judgmental of adults.

We talked with Julian when he transferred back to Seaside to finish his senior year, and his comments revealed his growing interest in a conventional future. He said: "I don't want to have to bust ass my whole life. Not caring about your education and not paying attention in school, later in life you have a shitty job. Later on all the things that you want, you can only buy so much. Versus, if you get your education and do what you gotta do, you can have a job and a house and you can have all the stuff you want. You can retire and relax instead of being the one who is still working and busting ass."

The problem for many independent teens like Angel, Benny, Keith, and Julian was that they could not imagine how they were going to cross the divide between their high school habits and the specific futures they desired.

CATCHING UP WITH TEENS: A BRIEF EPILOGUE

The fact that all of the teens in this study had been referred to counseling services meant that they faced some sort of challenge in their lives, and many of them confronted what we call chaotic or traumatic circumstances. Study members discussed family violence, victimization by family members, parental substance abuse, parental incarceration, and homelessness as traumatic experiences that dramatically interrupted their childhoods. Despite these challenges, the youth in this study were not remorseless criminals living by the "meanest codes of the meanest streets."

Moreover, none of the youth, as far as we have learned, had become involved in the adult criminal justice system. Given that Hawai'i, like many U.S. states, experienced an exponential increase in its prison population from the 1980s to the early 2000s, the ability to stay out of prison can be interpreted as a marker of adult success. Thus, the concluding finding of our study with youth is that, despite upheavals in the youth's lives, teens achieved many different types of success as young adults. In the following, we detail what happened to many of the teens when they became young adults.

Angel moved to California, lived with extended family members, and graduated from high school. At the time when this book was being written, Angel had completed two years of community college in California and was working in an entry-level position in California's technology industry. She was planning to transfer to a prestigious four-year college in the San Francisco Bay Area. She said that she was happy, although she noted that her life was hectic with work and school.

As we noted, Cassey dropped out of high school to help her mother and we heard nothing about her after she left school. Illeana, Trisha, and Annabelle were enrolled in community colleges in Hawai'i. Alika was also "doing very well," according to his parents, although we did not discover details about his work and college plans. We lost touch with Cornel and Masa, but according to teachers and other school staff, both students were "successful" in that they had earned good grades and graduated from high school.

Benny and Keith, whose foster father owned a construction company, found semi-stable employment as construction workers, and both successfully passed the General Education Development test. Given that 8 percent of Hawai'i's labor force is employed in construction occupations (U.S. Census 2000b), this was a steady employment track for some in Hawai'i, and these boys' connection through their foster father gave them an advantage in this field.

Benny's worries about alcoholism ended up being prescient, as he continued to drink heavily after high school. He stopped showing up for his job, leading his foster father to "let him go," although Benny did find semi-regular employment with another construction team. The work was physically difficult for Benny, and he wondered how long he could meet its physical demands. His unsteady work was particularly troublesome because, by the age of twenty-three, he had three children to support. He was an extremely proud father, but without a consistent job, he was not able to be the provider that he had hoped to become, although he showered his children with love.

Keith, who moved to the continental United States, led a team of heavy equipment operators. Going to work, drinking in bars, and going back to work was Keith's routine. As a team leader, he could avoid a daily routine of arduous labor. He did not have the physical aches and pains that plagued Benny. Because he was single, he did not have to grapple with the specter of being a father, provider, and head of the family. But while he had employment success, Keith did not achieve the "clean" and healthy life he had imagined for himself as a teenager. Remember that during his senior year of high school, Keith distanced himself from his friends who were drinking heavily and doing drugs, activities that Keith at the time felt would "destroy his body."

Indeed, this is one of the negative outcomes found in this study. Independent boys who had been confident and hopeful about their futures often found themselves falling into the behaviors that they had denounced as teenagers. Benny, who had looked down on his parents for being poor providers because they were unemployed and drug addicted, found himself on the precarious edge of alcoholism, joblessness, and absentee parenting in his twenties. Keith, who had wanted to live a healthy and "clean" life, found himself drinking heavily as an adult.

Joel found service sector work for a local company, although his employment, as we heard, was not well paid or stable. He seemed to work only off and on. Julian selected another route to adult stability. He joined the military—a move that provided economic security. In chapter 5, we noted that military personnel were usually associated with being "from the mainland" and were often seen as racist and as outsiders to Hawai'i. In addition, youth noted that military members misused their authority, disrespected locals, and sexually demeaned women in the community. In the boys' ideologies regarding who was dominant and who was submissive, who hurt others and who was hurt, it was often military men who were positioned as the aggressors. Joining the military, therefore, required some internal moral negotiations for the boys.

Young Men and the Military

To understand boys' military decisions, we need to examine the boys' views of military life more closely. Though many boys mistrusted the military, for some boys, being in the military translated into having a stable job. The cost of living in Hawai'i is extremely high, and employment was difficult for some boys to find. Also remember that teens looked at class and economic inequalities in terms of those who "worked hard" versus those who got things "handed to them" or who had things "easy." Military personnel were seen as privileged people who "get more stuff cheaper," especially housing, groceries, and gas—three costly expenses. The military life, therefore, appeared to many boys as a privileged life.

Julian mentioned many of the attractions of the military when he discussed his reasons for joining the Army. He said, "I signed up for the Army. My grandpa served in the Marines. Like, the economy is hard. It is hard to find a job. The Army is a guaranteed job. The benefits when you retire. I look at all that stuff. It is easier."

Kula's, Vinny's, and Wilson's narratives also reveal how military life held a visceral attraction for some boys. All three teens had had difficulty with schoolwork and especially with focusing their attention in the classroom. Kula, for example, was eventually referred to counseling for being unable to "calm down" and "focus" in class. "Focus" and "calm down" became common refrains in Kula's life, as Kula often became agitated and distraught at school, leading him to note that "no one in class can handle me." While several adults at school perceived that therapy and counseling would help him, Kula believed that he needed something more austere. He explained, "They put me in therapy. It is torture. My therapist tries to get me to share my feelings. I am not a feeling-sharing person. I would rather take a military person as my therapist." For boys who rejected "talk therapy," counseling, and psychiatry as being too demonstrative, the military offered advantages. Vinny, Wilson, and Kula explained:

Kula: Once I graduate, I'm joining it. Going into the Army.

Katy: What do you like about military?

Vinny: Military can lead people to the right path.

Wilson: It helps you hold in your anger. It helps you concentrate on what you have to do and not goofing off.

Kula: Discipline, respect, and attitude.

On the cusp of adulthood, boys like Julian, Kula, and Wilson sensed that they did not have the traits necessary to bring them stability on their own. For Wilson, it was the ability to concentrate and "hold in his anger" that he lacked, while Kula noted that he couldn't control his behavior. Also, the solutions to their problems were masculinized, in that the boys described their need to "hold in" emotions. What they needed was less "talk" and more "discipline."

A point of concern here is that it was often the boys in the study who had trouble with authority figures who were attracted to the military. As we saw in chapter 5, boys in general were very likely to fight in contexts where they sensed racist demoralization. Despite the many attempts to achieve racial equality in the U.S. military, research consistently notes that racial conflict persists within military ranks (Burk and Espinoza 2012). In a study of 1,737 veterans surveyed in 2001, Sohn and Harada (2008) found that 38 percent of veterans categorized as Asian American and Pacific Islander (AAPI) reported having experienced ethnic or racial discrimination during their most recent military service. Other studies have established that adverse race-related events are extremely traumatic events for AAPI veterans, significantly contributing to the high rates of PTSD among this population (Loo et al. 2001, 2005, 2007). In fact, researchers argue that these race-related stressors contribute to the fact that AAPI veterans tend to have poorer mental health than other veterans (Tsai and Kong 2012).

CONCLUSION

A few trends outlined in this chapter shed light on the fairly successful experiences of youth. The first trend was that, despite rampant poverty, persisting racialization, political alienation, and the numerous social service failures confronting these two communities, there were noteworthy adults who were helping youth achieve resiliency against difficult odds. More specifically, there were state-supported therapeutic services as well as a community-based safety net made up of capable and caring adults who assisted teens. The result was that many adults came together in makeshift teams to provide some youth with the patience, commitment, and support needed to help them avoid violence, substance abuse, and school failure.

This recipe for success seemed to require particular components, with counseling and talk therapy being common ingredients. Even for those youth who had been arrested, detained, or incarcerated, the decision to change was not entirely born out of a desire to avoid the "pain of imprisonment" and, instead, came from the teens' ability to talk about and reframe their experiences, especially to talk about the many violent provocations they experienced.

The second trend was that gender shaped how the youth imagined their futures and prepared for young adulthood. The boys who fared the best in this study were those who had the second line of defense on their side.[7] In other words, they were the boys who did not rely solely on themselves and their masculine independence to get by. Rather, these boys had a team of capable adults to help them and, in fact, they engaged in the feminized practices of "talking it out," processing emotions, and receiving "love." Masculinity standards often told boys to ignore, cover up, and overcome the traumas of their past; if they did not have a team of adults to help them, they did this on their own.[8]

Girls, on the other hand, did not often find sanctuary within the second line of defense, and this might have something to do with the fact that many families in these neighborhoods—as indeed in numerous neighborhoods throughout the United States—operate within patriarchal values and structure. Thus, girls faced unequal division of household labor and strict regulation and control in families.

There was an inherent irony in girls' experiences as they graduated from high school. Even though the girls faced numerous restrictions, pressures, and demands, self-reliant girls seemed to have an easier time than independent boys when transitioning into young adulthood. There were some key reasons for this. First, most girls learned an early lesson that adults were not likely to intervene and to solve problems in girls' lives: the girls knew early that they were "on their own." By their teen and early adult years, therefore, girls were accustomed to accomplishing tasks without much help from others. On a second and related note, the structure of young womanhood was not much different from the structure of girlhood. During childhood and adolescence, girls grew used to undertaking demanding work and, often, to completing thankless tasks. Thus, young adulthood, with its combined demands of school (for some), work, and family could be seen as "more of the same" for girls.[9]

8

___

Theoretical Conclusions

This book reveals what it is like to be an adolescent under colonial patriarchy—a system in which racial marginalization and male privilege are central organizing features of everyday life. In the introduction, we explored theories of patriarchy and racialization under colonialism, and we noted how they structure the economic, political, and social statuses available to youth—and their resulting life chances. One key feature of the colonial patriarchy perspective that we advanced is that it predicts a diversity of experiences based on what is called an individuals' positionality. In other words, adolescence is not a monolithic experience but rather, is differentially experienced according to a series of hierarchies and exclusions as well as supports and opportunities. Therefore, the life chances and challenges confronting the youth depended on their gendered identities, the history of racialization faced by members of their race and ethnic group, and their economic status. It is at the intersection of major dimensions of inequality that we can understand the vicissitudes of adolescence. The study also revealed the critical role of caring adults at the interface of youth and the institutions that train and discipline them, in making pathways available for adolescents to grow their capabilities and choices. Based on these findings, we extend critical studies perspectives on punishment, which tends to portray a monolithic punitive system rather than one in which institutional agents' compassion matters in meaningful ways.

In the following sections, we review the key features of gender and racialization, first for the girls and then for the boys. We then summarize the contributions that the girls' and boys' experiences can make to critical perspectives of youth and youth violence. After offering a view of youth's experiences through a colonial patriarchy lens, we explain how youth violence can be read in the colonial patriarchy scheme. We conclude with some notes on promising directions for future work with teens growing up at the axis of multiple inequalities.

RACIALIZED PATRIARCHY: THE GIRLS' STORY

Girls' experiences were among the most complicated ones to emerge in this study, because Native Hawaiian and other Pacific Islander girls confront a complex set of social and familial inequities. This study has told an implicit tale about the multiple contingencies in girls' experiences that we want to make explicit here, and that is how male privilege and racialization wove their way through the girls' lives to create specific obstacles, resistance strategies, and realities for the girls.

The girls' experiences can be understood in more detail by highlighting how Western patriarchal structure and meanings have been thrust on women and girls in ways that advance the processes of racialization as well as male privilege. Hegemonic femininity produces particular controlling images (Pyke and Johnson 2003) that are centered on women and girls with economic and racial privileges—the racial and economic elites—but are used to control, and to "other," women who are from subordinated racial and economic groups. Certainly the bourgeois images of the domesticated, self-sacrificing, nurturing, compliant, and dependent female are troubling enough for all women, privileged or not. Add to this the racially weighted institutional hierarchies dominated by Whites and Asians in Hawai'i, severe economic hardships, and the political alienation confronting families in this study, and we see that many women were asked to perform everyday miracles. Mothers were expected to create nurturing homes and lend support to extended family members with meager or nonexistent wages. They were also expected to contribute to building healthy and active communities while most of the political leaders in the state ignored their needs. These pressures created visible race and class disparities in the quality of health care, elder care, childcare services, and education. And given this reality, it was usually women rather than men or the state who filled the gaps in meeting the needs of families. These women had at least one resource on their side: their daughters.

Many girls in this study occupied a subordinate status that could be described as that of invisible laborers. As noted in chapter 3, the girls' domestic work was a cornerstone of family and community survival, but girls' efforts often went unacknowledged and unappreciated. Many girls in the study were perplexed by this reality, as most deeply loved their families, while also chaffing at the injustice. These family-based conflicts for girls were made especially keen by the relationships between girls and boys in families. Girls were routinely devalued and demoralized in the family, often by boys. Many boys, who had few status opportunities themselves, had an advantage over girls in the form of male privilege, with resulting autonomy, freedom from household labor, and leisure time.

Boys maneuvered to maintain these advantages, often by distancing themselves from all things feminine, including domestic labor. For some boys, distancing themselves from the taint of feminine domestic spheres also meant that these boys looked down on and denounced the girls in their families. This denigration from boys created another layer of stress and strain for the girls. Here, the gender line was drawn not only on the street, but also in the family, where it sometimes positioned the needs of girls against those of boys.

Chapter 4 highlights how colonial patriarchy produced complicated and often contradictory messages and statuses for girls in peer groups. As Jones (2010), Leitz (2003), and Ness (2004) note, girls struggling with racialization and poverty can craft alternative femininities, including tough and rugged violent personas, to survive in worlds where docility and meekness would be serious problems for them. In this book, we note that girls' social networks were not entirely defined by hegemonic or alternative versions of femininities, and girls negotiated conflicting demands. Girls were evaluated according to their moral strength, self-reliance, and outspokenness—traits that were necessary for family, community, and their own survival.

The girls in this study also had to negotiate hegemonic rules dictating the meaning of femininity. For example, girls were expected to be chaste, dependent on boys, demure, petite, pale, frail, and sexually attractive to and interested in boys. As reviewed in the introduction, Richie's (2012) perspective posits that the more distant one is from the dominant hegemonic norms, the more complicated and contingent a person's life and life chances become. Chapter 4 stands as a testament to the specific contingencies and contradictions that the Native Hawaiian, Samoan, and other Pacific Islander girls faced. On one hand, many girls felt pressure to fit the dominant, White, middle-class image of femininity (sexually modest, dependent on boys, and attractive to boys). On the other hand, those who conformed to this image were also at a disadvantage in standing up for themselves. Thus, we found that colonial patriarchy for girls meant that the rules facing girls were so narrow, complicated, and contradictory that girls could rarely meet the conflicting gender expectations thrust on them. Therefore, girls were rarely able to gain the respect that they sought to receive.

In chapters 3 and 4, we also saw girls developing resistance strategies to accommodate the unequal division of labor and gendered mistreatment that they received. The girls in this study learned at an early age that they needed to speak out and stand up for themselves—a situation that contributed to the fact that most of the girls in this study were very comfortable talking about their lives and their needs. It should be noted that the line between talking it out and striking out was rather thin at some points for girls. While girls were verbally skilled, there were times when they physically lashed out instead of speaking up.

In addition to tracing the childhood and adolescent pressures that girls faced, chapters 3 and 4 also uncovered circumstances that assisted them later in life.

Being able to accomplish difficult tasks, often without help from others, probably contributed to girls' sense of competence. As we saw in chapter 7, many girls in this study prepared for their post-high-school years by making plans for their futures and meeting difficult goals, some of which included applying to colleges and finding jobs to fit their school schedules. A couple of the girls made plans to graduate from high school early as an escape route from the enormous family strains that they faced.

In chapter 7, we found that age added another dimension to the story of colonial patriarchy. More specifically, patriarchy meant that girls did not develop a sense of gender privilege and the corresponding expectation that they would receive entitled treatment in families, at school, and with peers. While girls certainly did not enjoy being disrespected, they also did not expect special treatment and, therefore, they were less likely to feel overwhelmingly distraught when faced with disrespect as young adults. Here, we argue that girls tended to go through fewer status adjustments than boys when traversing the adolescent/adult divide.

Hawai'i's economy is heavily based on mass tourism that markets a service-oriented visitor experience. This industry has a history of selectively appropriating indigenous values of aloha and hospitality and promoting the imagery of the exotic, domesticated native (Trask 1999). For Native Hawaiian and other Pacific Islander girls who entered the service sector workforce in Hawai'i, the experience of being unappreciated, objectified, assigned thankless tasks, and having their dress, bodies, and demeanor policed did not necessarily come as a surprise. Both girls and young women were likely to be monitored, degraded, and overwhelmed with work.

MALE PRIVILEGE UNDER COLONIAL PATRIARCHY: THE BOYS' STORY

Boys experienced a mix of privilege and disadvantage. As noted, boys had autonomy and freedom from domestic responsibilities, but they also faced the fallout of racialization under settler colonialism. In essence, males were tasked with being protectors and providers while their families were relegated to some of the most precarious positions in the economy and the political system. The perspective of colonial patriarchy that we offer places boys' position between privilege and disadvantage in a larger context and points to how the boys were set up to face numerous difficulties when they became young men.

The structure of male privilege under colonial patriarchy not only positioned males in dominant roles in families but also meant that men were seen as having agency. In contrast, hegemonic notions of femininity tended to construct women and girls as being vulnerable and easily taken advantage of. Because of their age, most boys were not in the labor force and, therefore, the manly image of economic provider and head of the family was not one that they could take on as adolescents. Regardless, the boys did demonstrate concerns about having a role in public arenas, with a sense of public (or civic) life that was limited to school, neighborhoods, and teen "hangouts." When circulating in these public spaces, the boys tended to believe that they had a masculine duty to stand up for themselves as well as to defend against egregious wrongs or injustices that they witnessed.

One of their most pressing concerns, according to the boys, was the race-based demoralization that they confronted. Having masculine agency in a racialized society meant that boys were fighting multiple inequalities with few resources. In fact, when boys faced family traumas or when they were disrespected or abused, their sense of masculine agency created a visceral disdain for this vulnerability and their lack of control over their circumstances. In some ways, fighting was a way to take control over a situation and to act like "a man" rather than a fearful "child."

The masculine scripts of patriarchy melded together with a globally nested settler colonial regime of racial stratification to position boys in precarious no-win situations. Violent boys were seen as threatening and confirmed the fears of dominant groups. Survival tactics, such as fighting, that may have worked for them during adolescence only promised involvement in the criminal justice system in a state where the overrepresentation of Native Hawaiians and Pacific Islanders in jails and prisons had long been an intractable problem. Tracing gender schemes under colonialism, Tengan (2002, 245) argues that racially privileged men in colonial societies are often quick to "point out the violence and misogyny of hypermasculine practices" among Pacific Islanders as a way to reaffirm their own "superiority and dominance."

It should be noted here that there have been decades of colonial discourse about savage, violent, and primitive qualities among indigenous men. Because of this, powerful elites as well as a state apparatus of social control are (to some degree) expecting male violence. Violent young men were apt to be construed as even more frightening and dangerous than violent boys, because of their age. Seen as undisciplined, out of control, and possessing the full physical power of manhood, violent men were perceived as a serious social problem that, as mentioned earlier, translated into the likelihood that they would be heavily policed, arrested, and sent to prison. Indeed, this was the reality confronting many study members' fathers, older brothers, male cousins, and uncles. It was also a reality that reproduced the economic, political, and social marginalization already confronting families in this study.

Most boys who graduated from the lunch group program managed to stay out of prison, but their transition into manhood was difficult. As mentioned in chapter 7, boys who landed in the community safety net and who talked through difficult emotions with counselors and other supportive adults did fairly well. However, boys who avoided the feminized processes of discussing their feelings and emotionally depending on others faltered. There were a few masculinized professions in Hawai'i that boys attempted to enter after high school, namely manual labor and the military. We suggest that racialized gender, however, may have compromised young men's ability to thrive in these contexts.

Remember that boys were socialized to fight injustice, which they commonly viewed as being taken advantage of by others. It was likely that in both manual labor jobs and the military—two occupations many boys considered to be viable options—boys would confront authority figures who belittled and demoralized those in subordinate positions. It was likely that many of these young men would "react" and stand up against injustice, thus making their employment unstable. Also, if young men confronted racist slurs in these work worlds, they might be likely to feel compelled to stand up and fight, as they had when they were teenagers.

CONTRIBUTIONS TO THE LITERATURE

As noted in the introduction, the findings from this study of Pacific Islander youth can contribute to multiple theories pertaining to youth violence, interlocking oppressions, and critical theories of youth resilience. Moreover, we argued that there were several gaps in the youth violence and critical youth studies literatures, which we promised to fill. Below, we provide a summary of the theoretical and empirical contributions of the study.

Colonial Theories of Racial Domination

Previously we argued that, to date, theories of youth marginalization have not offered nuanced explanations of racism in the United States. More specifically, criminological explorations of violence tend to focus on racial residential segregation in the United States and on community stigma as key sources of racial oppression in young people's lives. In chapter 5, however, the youth told a different story. The teens, especially the boys, explained that they were growing up in a "jacked-up" American system, in which the odds were stacked against members of their racial and ethnic group.

The youth's arguments in chapter 5 introduce a theoretical challenge. For example, we often saw how dire economic conditions threatened family unity. Losing one's home, living in a car or a tent, sending children to live with other relatives or friends, having the state "take children," working multiple jobs, and being unable to afford health care and elder-care services were just some of the threats to family stability mentioned by the teens. Considering that poverty creates and exacerbates many of the challenges that teens faced, it would have been logical to argue that economic marginalization was a central problem limiting the youth's life chances. Explaining the strain in teens' lives as deriving only from their economic status, however, would have been a disservice to the youth featured in chapter 5, who told us that racism was their core concern.

Colonial frameworks allow us to examine the ways that the poverty confronting many of these families was created through racialization, racism, and race-making throughout American history. In the introduction, we outlined Tatum's (2000a, 2000b, 2002) theory of the racialized economic structure facing African Americans. A similar racialized understanding of poverty can also be applied to economic opportunity structures in Hawai'i, although it is beyond the scope of this study to detail the complicated history of racialized economic exclusion in Hawai'i.

To state it briefly, we offer a racialized economic perspective to note that poverty is racialized not just because members of some racial or ethnic groups are disproportionately poor or disproportionately reside in poor neighborhoods. Colonial theories outline how histories of racialization shape the way that groups have been differentially included and/or excluded in the U.S. economic system.[1] Moreover, such racially based economic exclusions have far-reaching effects across time and space; these effects should not be ignored.

Settler colonialism presented the teens in our study with a world in which the lion's share of privilege, power, prestige, and wealth lay disproportionately in the hands of Whites and members of some Asian ethnic groups, especially those in high positions with ties to global corporate networks or the upper echelons of the military industrial complex. Moreover, the constructed meanings and structure of life opportunities tethered to racial categories also meant that groups categorized as non-White or non-Asian, faced daily reminders of their compromised status. As boys recounted, because they were Brown and not White, because they were local and not from the mainland, or because they were Native Hawaiian or Samoan, and not Haole, they were seen as "stupid," "dumb," "ignorant," or "illiterate."

Boys interpreted economic inequalities through a racial lens and suggested that racially privileged groups were made up of those who "had more," "got more," and "had things handed to them." Elites were those who "did not work as hard" because of racial privilege. The image in boys' narratives about race is consistent with the racial formation explained earlier, in that it is not simply economic inequalities that determine one's advantages or disadvantages in life. In chapter 5, we saw the different ways that negative images of boys as passive and easily dominated or as violent and unintelligent led boys to embrace strategies that included self-presentation as being violently fearless or violently fearsome.

Regardless of whether boys were seen as passive and naïve or as physically powerful and intellectually weak, racist tropes constructed Native Hawaiians and Pacific Islanders in some similar ways: as ultimately lacking the ability to self-govern, either because they needed paternalistic protection (too fearful, passive, and naïve to govern themselves) or because they were "savage" (too fearsome, prone to violence, and not smart enough to govern themselves). The answer imposed in the end, in both cases, was the "civilizing force" of foreign influences. This outlook extended to the disciplinary policies of schools and the juvenile justice system, where paternalism often drove decisions about the form and length of disciplinary action.

As we noted in the introduction, the racist tropes that drove colonial control in the Pacific live on in the collective memory of youth. We drew from the images of collective trauma presented by Alexander et al. (2004) to assert that injustices of the past become embedded in the present through mass-mediated narratives, claims, metaphors, and analogies. Acknowledging that there are mediated images of collective trauma, our study focused close attention on how the youth used the images of past injustices to make sense of the world and, especially, of their place in it.

Using the colonial framework of race and racialization presented above, we assert that the search for respect that we saw boys undertaking in chapter 5 is not an epiphenomenon of neoliberalism, poverty, or institutional neglect. Nor is it a phenomenon that is located primarily in deindustrialized urban centers. We argue that the racial project of designating some racial or ethnic groups as superior and other groups as inferior has been a central project throughout American history and is ubiquitous, shaping opportunities for urban and nonurban youth alike.

The struggle for dignity, respect, and honor can be viewed, by extension, as a struggle against many forms of racial domination and against long racist histories. Moreover, we use colonial theory to note how White racial superiority has been stitched into the very fabric of American society and its national identity. Seen against a backdrop of colonial theory, therefore, chapter 5 stands as the youth's testimony to the destructiveness and persistence of racism in their lives and chapter 6 illustrates the ways racism manifests in institutions of social control. We assert that it is time to take the multifaceted nature and the long history of racial inequalities in America seriously in our theories.

Gender and Intersecting Inequalities in a Colonial Society

In our introduction, we noted that youth violence theories should account for the intersections of inequalities in youth's lives. We also wanted to offer images of teen violence that did not pathologize the youth in this study but, instead, allowed us to view the girls' and boys' resilience and resistance together with their violence. In other words, we advocated for a more holistic view of violent youth as individuals who live between the dichotomous categories of "good" or "ghetto" and "decent" or "violent."

In terms of accounting for intersecting inequalities, we turn to Patil's (2013) transnational gender theory. Patil argues that "patriarchy—and thereby gender— is always already imbricated within multiple axes of power that are advanced by, complicit in, and often the vehicle for various border crossings" (848). Border crossings in the context of this study comprise the intrusion of Western gender systems into Pacific lands.

Patil (2013) highlights two ways that Western gender order has been imposed in non-Western lands. First, Western gender schemes made "explicit connections between familial rule and political rule, arguing that the family is the source of all authority relationships in society" (854). Here, the colonist positioned himself as the patriarchal leader who was responsible for the "shaping up" of his children (colonial subjects) into proper citizens.[2] Second, Patil points to the modern gender order characterized by "the public/private divide and the relegation of the family and women to the private" (855). This public/private gender order generated divisions between men's and women's orientations, roles, labor, time, space, and even their bodies. Modern patriarchy also created the devaluation of feminized labor—which we explored in chapter 3—wherein childcare, cooking, cleaning, and managing other domestic tasks became the "lowly" responsibilities of women and girls. Conversely, taking an active role in the public sphere became highly revered and was masculinized.

Age inequalities and the disenfranchisement of young people also emerged in the modern Western gender order. The Western and domesticated gender ideologies, in which women were to care for and nurture children and men were to be leaders and economic providers, gave youth very little power. Children were emotionally, economically, and politically dependent on the family unit, with fathers making decisions on behalf of the entire family. Being dependent on the family unit also led to different forms of inequalities for girls and boys.

In Western gender schemes—and also within Western projects to "civilize" the colonies—female children and femininity were positioned in particular hierarchical relationships with men and masculinity. In the Western colonizers' human taxonomies, White men were positioned at the apex of civilized societies. And White male superiority could only be ensured through the inferior positioning of adult women and of girls (who occupied a more devalued status than women because of their age). In essence, "girls were *necessary* [emphasis in the original] to define manliness by virtue of their difference from and distance from manliness. *Fin-de-siècle* masculinity came to depend upon femininity (as well as on children and savages) to define itself" (Lesko 2001, 78).

In addition to disempowering women, children, and those residing in non-Western lands, the Western gender order is also heterosexist. Lesko (2001, 78) notes that G. Stanely Hall's (1903) work at the turn of the century became a dominant force in Western societies and specifically advanced a "developmental model" of human age progression. In Hall's vision, properly developed boys and girls needed to progress through important life-stages on their way to adulthood (Hall 1903, cited in Lesko 2001). Significantly, to achieve proper manhood, "boys had to pass through a *female stage* before they moved to a higher position . . . . Thus, within the very schema of adolescence as a *developmental stage,* femaleness loomed as an obstacle that had to be navigated and surpassed" (Lesko 2001, 78). The science of adolescence, therefore, led to ubiquitous fears that some boys would never "phase out" of the feminine stage and the consequence was the creation of rigid gender divisions within many institutions (e.g., schools, families, public programs). Boys, it was viewed, must be removed from girls, lest boys become permanently "tainted" by femininity, since the taint of childish femininity was especially keen. Therein lay the formula for a future in which homosexual males were seen as underdeveloped, childish, feminine and, therefore, a problem to the Western sex/gender order.

Here, we see the roots of girls' complaints in chapter 3, in which the double jeopardy of being young and female meant that girls were keenly devalued in all spheres of their lives. This age-gender system also led to the likelihood that working-class and poor girls would be overlooked and devaluated, even as they were taking on the heavy demands of domestic labor necessary for family survival.

This age-gender order in Western systems also explains why girls experienced some relief at reaching adulthood. While they still wrestled with the stigma of femininity, the young women we followed in chapter 7 gained more autonomy and decision-making ability once they graduated from high school. By crossing the youth-adulthood divide, they broke free from the girlish dependency models built into the Western family unit. Compared with the girls, the boys had been given more autonomy and latitude to participate in public life as teens (e.g., to spend time outside of the house). As the perspective of the Western gender and age order predicts, on becoming young men, boys did not gain a level of autonomy significantly above and beyond what they had already experienced as teenagers.

Violence and the Regulation of Colonial Patriarchy

Relying on colonial patriarchy, we can offer an intersectional theory of youth violence. We note that there are many ways that interpersonal youth violence maintains the gender, age, racial, and sexual system embedded in the Western nation-state.[3] In fact, boys' violence against feminine, weak, or otherwise "unmanly" boys in Pascoe's (2012) study, which we reviewed in the introduction, can be said to be violence that maintains the gender order. Similarly, Miller's (2008) study of the pervasive sexual harassment and violence launched against the African American, inner-city girls in her study can also be seen as violence that maintains the gender order.

We also found the gender-order-maintained violence in our study. In chapter 3, we noted that some girls were harassed by boys for not having the right looks and body size, for "bossing around" boys in the family, or for attempting to join boys' in leisure activities. Such violence supports and regulates the Western age and gender order by keeping girls "in their place."

Boys' violence, revealed in chapter 5, might also work to maintain the gender order. As noted in chapter 5, Lesko (2001) argues that boys' proper socialization in a Western nation-state has historically encouraged their violent potential.
Boys need to be willing to fight for their country while also being able to follow
a military chain of command. Importantly, the potential for violence encouraged
by Western nationalism is for a "disciplined" (Foucault 1979) type of violence, in
which a strong dose of "self control" is combined with a sense of civic duty (i.e.,
obligation to one's nation) in boys' violent potential. If great nations need great
military force, then boys must be properly socialized to fight for their country.

But what if some boys, like those discussed in chapter 5, believe that the country
in which they live is "jacked up"? Moreover, what are we to make of boys who feel
betrayed and let down, not only by their nation but also by youth-serving institutions (e.g., schools), politicians, and most of the adults around them? If Lesko
(2001) is correct that boys are socialized to be "willing to fight" as a part of their
civic duty, then alienated boys might be likely to channel this "violence-as-civic-
duty" toward other groups and in other directions. Instead of being dedicated to
protecting the nation, the boys in chapter 5 explained feeling a sense of affilia-
tion to themselves (e.g., their sense of masculine independence) and also to their
friends, neighborhoods, ethnic groups, and families.

Chapter 5 contains empirical support for the view of interpersonal male violence as misplaced "civic duty." Remember that boys explained using violence to
"stand up" to those who egregiously abused their power, said that they would fight
anyone who tried to dominate them, and told us that violence could restore a general balance of power among boys in their communities. Boys also said that they
respected another boy who fought to "stand his ground" regardless of whether
the other boy won or lost a fight. Such themes of resisting domination, violently
"standing up" for what is right, and using violence to maintain a balance of power
do not seem to be particularly deviant motivations. In fact, such motivations
appear to line up with national narratives about the justified use of military force.
The problem with boys' violent motivations, as explored in chapter 5, was that
the boys were practicing a type of "undisciplined" violence. In other words, their
physical aggression did not follow a military chain of command, although some
boys expressed a desire to join the military to gain a sense of discipline and self-
control.[4]

We specifically argue that some of the boys' violence grew out of their misplaced
sense of masculine, civic duty. It is also important to note that the boys were being
somewhat community-minded. Like the boys in Rios' (2011) study, Northward
and Stevens Heights boys had developed a keen critical consciousness, and they
could read the power structures around them. Moreover, the boys in the present
study expressed that, as boys, it was their job to protect those who were "weak"
and "vulnerable," although their constructions of weakness and vulnerability

reinforced Western gender hierarchies. Like Rios, we argue that one promising avenue for future work with boys is to channel boys' critical consciousness into collective action that has the potential to change the injustices that the boys and girls saw around them.

If historic perspectives of male socialization to military violence in the modern Western nation-state help us explain the boys' "street" violence as a misplaced masculine sense of civic duty, then what are we to make of the girls' violence? According to historic discourses about gender in Western nation-states, girls' duty is to the domestic sphere and to enacting what we have called hegemonic femininity.

Previously, we noted that the girls' experiences were complicated and contingent, as they faced multiple conflicting demands and impossible-to-meet expectations. While hegemonic femininity does not explicitly sanction girls' violence, the girls discussed in chapters 3 and 4 sometimes turned to violence to solve problems.

The girls' violence explored in this book falls into three overlapping categories. First, some of the girls' violence fits into a category that we call "gender-order-maintaining" violence, whereby teenage girls punished other girls who violated gender norms. During childhood, girls were harassed and bullied by boys in school. But we also noted that by their teen years, boys who publicly assaulted other girls were condemned.[5] Therefore, teenage girls took up the job of maintaining the gender order by violently policing and punishing girls who broke the narrow and complicated femininity expectations. Girls in this study also noted being harassed by boys in their families; thus, male-on-female violence during the teen years can be said to continue, but in family and intimate spheres.[6]

A second category of girls' violence can be said to be a reaction to institutional failures, racialized economic strains, the feminization of domestic labor, and the devaluation of all things feminine. In this study, violence was sometimes a way for the girls to stand up for themselves and obtain what had been systematically denied to them. Girls at the intersections of multiple inequalities learned to speak up and strike out to keep themselves from being overlooked, ignored, overworked, taken advantage of, or abused. In this way, violently standing up for themselves served an important instrumental goal, although violence usually only offered temporary solutions to entrenched problems in the girls' lives.

Third, consistent with feminist criminology perspectives (Brown 2003; Morash and Chesney-Lind 2009), some of the girls' violence also fell into the category of righteous anger at the pervasive inequalities in the girls' lives. Girls in this study had many reasons to be angry, and some of their violence stemmed from overwhelming emotional frustration. The line between verbalizing negative emotions like anger and acting out in anger was very thin. Hence, violence as righteous anger was similar to the instrumental violence that girls used to stand up for themselves. Both were responses to living at the axis of multiple inequalities. The difference, however, was that violence as righteous anger stemmed primarily from emotional turmoil and tumult in the girls' lives, while instrumental violence stemmed from the girls' efforts to meet their needs in situational contexts (e.g., to not be harassed, overworked, ignored, or abused).[7]

The insight about girls' violence as stemming from righteous anger points to another gap in the youth violence literature, one not mentioned in the introduction. As Schaffner (2006) aptly notes, when looking at violence, social scientists have often overlooked the turbid emotional world of adolescents, especially those who have experienced significant losses and traumas. While theories of colonial patriarchy have been keen to look at racial, economic, and political alienation as causes of violence, the emotional weight of worry, distress, sadness, frustration, irritability, outrage, self-hatred, depression, and disappointment (to name a few) also need to be added to the mix, as every girl and boy in this study experienced a few, if not all, of these emotions at some time during high school.

The patriarchal structure of and beliefs circulating throughout the United States meant that girls and boys had different sources of trauma, pain, loss, and hardships. Boys, as we saw in chapter 5, viscerally disdained being in a state of childlike vulnerability or lacking control over their lives. Boys were not likely to use terms such as trauma or vulnerability to describe their state, though many of the boys discussed devastating events in their young lives. Their response was to take control of their circumstances, with violence if necessary. Girls, on the other hand, did not have the same response as boys to the state of childlike vulnerability, and embraced a sense of self-reliance rather than independence, as discussed in chapter 7. Self-reliant girls did not attempt to control or govern just social relations in their communities and peer networks, as boys often did. Instead, they looked inward and especially to their own abilities to "get things done" to manage various challenges. The result for many girls was a feeling of being overwhelmed, isolated, and angry.

Our model sees violence as an impulsive act born out of micro-level and situational circumstances, as well as a response to macro structures. We are especially attuned to the fact that violence is often a situational response to an event with no better recourse in sight. Much of the violence in our study could be traced to youth's pasts, which were marked by trauma, racialized poverty, and alienation, and had to do with unrequited pain and suffering. A spurt of aggression related to some past experience sometimes exacerbated or triggered fighting among peers. Some teens also sensed that a set of abstract rules encouraged the use of violence in certain situations, especially for the boys. But these rules, we found, represented more of an imagined set of expectations than a clear code, and boys often disagreed about what were the "right" and "wrong" ways to approach and use violence.

Our model here is a holistic approach to understanding fighting and the use of violence, one that takes into account the history and the collective memory of place as well as the racial stratification, socioeconomic, gender, age, heterosexist, and political systems at the macro level that mediate social relations at the micro level. It includes the social processes that shape collective meanings at the intersections of multiple inequalities. Youth violence has many sources and is often contingent on multiple situational factors, just as physical fights between youth involve more than the immediate conflicts at hand. What we offer is an approach to understanding fighting among youth that captures these contextual, contingent, and situational influences, especially as they operate differently for girls versus boys and for groups that are experiencing the harsh realities of a colonial past and present.

Juvenile Justice, School Discipline, and the Theory of Punishment

Finally, we address the prevailing theories of punishment as they concern juvenile justice and school discipline. As we discussed in chapter 1, scholars have interrogated punitive trends in the U.S. criminal justice and education systems. Punishment can be seen as part of the colonial infrastructure, including the transportation of laws, institutions, and norms underpinned by class, race, and gender relations (Garland 2004; Wacquant 2001, 2009). Garland (1990) pressed for multidimensional analyses of punishment that avoid assuming a rational, cohesive, and strictly utilitarian penal strategy. He argued that public sentiments and human passions also shape the form and force of penal systems beyond the "controller and controlled." Certainly, many have examined the social processes involved in the rise of punitive institutions and policies, as in the "moral panic" that led to zero-tolerance legislation. But there is another side to the human and social element, as well as an additional cultural perspective, that we advance.

Like Garland (1990, 2004), we acknowledge the instrumental nature of punishment. Our study, however, demonstrates that there are sentiments intrinsic to the social relationships among and between actors in punitive institutions that do more than support the practice of punishment—they also subvert it. We argue that the role of caring individuals and their kindred networks complicates contemporary punishment theories, which instead imagine a rather monolithic and impenetrable system of discipline and control. In particular, in chapter 6 we examined an ethic of care that enjoyed expression in the "grey zone of discretion," during an era when criminal punishments were ratcheting upwards. This suggests that punitive policy can be undercut or moderated when collective sentiments side with those who are overpunished.

We found competing practices among criminal justice and education professionals, with agents adhering to different philosophical orientations, cultural lenses, and understandings of youth and violence. While some stuck by the punitive ethos of the time, others believed that the rules were harsh, unhelpful, and harmful. Such actors tended to embrace compassionate stances and did what was in their discretionary power to enact them. As much as they could, they avoided punitive responses and, instead, offered support along with mentorship. Such work blunted the edge of zero tolerance and took advantage of initiatives focusing on building capabilities and self-efficacy. This human interface between policies and institutional structures and the subjects of their control is critical to a multidimensional theory.

We also argue that there is a cultural dimension to the interface between youth-serving institutions and youth themselves that is integral to a system of colonial patriarchy. Native Hawaiian epistemology and knowledge systems are very much alive and present in local society in Hawai'i. Those who share these worldviews, whether they are of Native Hawaiian ancestry or not, are aware of the role that mainstream institutions such as schools and courts have played throughout Hawaiian history, as discussed in chapter 6.[8] Those who share an indigenous (not only Hawaiian) epistemology or sensibility about the settler colonial condition operate with a different stance towards violence and discipline, one informed by a more holistic perspective. So while the historical arc of colonialism remains in force, so too does the ethos of compassion as well as of political and cultural resistance. The stories told by youth and shared throughout this book underscore the positive difference that caring people played, especially at times when youths' fates hung in the balance.

9

Compassionate and Constructive
Policy and Practice

Each individual has to make that commitment. You can't teach that. On an
individual basis, there needs to be that sort of commitment and willingness
to do whatever it takes. I think that's fundamentally important.

—PROBATION OFFICER AND WIN MENTOR, HAWAI'I FAMILY COURT

The "second line of defense" of caring adults played a pivotal role for countless
youth, as stories in the previous chapters have highlighted. Youth were helped in
their positive transformations by the love and devotion that committed adults had
for them and tried to demonstrate in their everyday interactions. But what specifically did these adults impart to help youth navigate a more hopeful future and
avoid the negative use of violence? Are there promising practices that are more
restorative and empowering for youth and their families as they move forward in
life? And to what policy directions do such practices point?

We begin this chapter by juxtaposing the experience of a family who lost a child
to violence against a description of a traditional Native Hawaiian cultural practice
for resolving problems or conflicts, one that integrates healing, self-reflection, and
mediation. We then describe ways that mediation-oriented approaches were used
in school and court settings as opportunities for youth to get to the deeper roots
of the challenges they faced. We then turn to policy and summarize the major
critiques of zero-tolerance policies and share some of the changes in policies and
practices that are beginning to unfold in Hawai'i, at least in their early stages.

INSTITUTIONAL FAILURE TO EFFECTIVELY
ADDRESS VIOLENCE

Ramie lost her son, Corey, to violence. A recent high school graduate, he was a
gregarious, handsome, and well-loved young man. He had grown up in the local
rural neighborhood. He had loving parents who cared for him and provided him
a stable and nurturing home. But one Sunday morning, Corey intervened in a

domestic dispute between a man and a woman and was fatally stabbed in the heart by the man, who used a pocketknife. A friend delivered the news to Ramie as she was exiting the Sunday service at her church. She collapsed in grief. The individual who stabbed her son was reported to have over a dozen previous convictions. He was found guilty and handed a prison term. After six years, he was released on parole. While Ramie publicly expressed forgiveness soon after her son's death, the process that she and her family underwent highlights a serious problem in the way the justice system works to ignore rather than quell the cycle of violence and pain, which leads to greater infliction—and self-infliction—of harm.

Years after the incident, pain and suffering remained. While Ramie was able to come to a place of forgiveness, it was difficult for others close to Corey to do the same. Emotional pain, like a festering sore on the body, continued to weigh upon the emotional and physical health of many who were close to him. With the release of the perpetrator on parole, their pain was revisited, not only the anguish they had felt at the loss of their loved one, but also a feeling of injustice, that a killer could be freed without giving any indication that he had changed.

The underlying institutional problem here is that we do not have a justice system that is, broadly speaking, restorative—one that helps to restore the well-being of the survivors of violence, the victim's loved ones, the perpetrators of harm, and the broken relationships resulting from such events. Our institutions fail to "get to the root" of social problems, focusing more on symptoms than on their underlying causes. We have little institutional space for reconciling conflicts or healing the wounds of trauma. Institutions that can work together to holistically address the complexity of the problems usually do not. Each institution has its own set of powers, responsibilities, rules, regulations, and operating procedures. After a violent event, schools report incidents, issue sanctions, and handle any repercussions while returning the school to "normalcy." Police apprehend and investigate. Courts hear testimony, examine evidence, render decisions, and mete out sanctions. Medical examiners tend to the injured and determine the cause of death. Mental health professionals offer victims emotional and psychological assistance.

Besides punishment, where in all of this are the systematic efforts to resolve conflicts between parties to violence? How robust is the process for apology, restitution to victims, and forgiveness? Where are the adequate mental and behavioral health supports for perpetrators as well as victims? What resources are available to those on all sides for healing the hurt they are experiencing and for reining in their suffering? And how are perpetrators of violence integrated into schools and communities in ways that ensure greater safety while at the same time avoiding straitjacketing?

There has long been a restorative tradition within our schools and justice system, but it has never been the dominant one. "Restorative justice" models that have been more popular in other industrialized countries, such as Canada, Australia and Aotearoa, have never gained mainstream support in political debates over crime and punishment in the United States. It is common knowledge that that the majority of violence takes place between individuals who know each other. Violence is often a result of interpersonal or intergroup conflict that could be resolved constructively given different cultural and material circumstances. A major challenge to our society is to systemically increase the capacity of youth, as well as adults, to resolve problems in ways that minimize harmful violence while at the same time addressing the colonial conditions that breed violence. Can institutions equip and empower people to resolve conflicts, restore relationships, and allow the healing of the intergenerational trauma that both exacerbates violence and results from it?

In the case of Corey's violent death, institutions did nothing to address the tension that continued to plague the relationship between the perpetrator and the victim's family. There was no space created in the formal process for the perpetrator to express remorse, apologize, and deliver even a modest form of restitution. There was no assurance to the victim's family that the man would get help for the undisclosed problems that had led to his criminal record and violent outburst. Nor was evidence presented to the family that the perpetrator had received the help he needed while imprisoned. Also missing was adequate support for loved ones as they themselves struggled to live under the shadow of grief. We understand that violence in the United States results from a variety of factors, including social norms that reinforce violent behavior, easy access to weapons, and lack of peaceful conflict resolution skills, to name a few. We also know that a host of challenges face families affected by settler colonialism, such as household instability, alienation, domestic abuse, low self-esteem, substance abuse, and mental health challenges such as depression that complicate relationships.

So what would be a better way for us as a society to respond to fighting? What can be changed so that our current juvenile justice and educational systems stop perpetuating the cycle of violence and do more both to heal the sores and to address the underlying sources of discord? How can the compassionate adults effective in working within the juvenile justice, education, and youth services systems improve the structure and operation of the system itself? Rather than reinforcing patterns of social inequality and histories of injustice in our formal systems of governance, how can institutions take steps to allow healing and restoration, changing the trajectory to one that is more just and hopeful?

HO‘OPONOPONO: A PATH TOWARD HEALING
AND RECONCILIATION

One implication of colonial criminology theory is that while criminalized or problematized behavior can be understood in its colonial context, we might find effective solutions in precolonial practices. Ho'oponopono is one such practice that was used prior to Western contact in Hawai'i to handle problems leading to illness, unease, or conflict at the level of the 'ohana or family, often within the extended family. It was used to maintain social and spiritual harmony, not only in the family, but also in the broader community, by resolving problems at their source and not leaving lingering guilt, resentment or animosity to fester and grow. It represented a process and way of life, a path for dealing with social infractions and returning to a more harmonious state of mutual respect and appreciation. The practice continues to be grounded in a Hawaiian epistemology or way of knowing that is spiritually based, steeped in cultural knowledge, and tied to lifeways of old Hawai'i, but adapted to contemporary times. Though subject to colonial influence and rule since the late 1700s, numerous Hawaiian elders and their families continued the practice through the postcontact years and after the illegal overthrow in the late 1800s (Shook 1985).[1]

What is ho'oponopono and what promise does it hold for youth who become involved in physical fighting? The usage presented by Pukui, Haertig, and Lee (1972) is most relevant here. They defined ho'oponopono as "setting to right; to make right; to correct; to restore and maintain good relationships among family, and family-and-supernatural powers. The specific family conference in which relationships were 'set right' through prayer, discussion, confession, repentance, and mutual restitution and forgiveness" (60). Ho'oponopono commences with prayer, as the purpose of the process is to set things right not only between people, but also between the individuals involved and the greater spiritual power(s), in any form(s) the participants may see them.[2] It requires a sincere intention to correct wrongs and to be truthful and forthcoming about wrongdoing, grievances, grudges and resentments. Pukui, Haertig, and Lee pointed out that this quality was called 'oia'i'o, or the "very spirit of truth." Once the hala or transgressions are disclosed and responsibility for them is assumed, the parties can begin to release themselves from the negative entanglement they are experiencing. An important part of the process is the timely provision of restitution for any wrongs done. This sharing and restitution open the way for mihi, or forgiveness, and oki, or severance of any misgivings, tensions, and ill feelings. This allows for a fuller sense of resolution and peace. The steps of repenting, forgiving, and releasing are closed with prayer and oftentimes followed with heartfelt embrace (Pukui, Haertig, and Lee 1972; Shook 1985).

Ho'oponopono has been applied more formally in local social work practice by organizations serving Hawaiian families, such as the Queen Lili'uokalani Children's Center, starting in the 1960s (Shook 1985). And as early as the 1970s, it began to be a recognized method within the Western health sciences (Draguns 1981; Moku'au 1998; Pedersen 1979; Tseng and McDermott 1975, 1981). The power of ho'oponopono became evident to Western-trained professionals as they saw positive outcomes of the process among the youth and families they served. Shook (1985) studied how hoʻoponopono was applied in social work practice, noting that the adoption of this and other culturally based practices were part of an overall recognition that Western philosophical traditions based on rational, scientific thought had clear limitations in addressing health issues, particularly among ethnocultural groups who shared non-Western epistemologies. Whereas, she states, "the alternative is to consider other methods, including those based on more unifying philosophies that do not separate physical emotion, and spiritual factors in health and illness" (25).

In addressing the problem of fighting, hoʻoponopono has notable advantages as a practice for the prevention, intervention, and resolution of fighting. First, it offers a structured yet flexible way for all parties to uncover and understand the evolution of the problem and search jointly for a satisfying resolution. It allows people to give and receive forgiveness and make appropriate restitution. It is a dignified way to resolve conflicts within the safety and support of others, especially elders in a culture that accords respect to the older generations. It allows people to restore harmony in their relations. It can deepen emotional commitments to working things out in the future. And finally, while it may naturally resonate with Native Hawaiian cultural frameworks, those who participate in it can tailor it to different cultural frameworks, since it is a process rather than a program per se. In fact, similar processes can be found in many indigenous cultures. The basic process and underlying principles take the shape of those who are participating in it and the cultural meanings they bring with them. In the context of this study, one important exception to the beneficial use of hoʻoponopono is in the case of girls or boys who have been physically or sexually abused and who could be retraumatized by a face-to-face meeting with their abuser. This type of fighting is not the focus of this book and it is important to point out that hoʻoponopono is not appropriate for all situations.[3]

That said, efforts have been made to incorporate approaches modeled upon hoʻoponopono into criminal and juvenile justice processes in Hawaiʻi. Most were relatively short-lived despite evidence of their promise. The Kupuna Program, created by Alu Like, a major nonprofit organization serving Native Hawaiians, catered to those arrested for substance abuse offenses during early 1990s. An evaluation showed that of the 341 adults served by Kupuna, only 3 percent were rearrested for substance abuse violations (Napeahi et al. 1998; Mokuʻau 2002). Another program, called Huikahi Restorative Circles, was piloted in 2005 at the state men's minimum-security prison and later at the Women's Community Correctional Center (Walker and Greening 2013). And in 2011, the first restorative circle was held for a youth who was transitioning out of the HYCF, the only juvenile corrections facility in the state.

Outside the justice system, there have been numerous programs based on the model of hoʻoponopono. One notable program is Kahua Ola Hou, a substance abuse treatment program developed on the Hawaiian island of Molokaʻi by Wayde Lee and based on knowledge passed down from many of the elders with whom he studied.[4] This program was reestablished, under the name Wahi Kanaʻaho, as part of a juvenile justice reform initiative in 2015. Based on his many years as a cultural practitioner teaching youth the healing art of hoʻoponopono, Lee stresses the importance of helping the youth become healers. As he explained to us, his elders told him, "You cannot heal nobody, only akua [god] can. But you can teach them how to become healers." He explained, "Kūpuna [elders] also told me, 'Akua no make rubbish.' Every child is born 'perfect,' with god-given gifts. But somewhere along the way, something wen' broke." Lee has seen how structured environments can provide the foundation for healing, by continuing the healthy upbringing that may have been interrupted. And gaining experience in leading hoʻoponopono with one's own parents or guardians not only enables youth to heal themselves and their close relationships, but also empowers them to resolve future conflicts and to become more resilient.

RESTORATIVE DISCRETION AND CONFLICT MEDIATION

What if schools and courts gave youth the support they need to engage in processes of healing and reflection, to become more empowered in their lives, and to productively deal with conflicts and other life challenges? Here, we share the story of Kelly, which gives us a glimpse of a more positive response to fighting. Kelly was born and raised in Northward and had attended Seaside High. When she was ten years old, her parents began to use drugs, and by the time she reached fourteen, she and her siblings had been removed from their home by Child Welfare Services and placed under the custody of their grandmother. They were then moved again and placed with their aunt and uncle. Kelly was forced to take on the mother role for her younger brother and sisters. Though she expressed love for her auntie, she felt like a slave under her roof. She felt, at that time, that her aunt had taken them in for the monetary payment rather than out of any feeling of love.

The pain of childhood turned to anger and self-destructive behavior as Kelly grew older. Her anger became a shield against loving emotions and protected her from the deep pain she actually felt. As she shared with us, "I was that girl who never cared about getting hurt, about dying. Never cared. I was like, 'whatever.' I go out there and if I die, I die. If I kill somebody, I kill somebody. That's what my outlook on life was at the time." She admitted to having had anger issues and depression before the age of eighteen, but it was not until her senior year at Seaside that she actually got into her first physical fight. Her closest friend, Tesha, complained to Kelly one day that she was being bullied by Arlene, another girl at the school.

Kelly, coming to the defense of Tesha, proceeded to confront Arlene and fought with her on the campus grounds.

After Kelly was caught in the act of fighting, the school could have suspended her for some length of time, as the fight was a Class A Offense. In this case, however, the vice principal, Mr. Abe, decided to encourage Kelly and Arlene to get together to mediate the conflict under his facilitation. Mr. Abe spoke with both of them separately and had them reflect upon what had happened. He encouraged Kelly to take responsibility for her role in the confrontation. With their consent, he had them discuss what took place from their respective points of view. Kelly described what took place next: "He put us in a conference room and called our guardians. And so we sat there. I was on one end and she was on the other end of the table. And he was standing there and asking me, because he knows me personally, 'Why? Why did you guys fight? You're not known to fight. You never did have a fight record.'"

Kelly went on to describe the encounter: "He asked me to speak first because he knows I have a good talent speaking. So I did. I asked her, 'I had no problem before we fought; I have no problem with you now. I don't hate you. I don't even want anything to do with you. I don't care. There's no relationship or anything. I just want you to know that I apologize for what I have done.'" Kelly also wanted to take the opportunity to find out, from Arlene's point of view, why Arlene had threatened to beat up her best friend. Kelly recalled asking Arlene: "'All I want to know is why . . . . Why is there a reason you want to beat up my sister? Family is family,' I told her. And she said, 'Well, you know, she's the one who started it. Because I told everyone I'm the queen of Samoa and your fucking sister told me, "Oh, how are you the queen of Samoa when you look like that?"'" After hearing this from Arlene, Kelly realized there was another side to the story. She realized that it was actually Tesha who had initiated the conflict, by throwing an insult at Arlene. Kelly felt empathy toward Arlene and felt badly that she had attacked her, since she felt it had been wrong of Tesha to insult her in that way. She realized that by not finding out more about the problem from Arlene's point of view, she had jumped to a wrong conclusion.

Once she had understood the problem from both perspectives, Kelly felt that the fight reflected badly upon her, from the standpoint of what was just. She proceeded to apologize to Arlene for the admitted wrongdoing while also sharing her own point of view. She continued:

> So I felt even more worse because I was fighting this girl that my sister made fun of. So I looked like the bad person now. But I never meant for it to get to a fight, so when she told me that, I was like, I wanted to laugh but I kept it in because Mr. Abe said "Don't bring up your bad side." I said, "You know what? I apologize for my wrongdoings. I came up to you nice and you came back to me wrong and so that's why I stood up for my self. I wasn't fighting for her but I was fighting for what you had told me,

saying, 'You're nobody, who you?' And stuff like that." And she was like, "Well, how you gonna react to somebody when someone comes up to you asking why we like fight and stuff like that?' I said, "You're right. I would have done the same thing. But we both wrong."

Kelly also wanted Arlene and Tesha to make amends between them. This was, in part, out of a desire to protect Tesha from any retaliation from Arlene in the future. After Kelly accepted responsibility for hitting Arlene, she also let Arlene know that she would encourage Tesha to apologize to her as well. She said to Arlene:

> "I'm gonna admit to my wrong and you can keep your wrong. I don't care what you do with your wrong, but I admit to my wrong and I will just let you know that I will be the bigger person and will set down to whatever I did." She understood, and all I told her was, "I don't want you to go back to Tesha and try to do any wrong to her and beat her up because I'm gonna step in. And I'm gonna tell her out of her heart to apologize for what she said to you." And so she said, "Ok, that's cool."

This led to the settling of the conflict and the restoration of a mutual understanding and basic respect between Kelly and Arlene. The vice principal also explained to Arlene that Kelly could be kind, which Kelly appreciated. She recalled: "And Mr. Abe was like explaining to her and her brother—her brother's the guardian—how I can be very respectful and caring. He explained that in front of her. He explained a lot of my personality to her, to make her understand more because he knew she was still mad. You know, I would be mad too, for being called out. I look at that and I laugh, because it was stupid. It was the stupidest fight ever in my life because it was 'he said, she said.'"

The vice principal gave Kelly and Arlene each a one-day suspension and the police dismissed Kelly's arrest. Kelly avoided fights for the remainder of her senior year and went on to graduate.

The rapport and relationship that the vice principal and other support staff had with Kelly was critical to handling the incident in a way that squelched any risk of further fighting. But more importantly, Mr. Abe had played a supportive role in Kelly's own ongoing journey of growth and transformation. Kelly expressed appreciation for his listening ear and for the way he had helped her to learn from the experience:

> Yeah, he knew all that and what I was going through. It made a impact on me because nobody likes him in our school because he was so strict. But once you get to know him, like when you get to know somebody, he was cool, you know . . . . He never judged me, you know. He never did judge me. That's why I respected him a lot because of the things I went through, he never pitied it and he never judged me. . . . And he never did bring it up (again). It was always like, "Oh, what did you do today" or "Why are you in here?" and stuff like that.

Kelly pointed to other school staff, like the health aide, to whom she was also grateful for unwavering support. Together they had helped her to learn a different way of resolving a problem, one that enhanced her personal growth and averted negative repercussions.

HELPING TO STRENGTHEN YOUTH'S CAPABILITIES

There were many instances in which youth were encouraged to build their ability to reflect upon themselves and the larger situation, empathize with others, apply thoughtful judgment, resolve interpersonal conflicts, and see and act in new ways. Adults helped to strengthen these abilities by providing guidance along the way. Teachers, probation officers, outreach workers, mentors, and others had many opportunities to be this supportive figure in their daily interactions with youth. As youth and adults in the study reflected upon what had been most effective, a common theme was youth having a safe space in which to examine themselves and their lives and to grow into themselves, with guiding wisdom and positive support from adults and peers.

Brandon, one of the WIN mentors, shared an incident that illustrated how he leveraged learnable moments. Andy, one of the youth participants in the court restitution program, had "acted up" and gotten confrontational with one of the WIN mentors at a cleanup activity at a local beach park. Andy's angry outburst created a scene and he quickly walked off into the distance, in shallow water along the shoreline. Brandon and his probation coworker quickly assessed that Andy was of no danger to himself or others and let him release his energy in the immediate aftermath of the incident: "He walked off. He went back to the car. The walk from the parking area to the site where we were clearing algae was pretty far, maybe a half a mile. So he stormed back and he was wading in knee-deep water. So part of it was like, 'He's gonna do whatever he wants and that's fine as long as he's not gonna hurt anybody.' And, 'That's a lot of water with the long distance, so he's gonna burn it off.' So there's that awareness too."

Rather than reprimanding Andy on the spot, Brandon and the other mentors let the dynamics within the group unfold, waiting for the opportunity for engaged learning, not only for Andy but also for the rest of the group. As the group stopped for lunch, the mentors continued to engage with the youth, but let them come to their own understandings and lessons as they talked about the incident among themselves. Brandon held back to allow them to draw their own lessons without imposing his own, yet created space around that window of opportunity for learning: "I guess we never interrupted the momentum of that. And as people raised things we addressed it or we spoke about it. So it's still an engagement. Whatever the kids were saying, we were responding to that. But not so much in a "put out the fire" kind of way, but like, "Yeah, that's what happening" and "That's what he did." And it's really more about them and not so much about us. And that's a big thing."

Brandon would speak when he felt it was important to take a strong position, especially to make it clear if he thought something was not right—and he did so in the van ride back from the cleanup. But the mentoring was not focused on scolding. He and his coworker continued to talk with Andy over the next several weeks about how to deal with what had taken place and its underlying trigger. But they also wanted to see him come to a resolution on his own. Brandon shared how it was important to let Andy grow from this on his own time, with their support:

> He was apologetic, not right after I said what I said to them in the van, but he was on that trajectory of being remorseful. And I think for him that came after he was allowed that space . . . to do what he needed to. So I think he was able to get there pretty well on his own, you know? But we clearly see our roles as to make sure they know [what's right and wrong] but not so much when *we* want them to. 'Cause that's not easy to do. Restraint is good, too.

By practicing restraint and letting Andy come to his own realizations in his own time, albeit with some guidance, Brandon was able to help Andy change in a more internally meaningful way. Andy wrote three apology letters: one to the peer group, one to the service day host, and one to the organization that had organized the event. He also apologized to the staff with whom he had been confrontational and they eventually talked it through.

Through deeper conversation, it emerged that the trigger had to do with events in Andy's past. Brandon explained that the trust they had developed allowed Andy to reveal some of the underlying issues. They talked about his past and the need to move forward from it: "He said that 'nobody touches me.' That was his thing. When that grabbing happened, it triggered for him the feelings of the past . . . . Part of the conversation is to accept the fact that, yes, there is that issue that he has, but also that he's being nudged forward, too. You can still have those feelings and issues but maybe try dealing with them differently, yeah? 'How could you have done it differently?'" When caring adults posing such questions at opportune moments and allow youth to explore and understand their emotions and choices, youth can grow their own wisdom.

A CHANGING TIDE: A SHIFT TOWARD MORE COMPASSIONATE POLICIES AND PRACTICES

These examples of school and court staff handling conflicts and violence as growth and healing opportunities represent a set of philosophical beliefs and point to two important observations. One is that caring professionals, *regardless* of the policy environment they may find themselves in, can affect the lives of youth in meaningful and profoundly positive ways, especially as guides and mentors. These individuals described above, who went "against the grain" of punitive practices, were able to exercise their discretion and play a compassionate, supportive role while remaining within their professional bounds. Second, institutions like courts and schools that allow their staff to partner with grassroots groups offer unique opportunities for youth to discover their passions and to gain lifelong lessons in the company of positive community influences.

After three decades, the repressive policy tide had begun to cede some room to more compassionate and restorative initiatives such as this. In this section, we describe this unfolding shift, both nationally and locally.

National Shift in Thinking about Juvenile Justice

Controversy has grown over the years about the wisdom of the punitive, zero-tolerance approach. Nationally, dissatisfaction and protest have swelled, especially in response to growing evidence of the disproportionate impact of this approach on youth of color. A stockpile of policy-related research now underscores the need for a more restorative and therapeutic approach (Cullen 2007; Evans, McReynolds, and Wasserman 2006; Howell 2003; McGuire 2008). In 2005, the American Psychological Association, the largest national professional organization representing psychologists in the United States, surveyed the impact of zero tolerance policies in elementary and secondary schools and found little to support the assumptions upon which punitive approaches were founded. First, data did not support the fears used to justify zero tolerance measures to begin with; school violence had not been out of control nor had it increased since the mid 1980s. Second, mandated punishment for certain offenses did not lead to greater consistency in school discipline and, therefore, did not send out a definitive "zero tolerance" message to students. Third, there was no clear evidence that the removal of students who violated zero tolerance rules resulted in a more conducive learning environment. Fourth, the idea that swift and certain punishment would deter school misbehavior appeared to be mistaken; school suspension generally predicted higher rates of further infractions and suspensions. And finally, the use of harsh punishment did not necessarily create a sense of safety among parents and students. In addition to these faults in the basic assumptions, this report as well as other studies raised many questions about the efficacy of zero tolerance policies, such as their cost effectiveness and their appropriateness relative to other alternative approaches (Greenwood et al. 1998; Reynolds et al. 2008).

Researchers also found serious racial disparities, with an overrepresentation of African American and Latino and American Indian students in expulsions and suspensions (Reynolds et al. 2008). The harshest forms of school punishments were enacted in schools that also had the largest percentages of students of color (Irwin, Davidson, and Sanchez-Hall 2013; Kupchik and Ward 2014; Payne and

Welch 2010; Welch and Payne 2010). In Hawai'i, similar disparities existed for Native Hawaiian and Pacific Islander students. According to the U.S. Department of Education, Native Hawaiian and Pacific Islander youth comprised 33.6 percent of the state's public school population but received 50.2 percent of in-school suspensions, 49.2 percent of out-of-school suspensions, and 55.6 percent of expulsions in 2011 (U.S. Department of Education 2014).

Nationally, community leaders, parents, and even school administrators questioned these high suspension rates and mobilized for change. Some schools adopted alternative policies to zero tolerance, such as a system of graduated sanctions that pairs each level of offense with a level of punishment, along with better prevention strategies, such as counseling and mediation for student conflicts (Skiba 2000). Others eliminated the use of suspensions for relatively minor infractions, such as attendance problems. Some schools employed threat-assessment techniques, calibrating official responses to threats of violence according to the actual level of danger they pose. Other changes included lowering the number of suspension days, providing alternatives to suspension for first-time infractions, calling parent conferences, writing behavioral contracts, and requiring after-school sessions (St. George 2011).

At the national policy level, the U.S. Department of Education adopted the Positive Behavioral Interventions and Supports system in 1997, also known as Positive Behavior Support (PBS).[5] PBS is designed to leverage "teachable moments," a category that it broadened to include not only crises, but also the routine reinforcement of positive actions. Schools using PBS are expected to set and meet behavioral expectations in the same way they would approach any curricular subject.[6] Schoolwide education is to be used to clarify behavioral expectations and shape campus norms. Positive incentives for healthy social behaviors are to be favored over negative consequences for harmful behaviors. In PBS, collaboration between schools, community organizations, and families is seen as pivotal for assembling the most appropriate set of interventions for each type of student and for creating and sustaining the school environments that help youth thrive (Carr et al. 2002; Sugai et al. 1999).

In 2011, the U.S. Department of Justice and the U.S. Department of Education collaboratively launched the Supportive School Discipline Initiative to address the problem of the "school to prison pipeline." The main goal to was to build stakeholder collaboration in order "to ensure that school discipline policies and practices comply with the nation's civil rights laws and to promote positive disciplinary options to both keep kids in school and improve the climate for learning" (U.S. Department of Justice and the U.S. Department of Education 2014). The initiative included an enhanced Civil Rights Data Collection system that tracked school suspensions and expulsions according to students' racial background in order to identify racial disparities.

Within this tide of change, some have advocated for restorative justice. There is no uniform use of the term, but restorative justice is generally understood as "a process whereby all the parties with a stake in a particular offence come together to resolve collectively how to deal with the aftermath of the offence and its implications for the future" (Braithwaite 1999, quoted in Latimer, Dowden and Muise 2005, 128). There is growing recognition that restorative justice approaches are viable alternatives, as shown by meta-analyses among adults (Nugent, Williams, and Umbreit 2004) as well as juveniles (Bergseth and Bouffard 2013). Studies have shown that restorative justice approaches offer promising results, increasing community and victim involvement in the process of resolution, satisfaction of parties with the outcomes, offender compliance in case decisions, and perceptions of fairness, while lowering rates of recidivism (Bergseth and Bouffard 2013).[7]

Better than Punitive: Aligning Policy and People under an Ethic of Care

Some reform efforts in both the juvenile justice and education systems have been initiated in Hawai'i. One is focused on reducing the number of youth sent to the state's sole short-term detention facility. Changes were sought with the support and technical assistance of the Annie E. Casey Foundation's Juvenile Detention Alternatives Initiative (JDAI).[8] JDAI utilized a data-driven process to help jurisdictions develop standardized assessment tools and increase alternatives to detention through community partnerships. JDAI reached the state in 2009; the average number of those detained in Hawai'i plummeted between 2010 to 2014.[9] By the end of 2014, JDAI had spread to around three hundred counties nationwide, accounting for 25 percent of the nation's youth population, with similar success. Secondary benefits from the program have included a reduction in the numbers sent to correctional facilities and other residential placements with no reduction in public safety (Annie E. Casey Foundation 2014).

A second foundation-supported initiative in Hawai'i was led by the Pew Charitable Trusts' Public Safety Performance Project.[10] The result was passage of House Bill 2490, signed into law in 2014, which restricts long-term imprisonment to youth convicted of serious offenses, strengthens community-based probation supervision, and promotes greater interagency collaboration in order to help youth become successful and remain out of the juvenile justice system. Though the bill fell short of funding the requested amount for supportive programs, it was a first step at a legislative fix to identified problems within the juvenile justice system.

Individual reform champions within the system played a key role in these and other changes. For example, David Hipp of the Office of Youth Services and Judge Robert Browning of the family court played a leadership role in the drastic reduction in the number of youth sentenced to HYCF, even prior to the passage of the aforementioned legislation; commitments to the state's sole youth facility fell by

41 percent between 2004 and 2013, from 171 commitments to 101 commitments. Hipp and his staff assisted judges in finding appropriate alternatives to incarceration such as community-based services and facilities. Also important was a small but significant revision to eligibility requirements so that adjudicated youth could more easily access existing state-run mental health services. The Office of Youth Services also began to require many of their contracted service providers to serve court-involved youth, and, as limited as their funding was, shifted their resources towards aiding adjudicated youth in need of more intensive support.

Another significant reform effort was the Ho'opono Mamo Civil Citation Initiative, which was launched as a pilot program in early 2015 with the goal of diverting youth to appropriate support systems immediately upon police apprehension. Under this program, youth arrested for status offenses and first-time misdemeanor law violations are issued a citation and taken by police to an assessment center. There they are connected to supportive programs, ranging from substance abuse to educational services, depending on the needs and preferences of the youth and their families. This program provides eligible youth an opportunity to avoid an arrest record and increases the chances of connecting them with the appropriate support. The Ho'opono Mamo Civil Citation Initiative was framed as a paradigm shift, from the nationally dominant paradigm of punitive, top-down, institutionalized, and universal justice to a more restorative, collaborative, community-based, family-centered approach that is sensitive to the diverse range of ethnic groups in Hawai'i.

Moving forward, we believe it is important to develop a more holistic understanding of violence, as we have proposed in this book, and to abandon the misleading dichotomy between leniency and punishment. The more important question is how can we best support youth who confront violence and other problems at the intersection of race, gender, and class inequalities, given the conditions of colonialism. Tone deafness on the part of policy makers as well as the public about the lived experiences of these youth increases the neglect and injustice they face. This book has offered examples of culturally resonant approaches characterized by an ethic of care to illustrate the promise of a different paradigm—one that departs from the preoccupation with punishment and control and instead focuses on youths' capabilities to mend past wounds in order to successfully confront the challenges that remain. Taking a compassionate and emancipatory approach requires that youth and those who serve them not only get to the roots of personal problems but also understand the historical depths of current social problems. This approach challenges people to see the world through the eyes of others who have had very different experiences in life. Paradigmatic change demands a different type of professional practice as well as different rules and policies. At its foundation, it is dependent on asking everyone involved to live by an ethic of care. As Brandon, the WIN mentor, optimistically shared, "As an agency, we're moving toward being less punitive . . . maybe better than punitive."

APPENDIX 1

TABLE 1 Data Sources and Participant Demographics

Data type	Number of participants	Gender	Ethnicity**
Youth focus groups (10)*	45	24 Boys 21 Girls	18 Native Hawaiian; 16 Samoan; 11 Filipino
Youth interviews	42	28 Boys 14 Girls	22 Native Hawaiian; 10 White; 3 Samoan; 3 Mixed Asian; 2 Filipino; 1 Latino; 1 Mixed Pacific Islander
Adult focus groups (6)*	41	23 Men 18 Women	21 Samoan; 20 Native Hawaiian
High school staff interviews	11	6 Men 5 Women	5 Native Hawaiian; 4 White; 1 Portuguese; 1 Mixed Asian
Community adult and youth practitioner interviews	10	5 Women 5 Men	4 Native Hawaiian; 4 Asian/Mixed Asian; 1 Filipino; 1 Laotian
Youth observations	10	6 Girls 4 Boys	7 Native Hawaiian; 2 Samoan; 1 Other Pacific Islander
Total youth	97	56 Boys 41 Girls	47 Native Hawaiian; 21 Samoan; 13 Filipino; 10 White; 3 Mixed Asian; 1 Latino; 1 Mixed Pacific Islander; 1 Other Pacific Islander
Total participants	159	90 Male 69 Female	76 Native Hawaiian; 42 Samoan; 14 White; 14 Filipino; 8 Asian/Mixed Asian; 1 Latino; 1 Portuguese; 1 Laotian; 1 Mixed Pacific Islander; 1 Other Pacific Islander

* Focus group participants were split equally between Northward and Stevens Heights.
** Ethnic background was assessed using both teens' self-definition and school records.

TABLE 2 Demographics of Quoted Teens

Pseudonym	Gender	Ethnicity
Aaron	Male	Native Hawaiian
Alika	Male	Native Hawaiian
Angel	Female	Mixed Pacific Islander, including Tongan
Annabelle	Female	Native Hawaiian
Benny	Male	Native Hawaiian
Blake	Male	White
Cassey	Female	Native Hawaiian
Chad	Male	Native Hawaiian
Chevonne	Female	Native Hawaiian
Cornel	Male	Latino
Darren	Male	Filipino
Destiny	Female	Native Hawaiian
Erica	Female	Samoan
Illeana	Female	Native Hawaiian
Jared	Male	Native Hawaiian
Jay-Jay	Female	Filipino
Joanna	Female	Samoan
Joel	Male	Native Hawaiian
Johnna	Female	Samoan
Jules	Male	Samoan
Julian	Male	Native Hawaiian
Junior	Male	Native Hawaiian
Keith	Male	Native Hawaiian
Kula	Male	Native Hawaiian
Kyle	Male	Native Hawaiian

Pseudonym	Gender	Ethnicity
Luke	Male	Native Hawaiian
Mara	Female	Native Hawaiian
Marcus	Male	Samoan
Masa	Male	Mixed Asian
Mia	Female	Samoan
Mona	Female	Unknown
Palo	Male	Samoan
Phillip	Male	Native Hawaiian
Rae	Female	Native Hawaiian
Shawn	Male	Native Hawaiian
Travis	Male	Samoan
Trisha	Female	Native Hawaiian
Vinny	Male	Samoan
Wilson	Male	Native Hawaiian

NOTES

INTRODUCTION

1. We use pseudonyms for the names of people and places throughout this book. Exceptions include the names of programs, state offices, political leaders, Hawaiian islands, Honolulu, and the University of Hawai'i. Also, because the thesis of this book includes an understanding of how racialization contributes to challenges that youth faced, we did not want study members' race and ethnicity to be among the first pieces of information that readers learned about teens. Appendix 2 shows the gender and ethnic group membership of each quoted student.

2. None of the teens in this study identified themselves as transgender, genderqueer, or gender nonbinary. We use the girl/boy gender dichotomy because it reflects the way that the youth identified themselves. There were nonbinary gender teens in the schools, but they did not take part in this study.

3. According to the State of Hawai'i, Department of Public Safety (2008), Native Hawaiians and Samoans made up 39 percent and 5 percent of the incarcerated population (respectively) in 2008; those groups made up roughly 20 percent and 1.3 percent of the population of Hawai'i at the same time, according to census data. We note that census respondents were allowed to select two or more racial groups. The Department of Public Safety may have underestimated the incarceration rate of Native Hawaiians, because it often does not indicate cases when individuals are from two or more racial groups.

CHAPTER 1

1. The term *neoliberal* generally refers to a set of economic policies advocating for small government; open, competitive economic markets; government deregulation; and privatization in the economic sphere. Such neoliberal policies do not promote government support of social programs.

2. According to Russell-Brown's (1998) "criminalblackman" thesis, images of Black men and crime became so tightly coupled after the 1980s that male Blackness became equated with criminality in the public imagination.

3. In fact, many argue that after industrial jobs left the United States, America's economy was buoyed by the service sector. For an explanation of inner-city men's reaction to working in service sector jobs, see Bourgois (2003), especially the chapter "'Goin' Legit': Disrespect and Resistance at Work."

4. The fact that femininity is not traditionally associated with violence might be part of the reason why girls are generally less violent than their male counterparts (Chesney-Lind and Irwin 2008). Strain theory (Broidy and Agnew 1997) also predicts that girls and women (compared with boys and men) experience different types of strain, and have different responses to and coping mechanisms for it. Consequently, girls and women are less likely to respond to strain with crime and violence, when compared with their male counterparts.

5. Feminist treatments of girls' violence highlight that violent girls have been disproportionately exposed (as victims and witnesses) to violence, as compared with their male counterparts. Artz (1998, 2004), for example, notes that violent girls are exposed at high rates to male-on-female physical and sexual violence at home (see also Schaffner 2006). Joe and Chesney-Lind (1995) argue that girls join gangs as a way of coping with family abuse.

6. Using a framework of patriarchy to explain girls' violence clarifies girls' place in a violent street ethos. For example, some have advanced a masculinized girls thesis and noted that violent girls are taking on masculine traits (Baskin, Sommers, and Fagan 1993; Sommers and Baskin 1992, 1993). These researchers argue that the disadvantages concentrated in urban areas have minimized gender inequalities. The extreme economic oppression, political neglect, and racial stigma that exist in some communities are seen as overriding traditional gender relations and effectively rewriting the "gender line on the street" (Bourgois 2003). As a result, girls and women are liberated and free to take on traditionally masculine behaviors and traits such as violence (Baskin, Sommers, and Fagan 1993; Sommers and Baskin 1992, 1993).

7. Hey (1997) also documents how girls regulate the sexuality of other girls in schools.

8. There is a loose association between the critical youth studies tradition we review and the work of the Birmingham (UK) Centre for Contemporary Cultural Studies (CCCS), although CCCS researchers focused on subcultural forms of resistance among lower- and working-class youth (Clarke 1976; Cohen 1980; Hall and Jefferson 1976; Hebdige 1979; McRobbie 1981; Willis 1977). In the United States, by contrast, CCCS-inspired work often focuses on race (Rose 1994).

9. As Clay (2012, 3) notes, "Academic and popular constructions of youth of color portray them as gang affiliated, 'troubled,' and potentially dangerous." The concern has been that many of the researchers focusing on poor youth of color—criminologists especially (see Jones 2010)—were delivering findings that seemed to pathologize youth who did not have racial, class, gender, political, and other privileges.

10. Lopez (2003) documents how second-generation Caribbean girls assert themselves in schools and take a hopeful outlook on their chances of going to college and becoming independent women (see also Cammarota 2008). Lopez observes that girls develop a feminist orientation out of their deep respect for and love of the adult women in their families

as well as because "multiple generations of Caribbean women have historically engaged in feminist practices that have challenged male domination" (126).

11. For exceptions to the negative images of racialized masculinity, see Blount and Cunningham (1996) and Belton (1996).

12. Young African American men have historically borne the brunt of punitive institutions, making up 13 percent of the U.S. population but 40 percent of all inmates as of 2008 (Hartney and Vuong 2009). These disparities grew as the United States came to have the highest incarceration rate in the industrialized world, with over 1.5 million incarcerated in 2013 (Carson 2014). Many cite as evidence the statistic that approximately one in every three African American males is in prison, on parole, or on probation (Miller 1996; Roberts 2004).

13. There are, of course, African Americans who have entered the middle class, but they lag "far behind the White middle-class in regards to economic security, status, and wealth" (Tatum 2000b, 20).

14. Wun (2014) argues that theories resting too heavily on political-economic explanations of racial formation and racial inequality tend to obscure the independent and persistent role of racism as "an enduring social order" (1). Here, critical race theory provides a useful complement to theories of racial formation and colonial criminology. Critical race theorists similarly acknowledge the economic and political workings of inequality and the historic contexts within which the significance of race is shaped.

15. See, for example, Lilikalā Kameʻeleihiwa, *Native Lands and Foreign Desires: Pehea Lā E Pono Ai?* (1996), Jonathan Kay Kamakawiwoʻole Osorio, *Dismembering Lāhui: A History of the Hawaiian Nation to 1887* (2002), and Noenoe Silva, *Aloha Betrayed: Native Hawaiian Resistance to American Colonialism* (2004).

16. According to the U.S. Census Bureau (2010b), as of 2010 Native Hawaiians and other Pacific Islanders constituted 25.8 percent of the state population. Whites, Filipinos, Japanese, and Chinese were the other most populous groups, comprising, 25, 14.4, 13.6, and 4.18 percent, respectively, of the state population.

CHAPTER 2

1. Rios (2011) "shadowed" teens. Contreras (2013) drew on friendship networks from having grown up in the South Bronx to gain entrée into the lives of the "stick up kids." Jones (2010) and Black (2009), like us, gained access to the youth through programs. Unlike us, Black became like family to the boys as they became young men.

2. For criminologists, immersion in the field can include engaging in deviant or illegal activities with members of the studied setting (Adler 1993; Ferrell and Hamm 1998a, 1998b; Polsky 1967), although the ethics of such engagement, especially in reference to the work of Goffman (2014), have come under serious scrutiny in the 2010s (Lubet 2015). It is important to note, however, that engaging in illegal behaviors has been a part of ethnographies of crime since long before the controversies surrounding Goffman's work.

3. Ethnographers take great pains to decrease the social distance between themselves and the populations they study, by immersing themselves in core aspects of the lives of their "subjects." The impetus to decrease distance in the field of youth studies has produced several statements about the research roles that allow adults to minimize the adult/youth

divide (Adler and Adler 1998; Caputo 1995; Eder and Fingerson 2002; Fine and Sandstrom 1988; Nespor 1998; Punch 2002).

4. Hartford Connecticut's Institute for Community Research provides a center to support youth-based participatory action research (PAR). Elizabeth Chin (2001) used PAR on a smaller study while she was conducting her participant observation of youth and consumer culture.

5. Our stance, however, stopped short of being a critical pedagogy or PAR, in that students were not co-researchers. Also, the lunch bunch group might have been an alternative space, but it was not a pedagogically disruptive space. The lunch bunch was a therapeutic program that allowed students to discuss emotions, pain, trauma, turmoil, and routes to healing.

6. Here it is important to note that some of the research included in this book, especially the focus group study, was supported by an agency of the U.S. Department of Health and Human Services (DHHS). The contents of this book are solely the responsibility of the authors and do not necessarily represent the official views of the funding agencies. We are purposely not identifying which DHHS agency funded the violence prevention initiative to protect the real names of the schools, communities, and people in this study.

7. Importantly, the grant project (which ended in 2010) included numerous other researchers and personnel, and led to the participant observations and in-depth interviews gathered for this book, which were not part of the original violence prevention grant.

8. As noted in the acknowledgments, the names of people and places are pseudonyms, with the exception of the names of programs, state offices, political leaders, Hawaiian islands, Honolulu, and the University of Hawai'i.

9. Approximately one third of Northward's residents were Native Hawaiian, with the remaining population being categorized as mixed-race, White, or Asian (U.S. Census Bureau 2010a).

10. For example, most Northward community meetings included food, with community leaders and their children often cooking for and serving food to their fellow meeting attendees. After meetings, someone usually volunteered to bring leftover food to the homeless camp on the beach.

11. The remaining students at Cleveland and Seaside identified as Japanese, Chinese, Korean, and White.

12. While reporting the rate of suspensions per 1,000 students might be preferable, we are choosing not to do so, as part of our commitment to revealing approximate, rather than actual, school enrollment data.

13. Researchers often disagree about definitions of violence, with some noting that violence includes psychological and verbal attacks. During the DHHS study, teens were asked survey and qualitative questions about how they defined violence. Most agreed that violence included physical fights and occasions when individuals physically hurt someone else on purpose.

14. Collecting consent forms from adult participants and assent forms and parent consent forms from teens was a requirement during every phase of this study. Thus, all the youth and adults mentioned in this book turned in the required assent and consent forms (respectively).

15. We thank Carrie Shoda-Sutherland, who coined this phrase when she learned about the project.

16. The counselors communicated some ground rules for safety, which included asking students to respect and not judge one another when differences emerged. Also, counselors reminded students that adults at school were mandatory reporters, meaning that, among other things, adults were required to report any cases when a student might be seriously injured or might seriously injure another person.

17. Counselors selected teens to be included in the lunch bunch program using their professional experience to discern which teens they thought could benefit from a group-counseling environment.

18. Some may wonder how we kept track of who we could include in field notes. Katy usually started each field note with a list of the students (using only their fake names) who were part of the observation study that year. The lunch bunch only included about seven girls and seven boys in any given year, and of those teens, only about two girls and two boys (on average) had returned parent permission forms allowing them to be in the observation study. Chronicling the activities of two girls and two boys in weekly field notes was not difficult.

19. Many teens lost their free and reduced priced meal cards during the school year and some parents were not able to pay the replacement fee. Consequently, some students went without food for several hours a day.

20. We did not have access to school records, but the counselors were able to confirm if lunch group teens' self-reported race and ethnic background matched the data that the school had for teens—overwhelmingly, the school data matched students' self-reports.

CHAPTER 3

1. As noted in the introduction, Miller's (2001) work has been used to argue that some of women's and girls' crime (especially their violence) is linked to their efforts to take on masculinized roles in criminal settings, like gangs. We also cited Miller's (2001, 10) argument that gender's "significance is variable" (see also Grundetjern 2015). Our view of violent girls is not in agreement with Miller's (2001) thesis that deviant, delinquent, and violent girls in male-dominated settings attempt to be "one of the guys."

2. In sociology and education studies of youth from diverse class, ethnic, and racial backgrounds, there is an ongoing assumption that working-class girls are more verbally forthright than their middle-class counterparts (Fordham 1993; Glenn 2002; Grant 1984; Morris 2007; Goodwin 1982; Lesko 1988). One argument has been that girls who lack race and class privilege have to learn to stand up for themselves (Collins 2000; Hill 2002; Morris 2007; Ward 2000). It should be noted, however, that socializing children to have strong verbal skills and assert their opinions is also part of middle-class parenting, regardless of racial and ethnic background (Lareau 2011).

3. Miss Phillips was actually Mrs. Phillips, but "Miss" was a common term that youth used for teachers.

4. Miller (2008) also notes the pervasive and sexualized violence that inner-city African American girls face among peers.

5. Though there are many books that discuss girl-on-girl bullying, many of the girls in this study talked about being teased, tormented, and ridiculed by boys. This indicates that there are mean boys in the world, and we argue that researchers and the general public

should take note. A few researchers have also noted this trend (Miller 2008; Pastor et al. 2007).

6. There is a large body of work, too unwieldy to review here, on the language of youth. Some core assumptions, however, are that children ritually tease, gossip about, and insult one another as a form of creating solidarity and teaching one another to be "playful" (see Corsaro 2011; Corsaro and Eder 1990). In adolescent peer groups, however, language like teasing and gossip can reinforce hierarchies among and within peer groups, with girls having fewer status opportunities than boys (Eder 1995). Importantly, in the reproduction of inequalities research, talk and language are not apt to be seen as innocent or playful (Eckert and McConnell-Ginet 1992).

7. A-Plus is an after-school program in Hawai'i.

8. Miller (2008) found the same to be true among the African American girls in her study.

9. The lives of teens in our study are consistent with findings in the literature regarding children of incarcerated parents (Bernstein 2005; Siegel 2011; Wakefield and Wildeman 2014), in that they confirm that incarceration complicates children's lives. Our study is also consistent with the finding that it is difficult to untangle the effects of having an incarcerated parent from the effects of other challenges in youth's lives (see Raeder 2012). Wildeman, Wakefield, and Turney (2013) provide a well-argued review of the literature.

10. Given institutional review board restrictions, we did not include any questions designed to explore family violence. Individuals under eighteen are a vulnerable population, and we were required to put many protections and safety procedures in place so that youth would not be harmed during our study. The potential for distress when talking about family violence was a risk that we could not take with this group of teens. Adults and a few youth, however, sometimes brought up the topic.

11. "Ho" is a Pidgin expression often used at the start of a sentence to emphasize the importance of the statement that follows.

12. The findings that families keep girls of color close to home (Espiritu 1995) and that working-class girls of color face an unequal division of domestic labor have been documented elsewhere (Leadbeater and Way 2001; Mayeda, Pasko, and Chesney-Lind 2006; Williams, Alvarez, and Andrade Hauck 2002; Taylor, Veloria, and Verba 2007; Zhou and Bankston 1998).

13. These income calculations are based on information gleaned from interviews with teens and from the family income requirements for families to be eligible for the free and reduced priced meals program in the state.

14. Lee (2005, 106) found a similar pattern among Hmong girls in her study, one of whom announced, "No—I am not doing their [her brothers'] laundry, they are old enough to do their own laundry."

CHAPTER 4

1. Many researchers examining girls' experiences have noted pervasive sexual double standards among children and adolescents (Adler, Kless, and Adler 1992; Durham 1998; Kelly 1993; Thorne 1999). Lees (1997) found that there were many more derogatory names for sexually active girls than there were for sexually active boys.

2. Sociological studies of adolescence have established that girls police the behavior of other girls, often by spreading rumors about, shunning, or isolating girls who do not conform to traditional gender norms (Adler and Adler 1998; Adler, Kless, and Adler 1992; Eder and Parker 1987; Eder 1985, 1995; Hey 1997; Kelly 1993). Researchers also often point out that both the competition among girls and the policing behaviors result from a lack of opportunities for girls to achieve status in peer cultures (Adler and Adler 1998; Adler, Kless, and Adler 1992; Eder and Parker 1987; Merten 1997).

3. Here we draw a different image of boys than what Miller (2008) describes. We found that boys were not participating in an alternative and hypermasculine code. Instead, we argue that boys in our study were conforming to the same masculine expectations confronting most boys throughout the United States.

4. Angel was referring to a particular boy in the lunch group by using a racially charged term. It should be noted that the boy referred to was Native Hawaiian and that there were no African American boys in the lunch groups while Angel was participating in the program.

5. Teens did talk about examples of dating violence at school, and this intimate partner battering was an example of boy-on-girl violence. This study did not capture the nature of dating violence, first, because we did not receive institutional review board permission to examine this highly destructive form of aggression and, second, because teens did not bring it up often enough for us to analyze it.

6. We are not sure of Mona's ethnic background.

CHAPTER 5

1. Many of the teens in this study who were born and raised in Hawai'i spoke Pidgin, which is a language distinct from Standard American English and Hawaiian.

2. Other U.S. territories that are excluded from statehood include Guam, Puerto Rico, the U.S. Virgin Islands, Swains Island, and the Commonwealth of Northern Mariana Islands.

3. We depart here from the perspectives in the traditional American youth studies literature, many of which come from the symbolic interactionism tradition. Instead, we are examining how youth make sense of power imbalances. Doing so, we note how the micro-interactions among youth functioned within a macro context of racial, class, gender, age, and sexual inequalities. The youth themselves understood the distinction between the micro context and large-scale injustices.

CHAPTER 6

1. The idea of an ethic of care was advanced in educational philosophy by Noddings (2013) in a seminal book, *Caring: A Relational Approach to Ethics and Moral Education*. It can be traced to feminism in its focus on connection and relationship in interactions and decision-making and in its acknowledgment of women's ways of knowing (Gilligan 1982; Owens and Ennis 2005).

2. Though the proliferation of mentoring programs has tended to outpace empirical studies of their efficacy (Cavell et al. 2009), many mentoring programs have been found to

be effective when they adhere to "best practices" (DuBois et al. 2002). Studies have found that the closeness and stability of relationships with a trained, caring adult lasting over time leads to successful youth outcomes (Keller 2005; Rhodes 1994, 2002, 2005).

3. Interview with Probation 1, June 3, 2014, Honolulu.

4. The Anti-Drug Abuse Act of 1986 and the 1988 Omnibus Anti-Abuse Act put into place a framework of mandatory minimum penalties for a range of drug trafficking offenses.

5. For a memorandum on the subsequent amendment of the Three Strikes law, see Couzens and Bigelow 2016.

6. Hawai'i Sess. Laws 1965, Act 232, approved July 6, 1965. Cited in Corbett and King (1968).

7. According to FBI statistics, between 1996 and 2012, the rate of juvenile arrest declined 57 percent in the United States, from 9,252 to 3,969 arrests per 100,000 persons aged ten to seventeen, while Hawai'i's rate declined 49 percent, from 13,125 to 6,655 arrests per 100,000 juveniles. Hawai'i's higher arrest rate may be in part due to the fact that not all law enforcement jurisdictions in other states arrest juveniles for status offenses (i.e., offenses that are not classified within the adult crime index). However, as of 2012, Hawai'i's violent crime index arrests (191 per 100,000) as well as property crime arrests (1,064 per 100,000) remained slightly higher than the United States as a whole (184 and 888 per 100,000 respectively). For U.S. Office of Juvenile Justice and Delinquency Prevention data, see Puzzanchera and Kang (2014).

8. The Hawai'i Juvenile Justice Working Group was established in spring 2013 by the Governor Neil Abercrombie, whose term ended in 2015. It included twenty representatives from the executive, legislative, and judicial branches including law enforcement, prosecution, public defense, and community service providers.

9. This study examined a sample of 232 juveniles committed to HYCF during fiscal years 2005, 2006, and 2007 (State of Hawai'i, Department of the Attorney General 2010, 2012).

10. This 2003 memo from the American Civil Liberties Union of Hawai'i to Attorney General Mark Bennett was based on visits to the facility, an interview with the facility director, and individual meetings with approximately seventy wards (White 2003).

11. The Department of Justice outlined remedies and placed the facility under federal oversight from 2006 to 2011.

12. This mixed methods study involved an analysis of arrest data from 2000 to 2010, along with interviews with key informants related to the juvenile justice system and advocacy organizations. For more details, see Umemoto et al. 2012. The final report can be accessed at http://ag.hawaii.gov/cpja/files/2013/01/DMC-FINAL-REPORT-2012.pdf.

13. These findings in the study were based on reviews of 142 randomly sampled case files for adjudicated youth arrested in 2009.

14. David Hipp, "Problems and Reform Opportunities in Hawaii's Juvenile Justice system," Presentation to the Department of Urban and Regional Planning, University of Hawaii, Honolulu, September 4, 2014.

15. Interview with probation officer 3, June 10, 2014, Honolulu.

16. While local school districts were given discretion to shorten the length of expulsion on a case-by-case basis, reports on the implementation of the law showed that most students received the full one-year expulsion. For data from school years 2003–4, 2002–3, 2001–2, 2000–1, 1999–2000, 1998–99, 1997–98, and 1996–97, see U.S. Department of Educa-

tion, Reports on State Implementation of the Gun-Free Schools Act, www2.ed.gov/about /reports/annual/gfsa/index.html.

17. Chapter 19 originated with the original 1964 Department of Education "Rule 21, Relating to Student Discipline," the 1963 "Rule 3, Relating to Police Interviews and Arrest of Students During School Hours," and the 1964 "Rule 24, Relating to Students Smoking on School Premises." See State of Hawai'i Board of Education, n.d. HBOE policies concerning fighting and violence fall under the title "Student Misconduct, Discipline, School Searches and Seizures, Reporting Offenses, Police Interviews and Arrests, and Restitution for Vandalism." See Hawai'i Board of Education official website, accessed April 10, 2014, www .hawaiiboe.net/AdminRules/Pages/AdminRule19.aspx.

18. The rule designates four classes of offenses, from Class A offenses, which are considered most severe (e.g., homicide, firearms use or possession, robbery, drug sale, possession or use) to Class D offenses, which are considered least severe (e.g., public displays of affection, bringing pets or contraband items to school).

19. This rate included in-school and out-of-school suspensions for students without disabilities. See U.S. Department of Education, Office for Civil Rights 2014.

20. The word 'aina has various meanings, many of which are spiritual in nature. In this context, it refers to the "land that feeds" in mutual interdependence with humans and all living beings.

CHAPTER 7

1. The U.S. Supreme Court Roper v. Simmons (2004) declared the death penalty for juveniles to be unconstitutional. After 2004, life sentence in prison became the harshest punishment allowable for juveniles in the United States.

2. We cannot be sure how common it was for the teens' parents or other family members to have been under the surveillance of the criminal or juvenile justice systems. The theme of parental and family members' incarceration emerged during interviews and lunch bunch conversations and we never designed specific probes or questionnaires to obtain more precise information. Because the institutional review board requirements (IRB) were strict and very difficult to navigate (we had to go through a yearly IRB review at UH and a semiregular IRB review process with the Hawai'i State Department of Education), we did not want to add a host of additional questions, probes, or questionnaires to our original research proposal. We refer again to the parental incarceration literature that we cited previously (Bernstein 2005; Raeder 2012; Siegel 2011; Wakefield and Wildman 2014) to suggest that there are some similar themes in our findings regarding the upheaval, chaotic circumstances, and emotional upset that confront youth when their parents and other family members are involved in the criminal justice system.

3. *Kine* is a Pidgin word roughly meaning "thing" or "stuff."

4. Miller (2008) also noted that the African American girls in her study relied on themselves, although she argued that their self reliance was aimed at becoming "streetwise," "respecting themselves," and "protecting themselves" as routes to avoid victimization (146–47).

5. The girls in this study were not markedly different from working-class racialized girls in other studies, who see school as a way to secure their independent futures (Lee 2005; Lopez 2003; Morris 2007; Taylor et al. 2007).

6. Our findings seem to be in agreement with Harris's (2011) and Ungar's (2002) assertion that boys, even the most troubled and enmeshed in delinquent peer groups, do not want to fail in school. Overall, we agree that youth who sometimes use violence or who are criminalized (Rios 2011) can cling to conventional goals, including the desire to pass their classes, graduate from school (see also Carter 2005), and secure stable jobs.

7. By faring the best, we mean that these boys were the most likely boys in the study to receive good grades and express hopefulness about their futures. Also, the boys with the second line of defense on their side did not express worry or anxiety about future employment or education after high school. They were, in other words, confident that they would "do well" as young men.

8. Abrams and Anderson-Nathe (2012), while collecting data for their book *Compassionate Confinement: A Year in the Life of Unit C,* discovered a similar pattern whereby adherence to masculine hegemony (especially when masculinity is reinforced in institutional settings) was not helpful for boys. Thus, part of compassionate work with teens should probably emphasize educating all youth about the many harms that male domination presents to boys and girls alike. By extension, ending the devaluation of all things "feminine"—such as being loving and kind—can end the oppressive gender dichotomies forced on youth. In essence, resilience among youth should include assertiveness, leadership, and critical consciousness, along with kindness and the ability to love and care for others.

9. The ability of most girls in this study to weather difficult challenges needs to be tempered with a note about the troubling experiences of girls in the juvenile justice system. Decades of research on girls' experiences in the justice system remind us of what awaits unruly girls, or girls who act out, run away, talk back to parents, join gangs, or find themselves addicted to drugs or alcohol. Girls who are charged with status offenses are more likely than status-offending boys to be institutionalized (Chesney-Lind and Shelden 2004; Datesman and Scarppitti 1977) and the detention and incarceration of girls increased at faster rates than that of boys throughout the 1990s and early 2000s (Snyder and Sickmund 2006). There is ample evidence to suggest that these increased rates of institutionalization for girls were based on what is called "relabeling" or "upcriming" (see Chesney-Lind and Belknap 2004), meaning that girls seemed to be behaving as they always had, but in the 1990s and early 2000s, their minor offenses, like talking back and being unruly, were "relabeled" into criminal conduct and their assaults were "upcrimed" and taken more seriously than they had been before (Chesney-Lind and Irwin 2008).

CHAPTER 8

1. The racial and ethnic composition of those in positions of power in Hawai'i's schools, courts, workplaces, and political offices is skewed toward Whites and Asians—especially Japanese and Chinese, who are highly assimilated into the norms and epistemic worldviews of mainstream, capitalist, and White Western society. Though individuals in power may have been empathetic toward the needs and circumstances of the youth in this study, there was nonetheless a larger, macro-level disconnection stemming from colonization that left a great divide in understanding between an imposed Western system of knowledge, values, and lifeways and those of people indigenous to these and other Pacific Islands.

2. The extent to which an indigenous society was considered to be properly civilized depended in large part on whether indigenous "men took up their proper place as heads of households" (Patil 2013, 857). Civilized societies, in the Western mind, were gender asymmetrical, and societies in which there was gender power-sharing were considered "savage."

3. Inasmuch as theories of the Western gender order are also theories of "multiple axes of power" (Patil 2013, 848), when we discuss gender-order-maintaining violence, we are also discussing violence that maintains racial, sexual, age, economic, and other hierarchies of power and privilege in the Western nation-state.

4. At the same time that some boys highlighted the history of the overthrow of the last Hawaiian monarch by military force and their perceptions that military members "abused their" power, had material advantages over them, and acted inappropriately in Hawai'i, other boys respected the military as a means to gain a sense of "self-control" and to become more "disciplined." It was almost as if those boys who wanted to join the military sensed that their "acting out" and violent behaviors were problematic. The problem, according to the boys, was not their aggression and violence per se, but the lack of discipline and order in their violence.

5. Girls were not considered appropriate "sparring" partners for boys because they were seen as easily overpowered; thus, only a "weakling" would feel the need to attack a girl. It is important to note that Pascoe (2012) and Miller (2008) also document the many forms of male-on-female violence that are normalized and tolerated in adolescents' lives.

6. It might be true that the girls also experienced relationship violence, although it was beyond the scope of this study to examine this aspect of youth's lives.

7. As Schaffner (2006) notes, hegemonic femininity creates contexts in which girls have an ambivalent relationship with anger. White, middle-class, "domesticated" girls are not supposed to show anger. But the girls in this study were denied the material and symbolic resources afforded to White, middle-class Americans.

8. To think there that is a single "Hawaiian knowledge system" would be too simplistic (see Meyer 1995, 1998).

CHAPTER 9

1. Knowledge about ho'oponopono was also preserved in texts, most notably by Hawaiian scholar, educator, and cultural practitioner Mary Kawena Pukui and her colleagues in *Nānā I Ke Kumu* (Pukui, Haertig, and Lee 1972), a seminal source on Hawaiian customs and traditions. Other scholars and practitioners have also described or documented the process in published works and in educational curricular materials (Andrade et al. 1994; Chun 1995; Ito 1983; Lee 2013; Meyer 1995; Nishihara 1978; Paglinawan 1976; Shook 1985; Stodden, Stodden, and Napoleon 2000).

2. See Napeahi et. al. (1998) for a description of ten steps in the process of ho'oponopono.

3. This book section is in no way intended to provide any instruction in ho'oponopono, which should be learned under the apprenticeship of experienced practitioners.

4. Wayde Lee acknowledges the following kūpuna for his development and that of Kahua Ola Hou and the Pono Lōkahi curriculum: Mary Wahineokalani Lee, Abby Napeahi, Malia Craver, Anita Arce, Malia Poepoe, Vanda Hanakahi, Harriet Ne, Ivy Hanakahi Woo, and his mother, Jane Pahula Lee (see Withy, Lee, and Renger 2007).

5. For background on PBS, see Sugai et al. (1999).

6. See the Technical Assistance Center on Positive Behavioral Interventions and Supports, at pbis.org. This center was established by the U.S. Department of Education's Office of Special Education Programs (OSEP) "to define, develop, implement, and evaluate a multi-tiered approach to Technical Assistance that improves the capacity of states, districts and schools to establish, scale-up and sustain the PBIS framework."

7. Many of these initiatives cite studies of adolescent brain development and peer influence, attitudes toward risk and perception of risk, degree of future orientation, and locus of control. See the National Research Council of the National Academies' Committee on Law and Justice report, *Reforming the Juvenile Justice System: A Developmental Approach* (Bonnie et al. 2013).

8. Launched in the 1990s and brought to the Hawaiian islands in 2009, JDAI fostered collaboration between various government agencies and community organizations in order to reduce or eliminate the detention stay using objective screening methods and community-based alternatives to detention.

9. Carol Matsuoka, Powerpoint data presentation, Hawai'i members of JDAI, 2013.

10. Staff from the Pew worked with Governor Neil Abercrombie, Chief Justice Mark Recktenwald, Senate President Donna Mercado Kim, and House Speaker Joseph Souki to establish the Hawai'i Juvenile Justice Working Group.

Abrams, Laura S., and Ben Anderson-Nathe. 2012. *Compassionate Confinement: A Year in the Life of Unit C.* New Brunswick, NJ: Rutgers University Press.

Adams, Natalie G. 1999. "Fighting to Be Somebody: Resisting Erasure and the Discursive Practices of Female Adolescent Fighting." *Educational Studies* 30 (2): 115–39.

Adler, Patricia. 1993. *Wheeling and Dealing: An Ethnography of an Upper-Level Drug Dealing and Smuggling Community.* New York: Columbia University Press.

Adler, Patricia A., and Peter Adler. 1998. *Peer Power: Preadolescent Culture and Identity.* New Brunswick, NJ: Rutgers University Press.

———. 1987. *Membership Roles in Field Research.* Newbury Park, CA: Sage.

Adler, Patricia, Steven J. Kless, and Peter Adler. 1992. "Socialization to Gender Roles: Popularity among Elementary School Boys and Girls." *Sociology of Education* 65 (3): 169–87.

Ah Nee-Benham, Maenette Kape'ahiokalani P., and Joanne Elizabeth Cooper, eds. 2000. *Indigenous Educational Models for Contemporary Practice: In Our Mother's Voice.* New York: Routledge.

Akom, A. A., Shawn Ginwright, and Julio Cammarota. 2008. "Youthtopias: Towards a New Paradigm of Critical Youth Studies." *Youth Media Reporter: The Professional Journal of the Youth Media Field* 2 (4): 1–30.

Alexander, Jeffrey C., Ron Eyerman, Bernhard Giesen, Neil J. Smelser, eds. 2004. *Cultural Trauma and Collective Identity.* Berkeley: University of California Press.

Alexander, Michelle. 2012. *The New Jim Crow: Mass Incarceration in the Age of Colorblindness.* New York: The New Press.

Anderson, Elijah. 1999. *Code of the Street: Decency, Violence, and the Moral Life of the Inner City.* New York: Norton.

———. 1990. *Streetwise: Race, Class, and Change in an Urban Community.* Chicago: University of Chicago Press.

Andrade, N. N., R. C. Johnson, J. Edman, G. P. Danko, L. B. Nahulu, G. K. Makini Jr., N. Yuen, J. A. Waldron, A. Yates, and J. F. McDermott Jr. 1994. "Non-Traditional and Traditional Treatment of Hawaiian and Non-Hawaiian Adolescents." *Hawai'i Medical Journal* 53 (12): 344–47.

Annie E. Casey Foundation. 2014. *Juvenile Detention Alternatives Initiative Progress Report, 2014.* Baltimore: Annie E. Casey Foundation. Available at www.aecf.org/resources/2014-juvenile-detention-alternatives-initiative-progress-report/.

Artz, Sibylle. 2005. "To Die For: Adolescent Girls' Search for Male Attention." In *Development and Treatment of Girlhood Aggression,* edited by D. Pepler, K. Madesn, C. Webster, and K. Levene, 137–59. Hillsdale, NJ: Lawrence Erlbaum Associates.

———. 2004. "Violence in the Schoolyard: School Girls' Use of Violence." In *Girls' Violence: Myths and Realities,* edited by C. Alder and A. Worrall, 151–66. New York: State University of New York Press.

———. 1998. *Sex, Power, and the Violent School Girl.* Toronto: Trifolium Books.

Arum, Richard. 2005. *Judging School Discipline: The Crisis of Moral Authority.* Cambridge, MA: Harvard University Press.

Austin, Roy L. 1983. "The Colonial Model, Subcultural Theory and Intragroup Violence." *Journal of Criminal Justice* 11 (2): 93–104.

Barker, Olivia. 2003. "Scantily-Clad Teachers Compel Schools to Consider Dress Codes." *Honolulu Advertiser,* Sept. 8. http://the.honoluluadvertiser.com/article/2003/Sep/08/il/il03a.html.

Baskin, Deborah, and Ira B. Sommers. 1993. "Females' Initiation into Violent Street Crime." *Justice Quarterly* 10 (4): 559–81.

Batchelor, Susan, Michele Burman, and Jane Brown. 2001. "Discussing Violence: Let's Hear It from the Girls." *Probation Journal* 48 (2): 125–34.

Belknap, Joanne. 2015. "The 2014 American Society of Criminology Presidential Address: Activist Criminology: Criminologists' Responsibility to Advocate for Social and Legal Justice." *Criminology* 53 (1): 1–22.

Belton, Don. 1996. *Speak My Name: Black Men on Masculinity and the American Dream.* Boston: Beacon Press.

Bergseth, Kathleen J., and Jeffrey A. Bouffard. 2013. "Examining the Effectiveness of a Restorative Justice Program for Various Types of Juvenile Offenders." *International Journal of Offender Therapy and Comparative Criminology* 57 (9): 1054–75.

Bernstein, Nell. 2005. *All Alone in the World: Children of the Incarcerated.* New York: The New Press.

Best, Amy L. 2000. *Prom Night: Youth, Schools and Popular Culture.* New York: Routledge.

———, ed. 2007. *Representing Youth: Methodological Issues in Critical Youth Studies.* New York: New York University Press.

Biernacki, Patrick, and Dan Waldorf. 1981. "Snowball Sampling: Problems and Techniques of Chain Referral Sampling." *Sociological Methods and Research* 10 (2): 141–63.

Bishop, Donna M., and Charles E. Frazier. 1996. "Race Effects in Juvenile Justice Decision-Making: Findings of a Statewide Analysis." *Journal of Criminal Law and Criminology* 86 (2): 392–414.

Black, David. 1993. *The Social Structure of Right and Wrong.* San Diego: Academic Press.

———. 1983. "Crime as Social Control." *American Sociological Review* 48 (1): 34–45.

Black, Timothy. 2009. *When a Heart Turns Rock Solid: The Lives of Three Puerto Rican Brothers on and off the Streets.* New York: Pantheon Books.

Blaisdell, Kekuni, and Noreen Moku'au. 1994. "I Hea Nā Kānaka Maoli? Whither the Hawaiians." *Huili* 2: 9–18.

Blauner, Robert. 1972. *Racial Oppression in America.* New York: Harper and Row.

Block, Fred, Richard A. Cloward, Barbara Ehrenreich, and Frances Scott Piven. 1987. *The Mean Season: The Attack on the Welfare State.* New York: Pantheon.

Blount, Marcellus, and George P. Cunningham, eds. 1996. *Representing Black Men.* New York: Routeledge.

Bonnie, Richard J., Robert L. Johnson, Betty M. Chemers, and Julie Schuck. 2013. *Reforming Juvenile Justice: A Developmental Approach.* Washington, D.C.: National Academies Press.

Bottrell, Dorothy. 2009. "Dealing with Disadvantage: Resilience and the Social Capital of Young People's Networks." *Youth and Society* 40 (4): 476–501.

Bowditch, Christine. 1993. "Getting Rid of Troublemakers: High School Disciplinary Procedures and the Production of Dropouts." *Social Problems* 40 (4): 493–509.

Bowles, Samuel, and Herbert Gintis. 1976. *Schooling in Capitalist America.* New York: Basic Books.

Bourgois, Philippe. 2003. *In Search of Respect: Selling Crack in El Barrio.* New York: Cambridge University Press.

Boyd, Tona M. 2009. "Confronting Racial Disparity: Legislative Responses to the School-to-Prison Pipeline." *Harvard Civil Rights-Civil Liberties Law Review* 44 (2): 571–80.

Braithwaite, John. 1999. "Restorative Justice: Assessing Optimistic and Pessimistic Accounts." In *Crime and Justice: A Review of Research,* edited by M. Tonry, 1–127. Chicago: University of Chicago Press.

Bridges, George S., and Sara Steen. 1998. "Racial Disparities in Official Assessments of Juvenile Offenders: Attributional Stereotypes as Mediating Mechanisms." *American Sociological Review* 63 (4): 554–70.

Broidy, Lisa, and Robert Agnew. 1997. "Gender and Crime: A General Strain Theory Perspective. *Journal of Research in Crime and Delinquency* 34 (3): 275–306.

Brown, Lyn Mikel. 2003. *Girlfighting: Betrayal and Rejection among Girls.* New York: New York University Press.

———. 1998. *Raising Their Voices: The Politics of Girls' Anger.* Cambridge, MA: Harvard University Press.

Brown, Paul W. 1987. "Probation Officer Burnout." *Federal Probation Journal* 51 (3): 17–21.

Burgess-Proctor, Amanda. 2006. "Intersections of Race, Class, Gender, and Crime: Future Directions for Feminist Criminology." *Feminist Criminology* 1 (1): 27–47.

Burk, James, and Evelyn Espinoza. 2012. "Race Relations within the U.S. Military." *Annual Review of Sociology* 38 (2): 401–22.

Burman, Michele, Jane Brown, and Susan Batchelor. 2003. "'Taking It to Heart': Girls and the Meanings of Violence." In *The Meanings of Violence,* edited by E. A. Stanko, 71–89. New York: Routledge.

Cabaniss, Emily R., James M. Frabutt, Mary H. Kendrick, and Margaret B. Arbuckle. 2007. "Reducing Disproportionate Minority Contact in the Juvenile Justice System: Promising Practices." *Aggression and Violent Behavior* 12 (4): 393–401.

Cammarota, Julio. 2008. *Suenos Americanos: Barrio Youth Negotiating Social and Cultural Identities*. Tuscon: University of Arizona Press.

Cammarota, Julio, and Michelle Fine, eds. 2008. *Revolutionizing Education: Youth Participatory Action Research in Motion*. New York: Routledge.

Campbell, Anne. 1984. *The Girls in the Gang*. London: Basil Blackwell.

Caputo, Virginia. 1995. "Anthropology's Silent 'Others': A Consideration of Some Conceptual and Methodological Issues for the Study of Youth and Children Cultures." In *Youth Cultures: A Cross-Cultural Perspective*, edited by V. Amit-Talai and H. Wulff, 19–42. London: Routledge.

Carr, Edward G., Glen Dunlap, Robert H. Horner, Robert L. Koegel, Ann P. Turnbull, Wayne Sailor, Jacki L. Anderson, Richard W. Albin, Lynn Kern Koegel, and Lise Fox. 2002. "Positive Behavior Support Evolution of an Applied Science." *Journal of Positive Behavior Interventions* 4 (1): 4–16.

Carson, E. Ann. 2014. "Prisoners in 2013." *Bureau of Justice Statistics*, Sept. 2014. www.bjs .gov/content/pub/pdf/p13.pdf.

Carter, Prudence L. 2005. *Keepin' It Real: School Success beyond Black and White*. New York: Oxford University Press.

Cavell, Timothy A., L. Christian Elledge, Kenya T. Malcolm, Melissa A. Faith, and Jan N. Hughes. 2009. "Relationship Quality and the Mentoring of Aggressive, High-Risk Children." *Journal of Clinical Child and Adolescent Psychology* 38 (2): 185–98.

Chesney-Lind, Meda. 2001. "Are Girls Closing the Gender Gap in Violence?" *Criminal Justice* 16 (1): 18–23.

Chesney-Lind, Meda, and Joanne Belknap. 2004. "Trends in Delinquent Girls' Aggression and Violent Behavior: A Review of the Evidence." In *Aggression, Antisocial Behavior and Violence among Girls: A Developmental Perspective*, edited by M. Putallaz and P. Bierman, 203–22. New York: Guilford Press.

Chesney-Lind, Meda, and Katherine Irwin. 2008. *Beyond Bad Girls: Gender, Violence, and Hype*. New York: Routledge.

Chesney-Lind, Meda, and Merry Morash. 2013. "Transformative Feminist Criminology: A Critical Re-Thinking of a Discipline." *Critical Criminology* 21 (3): 287–304.   •

Chesney-Lind, Meda, and Randall G. Shelden. 2004. *Girls, Delinquency, and Juvenile Justice*. Belmont, CA: Thompson/Wadsworth.

Chin, Elizabeth. 2001. *Purchasing Power: Black Kids and American Consumer Culture*. Minneapolis: University of Minnesota Press.

Chun, Malcolm Naea. 1995. *Making Peace: Ho'oponopono Then and Now*. Honolulu: Queen Lili'uokalani Children's Center and the Liliuokalani Trust.

Clarke, John. 1976. "The Skinheads and the Magical Recovery of Community." In *Resistance through Rituals: Youth Subcultures in Post-War Britain*, edited by S. Hall and T. Jefferson, 99–102. London: Hutchinson.

Clay, Andreana. 2012. *The Hip-Hop Generation Fights Back: Youth Activism, and Post-Civil Rights Politics*. New York: New York University Press.

Cloward, Richard A., and Lloyd E. Ohlin. 1960. *Delinquency and Opportunity: A Theory of Delinquent Gangs*. Glencoe, IL: Free Press.

Cohen, Albert K. 1955. *Delinquent Boys: The Culture of the Gang*. Glencoe, IL: Free Press.

Cohen, Phil. 1980. "Subcultural Conflict and Working Class Community." In *Culture, Media, Language: Working Papers in Cultural Studies*, edited by S. Hall, D. Hobson, A. Lowe, and P. Willis, 66–75. New York: Routledge.

Collins, Patricia Hill. 2000. *Black Feminist Thought: Knowledge, Consciousness, and the Politics of Empowerment*. 2nd ed. New York: Routledge.

Connell, R. W. 2005. *Masculinities*. Berkeley: University of California Press.

———. 1987. *Gender and Power: Society, the Person and Sexual Politics*. Cambridge, MA: Polity Press.

Contreras, Randol. 2012. *The Stickup Kids: Race, Drugs, Violence, and the American Dream*. Berkeley: University of California Press.

Cook, Bud, Lucia Tarallo-Jensen, Kelly Withy, and Shawn P. Berry. 2005. "Changes in Kanaka Maoli Men's Roles and Health: Healing the Warrior Self." *International Journal of Men's Health* 4 (2): 115–30.

Corbett, Gerald R., and Samuel P. King. 1968. "The Family Court of Hawai'i." *The Family Law Quarterly* 2 (1): 32–39.

Corsaro, William A. 2011. "Peer Culture." In *The Palgrave Handbook of Childhood Studies*, edited by J. Qvortrup, W. A. Corsaro, and M. Honig, 301–15. New York: Palgrave.

———. 2003. *We're Friends, Right? Inside Kids' Culture*. Washington, D.C: Joseph Henry Press.

Corsaro, William A., and Donna Eder. 1990. "Children's Peer Cultures." *Annual Review of Sociology* 16 (4): 197–220.

Couzens, J. Richard, and Tricia A. Bigelow. 2016. "The Amendment of the Three Strikes Sentencing Law." Updated February 2016, www.courts.ca.gov/documents/Three-Strikes-Amendment-Couzens-Bigelow.pdf.

Crabbe, Kamana'opono M. 1997. Hui Kū Ha'aheo Men's Group: A Pilot Project for Adult Native Hawaiian Males Utilizing a Cultural Approach towards Healing Problems of Alcohol/Substance Abuse and Family Violence. Unpublished manuscript. Honolulu: Hale Na'au Pono and Ho'omau Ke Ola.

Crenshaw, Kimberle. 1991. "Mapping the Margins: Intersectionality, Identity Politics, and Violence against Women of Color." *Stanford Law Review* 43 (6): 1241–99.

Cullen, Francis T. 2013. "Rehabilitation: Beyond Nothing Works." *Crime and Justice* 42 (1): 299–376.

———. 2007. "Make Rehabilitation Corrections' Guiding Paradigm." *Criminology and Public Policy* 6 (4): 717–27.

Daly, Kathleen. 2000. "Revisiting the Relationship between Retributive and Restorative Justice." In *Restorative Justice: Philosophy to Practice*, edited by H. Strang and J. Braithwaite, 33–54. Aldershot; Burlington, VT: Ashgate.

———. 1989. "Neither Conflict nor Labeling nor Paternalism Will Suffice: Intersections of Race, Ethnicity, Gender, and Family in Criminal Court Decisions." *Crime and Delinquency* 35 (1): 136–68.

Darling-Hammond, Linda. 2007. "Race, Inequality, and Educational Accountability: The Irony of 'No Child Left Behind.'" *Race Ethnicity and Education* 10 (3): 245–60.

Datesman, Susan, and Frank Scarppitti. 1977. "Unequal Protection for Males and Females in the Juvenile Court." In *Juvenile Delinquency: Little Brother Grows Up*, edited by T. N. Ferdinand, 59–77. Newbury Park, CA: Sage.

Delgado, Melvin, and Lee Staples. 2008. *Youth-Led Community Organizing Theory and Action*. New York: Oxford University Press.

Delgado, Richard, and Jean Stefancic. 2012. *Critical Race Theory: An Introduction*. New York: New York University Press.

DeMitchell, Todd A., and Casey D. Cobb. 2003. "Policy Responses to Violence in Our Schools: An Exploration of Security as a Fundamental Value." *Brigham Young University Education and Law Journal* 2 (2): 459–84.

Dilulio, John J. 1995. "The Coming of the Super-Predators." *The Weekly Standard* 27 (11): 23.

Dougherty, Michael. 1992. *To Steal a Kingdom: Probing Hawaiian History*. Waimanalo, HI: Island Style Press.

Draguns, Juris. 1981. "Cross-Cultural Counseling and Psychotherapy: History, Issues and Current Status." In *Cross-Cultural Counseling and Psychotherapy: Foundations, Evaluation and Cultural Considerations,* edited by A. J. Marsella and P. B. Pedersen, 3–27. New York: Pergamon Press.

DuBois, David L., Bruce E. Holloway, Jeffrey C. Valentine, and Harris Cooper. 2002. "Effectiveness of Mentoring Programs for Youth: A Meta-Analytic Review." *American Journal of Community Psychology* 30 (2): 157–97.

Durham, Meenakshi G. 1998. "Dilemmas of Desire: Representations of Adolescent Sexuality in Two Teen Magazines." *Youth and Society* 29 (3): 369–89.

Durkheim, Emile. 1961. *Moral Education: A Study in the Theory and Application of the Sociology of Education*. New York: Free Press of Glencoe.

Eckert, Penelope, and Sally McConnell-Ginet. 1992. "Think Practically and Look Locally: Language and Gender as Community-Based Practice." *Annual Review of Anthropology* 21: 461–90.

Eder, Donna. 1995. *School Talk: Gender and Adolescent School Culture*. With Catherine C. Evans and Stephen Parker. New Brunswick, NJ: Rutgers University Press.

———. 1985. "The Cycle of Popularity: Interpersonal Relations among Female Adolescents." *Sociology of Education* 58 (3): 154–65.

Eder, Donna, and Laura Fingerson. 2002. "Interviewing Children and Adolescents." In *Handbook of Interview Research,* edited by J. Gubrium and J. Holstein, 181–201. Thousand Oaks, CA: Sage.

Eder, Donna, and Stephen Parker. 1987. "The Cultural Production and Reproduction of Gender: The Effect of Extracurricular Activities on Peer-Group Culture." *Sociology of Education* 60 (3): 200–13.

Engen, Rodney L., Sara Steen, and George S. Bridges. 2002. "Racial Disparities in the Punishment of Youth: A Theoretical and Empirical Assessment of the Literature." *Social Problems* 49 (2): 194–220.

Erikson, Erik. 1950. *Childhood and Society*. New York: Norton.

Espiritu, Yen Le. 1995. *Filipino American Lives*. Philadelphia: Temple University Press.

Evans, Alison C., Larkin S. McReynolds, and Gail A Wasserman. 2006. "A Cure for Crime: Can Mental Health Treatment Diversion Reduce Crime among Youth?" *Journal of Policy Analysis and Management* 25 (1): 197–214.

Fanon, Frantz. 1967. *Black Skin, White Masks*. New York: Grove Press.

———. 1963. *The Wretched of the Earth*. New York: Grove Press.

Feld, Barry C. 1999. *Bad Kids: Race and the Transformation of the Juvenile Court. Studies in Crime and Public Policy.* New York: Oxford University Press.

Fenning, Pamela, and Jennifer Rose. 2007. "Overrepresentation of African American Students in Exclusionary Discipline the Role of School Policy." *Urban Education* 42 (6): 536–59.

Ferguson, Ann Arnett. 2001. *Bad Boys: Public Schools in the Making of Black Masculinity.* Ann Arbor: University of Michigan Press.

Ferrell, Jeff, and Mark S. Hamm, eds. 1998a. *Ethnography at the Edge: Crime, Deviance, and Field Research.* Boston: Northeastern University Press.

———. 1998b. "True Confessions: Crime, Deviance, and Field Research." In *Ethnography at the Edge: Crime, Deviance, and Field Research,* edited by J. Ferrell and M. S. Hamm, 2–19. Boston: Northeastern University Press.

Fine, Gary A., and Kent L. Sandstrom. 1988. *Knowing Children: Participant Observation with Minors.* Newbury Park, CA: Sage.

Fine, Michelle. 2006. "Bearing Witness: Methods for Researching Oppression and Resistance: A Textbook for Critical Research." *Social Justice Research* 19 (1): 83–108.

Fine, Michelle, Janice Bloom, April Burns, Lori Chajet, Monique Guishard, Tiffany Perkins-Munn, and Maria Elena Torre. 2004. "Dear Zora: A Letter to Zora Neale Hurston Fifty Years After Brown." In *Working Method: Research and Social Justice,* edited by L. Weis and M. Fine, 3–26. New York: Routledge.

Fine, Michelle, and Lois Weis. 1998. *The Unknown City: Lives of Poor and Working Class Young Adults.* Boston: Beacon Press.

Finley, Laura L. 2006. "Examining School Searches as Systemic Violence." *Critical Criminology* 14 (2): 117–35.

Finney, Ben. 2003. *Sailing in the Wake of the Ancestors: Reviving Polynesian Voyaging.* Honolulu: Bishop Museum Press.

Fischer, Claude S. 1980. "The Spread of Violent Crime from City to Countryside, 1955–1975." *Rural Sociology* 45 (3): 230–46.

Fordham, Signithia. 1993. "'Those Loud Black Girls': (Black) Women, Silence, and Gender 'Passing' in the Academy." *Anthropology and Education Quarterly* 24 (1): 3–31.

Foucault, Michel. 1979. *Discipline and Punish: The Birth of the Prison.* Translated by Alan Sheridan. New York: Vintage Books.

Freire, Paulo. [1970] 1993. *Pedagogy of the Oppressed.* New York: Continuum Publishing Company.

Fuatagavi, Lydia, and Paul Perrone. 2008. *Crime in Hawai'i, 2007: A Review of Uniform Crime Reports.* Honolulu: Attorney General, State of Hawai'i, Research and Statistics Branch, Crime Prevention, and Justice Assistance Division.

Fujikane, Candace. 2008. "Asian Settler Colonialism in the U.S. Colony of Hawai'i." In *Asian Settler Colonialism: From Local Governance to the Habits of Everyday Life in Hawai'i,* edited by C. Fujikane and J. Y. Okamura, 1–42. Honolulu: University of Hawai'i Press.

———. 2000. "Between Nationalisms: Hawai'i's Local Nation and Its Troubled Racial Paradise." *Critical Mass: A Journal of Asian American Cultural Criticism* 1 (2): 23–57.

Gabbidon, Shaun L. 2010. *Race, Ethnicity, Crime and Justice: An International Dilemma.* Thousand Oaks, CA: Sage.

Galtung, Johan. 1969. "Violence, Peace, and Peace Research." *Journal of Peace Research* 6 (3): 167–91.

Garcia, Lorena. 2012. *Respect Yourself, Protect Yourself: Latina Girls and Sexual Identity.* New York: New York University Press.

Garland, David. 2004. *The Culture of Control: Crime and Social Order in Contemporary Society.* Chicago: University of Chicago Press.

———. 1990. "Frameworks of Inquiry in the Sociology of Punishment." *British Journal of Sociology* 41 (1): 1–15.

Geertz, Clifford. 1973. "Thick Description: Toward an Interpretive Theory of Culture." In *The Interpretation of Cultures: Selected Essays,* edited by C. Geertz, 1–30. New York: Basic Books.

Gilligan, Carol. 1982. *In a Different Voice.* Cambridge, MA: Harvard University Press.

Gilligan, James. 1997. *Violence: Reflections on a National Epidemic.* New York: Vintage Books.

Gillis, John R. 1974. *Youth and History: Tradition and Change in European Age Relations, 1770 –Present.* New York: Academic Press.

Ginwright, Shawn, and Julio Cammarota. 2006. "Introduction." In *Beyond Resistance! Youth Activism and Community Change,* edited by S. Ginwright, P. Noguera, and J. Cammarota, xiii–xxii. New York: Routledge.

Ginwright, Shawn, Pedro Noguera, and Julio Cammarota, eds. 2006. *Beyond Resistance! Youth Activism and Community Change.* New York: Routledge.

Giroux, Henry. 2003. "Racial Injustice and Disposable Youth in the Age of Zero Tolerance." *International Journal of Qualitative Studies in Education* 16 (4): 553–65.

———. 1983. "Theories of Reproduction and Resistance in the New Sociology of Education: A Critical Analysis." *Harvard Educational Review* 53 (4): 257–93.

Glaze, Lauren, and Laura M. Maruschak. 2008. "Parents in Prison and Their Minor Children." *Bureau of Justice Statistics Special Report.* U.S. Department of Justice, Office of Justice Programs. August 2008, Revised March 30, 2010.

Glenn, Evelyn N. 2002. *Unequal Freedom: How Race and Gender Shaped American Citizenship and Labor.* Cambridge, MA: Harvard University Press.

Goffman, Alice. 2014. *On the Run: Fugitive Life in an American City.* Chicago: The University of Chicago Press.

Goodwin, Marjorie. H. 1982. *He-Said-She-Said: Talk as Social Organization among Black Children.* Bloomington: Indiana University Press.

Goodyear-Kaʻōpua, Noelani. 2013. *The Seeds We Planted: Portraits of a Native Hawaiian Charter School.* Minnesota: University of Minnesota Press.

———. 2009. "Rebuilding the Auwai: Connecting Ecology, Economy and Education in Hawaiian Schools." *AlterNative,* 5 (2): 47–77.

Gotanda, Neil. 1991. "A Critique of 'Our Constitution Is Color-Blind.'" *Stanford Law Review* 44 (1): 1–68.

Grant, Linda. 1984. "Black Females' 'Place' in Desegregated Classrooms." *Sociology of Education* 57 (2): 98–111.

Greenwood, Peter W., Karyn Model, C. Peter Rydell, and James Chiesa. 1998. *Diverting Children from a Life of Crime: Measuring Costs and Benefits.* Los Angeles: RAND Corporation.

Gregory, Anne, Russell J. Skiba, and Pedro A. Noguera. 2010. "The Achievement Gap and the Discipline Gap: Two Sides of the Same Coin?" *Educational Researcher* 39 (1): 59–68.

Griffiths, Vivienne. 1995. *Adolescent Girls and Their Friends: A Feminist Ethnography.* Aldershot, UK: Avebury.

Grundetjern, Heidi. 2015. "Women's Gender Performances and Cultural Heterogeneity in the Illegal Drug Economy." *Criminology* 53 (2): 253–79.

Hacking, Ian. 1999. *The Social Construction of What?* Cambridge, MA: Harvard University Press.

Hall, G. Stanley. 1903. "Coeducation in the High School." *National Education Association Journal of Proceedings and Addresses* 42: 442–55.

Hall, Stuart, and Tony Jefferson. 1976. *Resistance through Rituals: Youth Subcultures in Post-War Britain.* New York: Routledge.

Harcourt, Bernard E. 2008. *Against Prediction: Profiling, Policing, and Punishing in an Actuarial Age.* Chicago: University of Chicago Press.

Harris, Angela. 2011. *Kids Don't Want to Fail: Oppositional Culture and the Black-White Achievement Gap.* Cambridge, MA: Harvard University Press.

Harris, Anita. 2004. *All about the Girl: Culture, Power and Identity.* New York: Routledge.

Hartney, Christopher, and Linh Vuong. 2009. *Created Equal: Racial and Ethnic Disparities in the U.S. Criminal Justice System.* Oakland, CA: National Council on Crime and Delinquency.

Hawai'i Juvenile Justice Working Group. 2013. *Hawai'i Juvenile Justice Working Group Final Report.* Honolulu: State of Hawai'i, Office of the Governor.

Hawai'i State Department of Education. 2008. *School Status and Improvement Report: School Year 2006–07.* Honolulu: System Evaluation and Reporting Section, Systems Accountability Office, Office of the Superintendent.

Hawkins, Darnel F. 2011. "Things Fall Apart: Revisiting Race and Ethnic Differences in Criminal Violence amidst a Crime Drop." *Race and Justice* 1 (1): 3–48.

Heath, Shirley Brice, and Milbrey W. McLaughlin, eds. 1993. *Identity and Inner-City Youth: Beyond Ethnicity and Gender.* New York: Teachers College Press.

Heaviside, Sheila, Cassandra Rowand, Catrina Williams, and Elizabeth Farris. 1998. *Violence and Discipline Problems in U.S. Public Schools: 1996–97.* Washington, D.C.: National Center for Education Statistics.

Hebdige, Dick. 1979. *Subculture: The Meaning of Style.* New York: Routledge.

Hendrick, Harry. 2011. "The Evolution of Childhood in Western Europe c. 1400–c. 1750." In *The Palgrave Handbook of Childhood Studies,* edited by J. Qvortrup, W. A. Corsaro, and M. Honig, 99–113. New York: Palgrave.

Henry, Stuart, and Werner J. Einstadter. 2006. *Criminological Theory: An Analysis of Its Underlying Assumptions.* Lanham, MD: Rowman and Littlefield Publishers.

Hey, Valerie. 1997. *The Company She Keeps: An Ethnography of Girls' Friendship.* Buckinghan, UK: Open University Press.

Hill, Shirley A. 2002. "Teaching and Doing Gender in African American Families." *Sex Roles: A Journal of Research* 47 (11): 493–506.

Hirschfield, Paul J. 2008. "Preparing for Prison? The Criminalization of School Discipline in the USA." *Theoretical Criminology* 12 (1): 79–101.

Hondagneu-Sotelo, Pierrette. 1994. *Gendered Transitions: Mexican Experiences of Immigration.* Berkeley: University of California Press.

Howell, James C. 2003. "Diffusing Research into Practice Using the Comprehensive Strategy for Serious, Violent, and Chronic Juvenile Offenders." *Youth Violence and Juvenile Justice* 1 (3): 219–45.

Hurtado, Aida. 1996. *The Color of Privilege: Three Blasphemies on Race and Feminism.* Ann Arbor: University of Michigan.

Iadicola, Peter, and Anson Shupe. 2012. *Violence, Inequality, and Human Freedom.* New York: Rowman and Littlefield.

Inciardi, James A., and Lana D. Harrison, eds. 1998. *Harm Reduction: National and International Perspectives.* Thousand Oaks, CA: Sage.

Irwin, Katherine, Janet Davidson, and Mandy Sanchez-Hall. 2013. "The Race to Punish in American Schools: Class and Race Predictors of Punitive School-Crime Control." *Critical Criminology* 21 (1): 47–71.

Ito, Karen L. 1983. "Hoʻoponopono and the Ties That Bind: An Examination of Hawaiian Metaphoric Frames, Conflict Resolution and Indigenous Therapy." Undergraduate thesis, Pitzer College, Claremont, CA.

James, Allison, Chris Jenks, and Alan Prout. 1998. *Theorizing Childhood.* Cambridge, UK: Polity.

Joe, Karen A., and Meda Chesney-Lind. 1995. "'Just Every Mother's Angel': An Analysis of Gender and Ethnic Variations in Youth Gang Membership." *Gender and Society* 9 (4): 408–31.

Jones, Nikki. 2010. *Between Good and Ghetto: African American Girls and Inner City Violence.* New Brunswick, NJ: Rutgers University Press.

———. 2008. "Working 'The Code': On Girls, Gender, and Inner-City Violence." *Australian and New Zealand Journal of Criminology* 41 (1): 63–83.

———. 2004. "'It's Not Where You Live, It's How You Live': How Young Women Negotiate Conflict and Violence in the Inner City. In *Being Here and Being There: Fieldwork Encounters and Ethnographic Discoveries: Annals of the American Academy of Political and Social Science,* edited by E. Anderson, S. N. Brooks, R. Gunn, and N. Jones, 49–62. Thousand Oaks, CA: Sage.

Kāmauʻu, M. 1998. "Host Culture (Guava Juice on a Tray)." *ʻŌiwi: A Native Hawaiian Journal* 1: 135–36.

Kameʻeleihiwa, Lilikalā. 1996. *Native Land and Foreign Desires: Pehea Lā E Pono Ai?* Honolulu: Bishop Museum Press.

Kang-Brown, Jacob, Jennifer Trone, Jennifer Fratello, and Tarika Daftary-Kapur. 2013. *A Generation Later: What We've Learned about Zero Tolerance in Schools.* New York: Vera Institute of Justice.

Katz, Jack. 1988. *Seductions of Crime: Moral and Sensual Attractions in Doing Evil.* New York: Basic Books.

Katz, Michael B. 1989. *The Undeserving Poor: From the War on Poverty to the War on Welfare.* New York: Pantheon.

Keahiolalo-Karasuda, RaeDeen. 2010. "A Genealogy of Punishment in Hawaiʻi: The Public Hanging of Chief Kamanawa II." *Hūlili: Multidisciplinary Research on Hawaiian Well-Being* 6: 147–67.

Keller, Thomas E. 2005. "A Systemic Model of the Youth Mentoring Intervention." *Journal of Primary Prevention* 26 (2): 169–88.

Kelly, Deirdre M. 1993. *Last Chance High: How Girls and Boys Drop in and out of Alternative Schools.* New Haven, CT: Yale University Press.

Kimmel, Michael. 1996. *Manhood in America: A Cultural History.* New York: Free Press.

Kohlberg, Lawrence. 1981. *The Psychology of Moral Development*. New York: Harper and Row.

Kuhn, Jeffrey A. 1998. "A Seven-Year Lesson on Unified Family Courts: What We Have Learned since the 1990 National Family Court Symposium." *Family Law Quarterly* 32 (1): 67–93.

Kupchik, Aaron, and Geoff Ward. 2014. "Race, Poverty, and Exclusionary School Security: An Empirical Analysis of U.S. Elementary, Middle, and High Schools." *Youth Violence and Juvenile Justice* 12 (4): 332–54.

Lareau, Annette. 2011. *Unequal Childhoods: Class, Race, and Family Life*. 2nd ed. Berkeley: University of California Press.

Lasley Barajas, Heidi, and Jennifer Pierce. 2001. "The Significance of Race and Gender in School Success among Latinas and Latinos in College." *Gender and Society* 15 (6): 859–78.

Latimer, Jeff, Craig Dowden, and Danielle Muise. 2005. "The Effectiveness of Restorative Justice Practices: A Meta-Analysis." *Prison Journal* 85 (2): 127–44.

Lawrence, Charles, III. 2007. "Unconscious Racism Revisited: Reflections on the Impact and Origins of the Id, the Ego, and Equal Protection." *Connecticut Law Review* 40 (4): 931–77.

Leadbeater, Bonnie J. R. 2007. "Introduction: Urban Girls: Building Strengths, Creating Momentum." In *Urban Girls Revisited: Building Strengths*, edited by B. J. R. Leadbeater and N. Way, 1–18. New York: New York University Press.

Leadbeater, Bonnie J. R., and Niobe Way, eds. 2007. *Urban Girls Revisited: Building Strengths*. New York: New York University Press.

————. 2001. *Growing Up Fast: Early Adult Transitions of Inner-City Adolescent Mothers*. Mahway, NJ: Erlbaum.

Lee, Matthew R. 2008. "Civic Community in the Hinterland: Toward a Theory of Rural Social Structure and Violence." *Criminology* 46 (2): 447–78.

Lee, Stacy J. 2005. *Up against Whiteness: Race, School, and Immigrant Youth*. New York: Teachers College Press.

Lee, Wayde. 2013. *Pono Lōkahi Curriculum*. Honolulu: Kahua Ola Hou.

Lees, Sue. 1997. *Ruling Passions: Sexual Violence, Reputation and the Law*. Philadelphia: Open University Press.

Leiber, Michael J., Joseph Johnson, Kristan Fox, and Robyn Lacks. 2007. "Differentiating among Racial/Ethnic Groups and Its Implications for Understanding Juvenile Justice Decision Making." *Journal of Criminal Justice* 35 (5): 471–84.

Leiber, Michael J., and Kristin Y. Mack. 2003. "The Individual and Joint Effects of Race, Gender, and Family Status on Juvenile Justice Decision-Making." *Journal of Research in Crime and Delinquency* 40 (1): 34–70.

Leitz, Lisa. 2003. "Girl Fights: Exploring Females' Resistance to Educational Structures." *The International Journal of Sociology and Social Policy* 23 (11): 15–46.

Lesko, Nancy. 2001. *Act Your Age! A Cultural Construction of Adolescence*. New York: Routledge.

————. 1988. *Symbolizing Society: Stories, Rites and Structure in Catholic High School*. Philadelphia: Falmer.

Linnekin, Jocelyn. 1991. "Ignoble Savages and Other European Visions: The La Pérouse Affair in Samoan History." *The Journal of Pacific History* 26 (1): 3–26.

Lipsky, Michael. 1980. *Street-Level Bureaucracy: Dilemmas of the Individual in Public Service*. New York: Russell Sage Foundation.

Loo, Chalsa M., John A. Fairbank, and Claude M. Chemtob. 2005. "Adverse Ethnic-Related Events as a Risk Factor for Posttraumatic Stress Disorder in Asian American Vietnam Veterans." *Journal of Nervous Mental Disorders* 193 (7): 455–63.

Loo, Chalsa M., John A. Fairbank, Raymond M. Scurfield, Libby O. Ruch, Daniel W. King, Lily J. Adams, and Claude M. Chemtob. 2001. "Measuring Exposure to Racism: Development and Validation of a Race-Related Stressor Scale (RRSS) for Asian American Vietnam Veterans." *Psychological Assessment* 13 (4): 503–20.

Loo, Chalsa M., Brian R. Lim, Gabriel Koff, Robert K. Morton, and Peter N. C. Kiang. 2007. "Ethnic-Related Stressors in the War Zone: Case Studies of Asian American Vietnam Veterans." *Military Medicine* 172 (9): 968–71.

Lopez, Nancy. 2003. *Hopeful Girls and Troubled Boys: Race and Gender Disparity in Urban Education*. New York: Routledge.

Lopez, Nancy, and Chalane E. Lechuga. 2007. "They Are Like a Friend: Othermothers Creating Empowering, School-Based Community Living Rooms in Latina and Latino Middle Schools." In *Urban Girls Revisited: Building Strengths*, edited by B. J. R. Leadbeater and N. Way, 97–120. New York: New York University Press.

Lubet, Steven. 2015. "Did this Acclaimed Sociologist Drive the Getaway Car in a Murder Plot? The Questionable Ethics of Alice Goffman's *On the Run*." *New Republic* May 27. www.newrepublic.com/article/121909/did-sociologist-alice-goffman-drive-getaway-car-murder-plot.

Mac an Ghail, Mairtin. 1994. *The Making of Men: Masculinities, Sexualities, and Schooling*. Philadelphia: Open University Press.

Males, Mike A. 1996. *The Scapegoat Generation: America's War on Adolescents*. Monroe, ME: Common Courage Press.

Mandell, Nancy. 1988. "The Least-Adult Role in Studying Children." *Journal of Contemporary Ethnography* 16 (4): 433–67.

Massey, Douglas S., and Nancy A. Denton. 1993. *American Apartheid: Segregation and the Making of the Underclass*. Boston: Harvard University Press.

———. 1987. Trends in the Residential Segregation of Blacks, Hispanics, and Asians: 1970–1980. *American Sociological Review* 52 (4): 802–25.

Matsueda, Ross L., Kevin Drakulich, and Charis Kubrin. 2006. "Race and Neighborhood Codes of Violence." In *The Many Colors of Crime: Inequalities of Race, Ethnicity, and Crime in America*, edited by R. D. Peterson, L. J. Krivo, and J. Hagan, 334–56. New York: New York University Press.

Mauer, Marc, and Meda Chesney-Lind. 2003. *Invisible Punishment: The Collateral Consequences of Mass Imprisonment*. New York: The New Press.

Mayeda, David T., and Lisa Pasko. 2011. "Youth Violence and Hegemonic Masculinity among Pacific Islander and Asian American Adolescents." *Critical Criminology* 20 (2): 121–39.

Mayeda, David T., Lisa Pasko, and Meda Chesney-Lind. 2006. "'You Got to Do So Much to Actually Make It': Gender, Ethnicity and Samoan Youth in Hawai'i." *AAPI Nexus: Asian Americans and Pacific Islanders: Policy, Practice and Community* 4 (2): 69–93.

McGregor, Daviana P. 2007. *Nā Kuaʻāina: Living Hawaiian Culture*. Honolulu: University of Hawaiʻi Press.

McGuire, James. 2008. "A Review of Effective Interventions for Reducing Aggression and Violence." *Philosophical Transactions of the Royal Society B: Biological Sciences* 363 (1503): 2577–97.

McIntyre, Alice. 2000. *Inner-City Kids: Adolescents Confront Life and Violence in an Urban Community.* New York: New York University Press.

McRobbie, Angela. 1981. *Feminism for Girls: An Adventure Story.* New York: Routledge.

Meiners, Erica R. 2010. *Right to Be Hostile: Schools, Prisons, and the Making of Public Enemies.* New York: Routledge.

Merry, Sally Engle. 2001. *Colonizing Hawai'i: The Cultural Power of Law.* Princeton, NJ: Princeton University Press.

Merten, Don E. 1997. "The Meaning of Meanness: Popularity, Competition, and Conflict among Junior High School Girls." *Sociology of Education* 70 (3): 175–91.

Merton, Robert K. 1957. *Social Theory and Social Structure.* Glencoe, IL: Free Press.

Messerschmidt, James. 1986. *Capitalism, Patriarchy, and Crime: Toward a Socialist Feminist Criminology.* Totowa, NJ: Rowman and Littlefield.

Meyer, Manu Aluli. 1998. "Native Hawaiian Epistemology: Sites of Empowerment and Resistance." *Equity and Excellence* 31 (1): 22–28.

———. 1997. "Hermeneutics and Membership: One Local Girl's Version." Paper Presented at the Association of College Unions International, University of Hawai'i, Manoa, Hawai'i. October 18, 1997.

———. 1995. "To Set Right: Ho'oponopono: A Native Hawaiian Way of Peacemaking." *Compleat Lawyer* 12 (4): 30–34..

Miller, Jerome G. 1996. *Search and Destroy: African-American Males in the Criminal Justice System.* New York: Cambridge University Press.

Miller, Jody. 2008. *Getting Played: African American Girls, Urban Inequality, and Gendered Violence.* New York: New York University Press.

———. 2001. *One of the Guys: Girls, Gangs, and Gender.* New York: Oxford University Press.

Miller, Jody, and Christopher W. Mullins. 2006. "Stuck up, Telling Lies, and Talking Too Much: The Gendered Context of Young Women's Violence." In *Gender and Crime: Patterns in Victimization and Offending,* edited by K. Heimer and C. Kruttschnitt, 41–66. New York: New York University Press.

Miller, Walter. 1958. "Lower Class Culture as a Generating Milieu of Gang Delinquency." *Journal of Social Issues* 14 (3): 5–19.

Moku'au, Noreen. 2002. "Culturally Based Interventions for Substance Use and Child Abuse among Native Hawaiians." *Association of Schools of Public Health* 117 (1): S82–S87.

———. 1998. *Responding to Pacific Islanders: Culturally Competent Perspectives for Substance Abuse Prevention.* Washington, D.C.: U.S. Department of Health and Human Services, Center for Substance Abuse Prevention.

Monroe, Carla R. 2005. "Why Are 'Bad Boys' Always Black?: Causes of Disproportionality in School Discipline and Recommendations for Change." *The Clearing House: A Journal of Educational Strategies, Issues and Ideas* 79 (1): 45–50.

Morash, Merry, and Meda Chesney-Lind. 2009. "Girls' Violence in Context." In *The Delinquent Girl,* edited by M. Zahn, 182–206. Philadelphia: Temple University Press.

Morrell, Ernest. 2006. "Youth-Initiated Research as a Tool for Advocacy and Change in Urban Schools." In *Beyond Resistance! Youth Activism and Community Change,* edited by S. Ginwright, P. Noguera, and J. Cammarota, 111–29. New York: Routledge.

Morris, Edward W. 2007. "'Ladies' or 'Loudies'? Perceptions and Experiences of Black Girls in Classrooms." *Youth and Society* 38 (4): 490–515.

Moyo, Otrude N., and Saliwe M. Kawewe. 2002. "The Dynamics of a Racialized, Gendered, Ethnicized, and Economically Stratified Society: Understanding the Socio-Economic Status of Women in Zimbabwe." *Feminist Economics* 8 (2): 163–81.

Nadelman, Ethan A. 1998. "Commonsense Drug Policy." *Foreign Affairs* 77 (1): 111–26.

Napeahi, Abbie, Terry Kelly, Paula-Ann Burgess, David Kamiyama, and Noreen Moku'au. 1998. "Culture as a Protective Factor in Two Prevention Programs for Hawaiians." In *Responding to Pacific Islanders: Culturally Competent Perspectives for Substance Abuse Prevention,* edited by N. Moku'au, 97–116. Washington, D.C.: U.S. Department of Health and Human Services, Center for Substance Abuse Prevention.

Nespor, Jan. 1998. "The Meaning of Research: Kids as Subjects and Kids as Inquirers." *Qualitative Inquiry* 4 (3): 221–44.

Ness, Cindy D. 2010. *Why Girls Fight: Female Youth Violence in the Inner City.* New York, NY: New York University Press.

———. 2004. "Why Girls Fight: Female Youth Violence in the Inner City. In *Being Here and Being There: Fieldwork Encounters and Ethnographic Discoveries: Annals of the American Academy of Political and Social Science,* edited by E. Anderson, S. N. Brooks, R. Gunn, and N. Jones, 32–48. Thousand Oaks, CA: Sage.

Nicholson-Crotty, Sean, Zachary Birchmeier, and David Valentine. 2009. "Exploring the Impact of School Discipline on Racial Disproportion in the Juvenile Justice System." *Social Science Quarterly* 90 (4): 1003–18.

Nishihara, Dennis P. 1978. "Culture, Counseling, and Ho'oponopono: An Ancient Model in a Modern Context." *The Personnel and Guidance Journal* 56 (9): 562–66.

Noddings, Nel. 2013. *Caring: A Relational Approach to Ethics and Moral Education.* Berkeley: University of California Press.

Noguera, Pedro A. 2003. "Schools, Prisons, and Social Implications of Punishment: Rethinking Disciplinary Practices." *Theory into Practice* 42 (4): 341–50.

Nugent, William R., Mona Williams, and Mark S. Umbreit. 2004. "Participation in Victim-Offender Mediation and the Prevalence of Subsequent Delinquent Behavior: A Meta-Analysis." *Research on Social Work Practice* 14 (6): 408–16.

Office of Hawaiian Affairs. 2010. *The Disparate Treatment of Native Hawaiians in the Criminal Justice System.* Honolulu: State of Hawai'i, Office of Hawaiian Affairs.

Okamura, Jonathan. 2008. *Ethnicity and Inequality in Hawai'i.* Philadelphia: Temple University Press.

———. 1994. "Why Are There No Asian Americans in Hawai'i? The Continued Significance of Local Identity." *Social Process in Hawai'i* 35: 161–78.

———. 1980. "Aloha Kanaka Me Ke Aloha Aina: Local Culture and Society in Hawai'i." *Amerasia Journal* 7 (2): 119–37.

O'Kane, Claire. 2000. "The Development of Participatory Techniques: Facilitating Children's Views about Decisions Which Affect Them." In *Research with Children: Perspectives and Practices,* edited by P. Christensen and A. James, 136–59. New York: Falmer.

Omi, Michael, and Howard Winant. 2015. *Racial Formation in the United States*. 3rd ed. New York: Routledge.

Osgood, D. Wayne, and Jeff M. Chambers. 2000. "Social Disorganization Outside the Metropolis: An Analysis of Rural Youth Violence." *Criminology* 38 (1): 81–115.

Osorio, Jonathan Kamakawiwoʻole. 2002. *Dismembering Lāhui: A History of the Hawaiian Nation to 1887.* Honolulu: University of Hawaiʻi Press.

Owens, Lynn M., and Catherine D. Ennis. 2005. "The Ethic of Care in Teaching: An Overview of Supportive Literature." *Quest* 57 (4): 392–425.

Paglinawan, Lynette. 1976. "Hoʻoponopono: Problem Solving Hawaiian Style." *Honolulu* 11 (5): 89–108.

Pascoe, C. J. 2012. *Dude, You're a Fag: Masculinity and Sexuality in High School*. Berkeley: University of California Press.

Pastor, Jennifer, Jennifer McCormick, Michelle Fine, Ruth Andolsen, Nora Friedman, Nikki Richardson, Tanzania Roach, and Marina Tavares. 2007. "Makin' Homes: An Urban Girl Thing." In *Urban Girls Revisited: Building Strengths*, edited by B. J. R. Leadbeater and N. Way, 75–96. New York: New York University Press.

Patil, Vrushali. 2013. "From Patriarchy to Intersectionality: A Transnational Feminist Assessment of How Far We've Really Come." *Signs* 38 (4): 847–67.

Payne, Allison A., and Kelly Welch. 2010. Modeling the Effects of Racial Threat on Punitive and Restorative School Discipline Practices." *Criminology* 48 (4): 1019–62.

Pedersen, Paul B. 1979. "Perspectives on Cross-Cultural Psychology." In *Cross-Cultural Counseling and Psychotherapy: Foundations, Evaluation and Cultural Considerations*, edited by A. J. Marsella, R. G. Tharp, and T. J. Cibrorowski, 77–98. New York: Academic Press.

Piaget, Jean. 1965. *The Moral Judgment of the Child*. New York: Free Press.

Polsky, Ned. 1967. *Hustlers, Beats, and Others*. Chicago: Aldine.

Pope, C. E., R. D. Lovell, and H. M. Hsia. 2002. *Disproportionate Minority Confinement: A Review of the Research Literature from 1989 through 2001*. Washington, DC: U.S. Dept. of Justice, Office of Justice Programs, Office of Juvenile Justice and Delinquency Prevention.

Pukui, Mary Kawena, E. W. Haertig, and Catherine A. Lee. 1972. *Nānā I Ke Kumu* (Look to the Source). Vols. 1–2. Honolulu: Queen Liliʻuokalani Children's Center.

Punch, Samantha. 2002. "Research with Children: The Same or Different from Research with Adults?" *Childhood: A Global Journal of Child Research* 9 (3): 321–41.

Puzzanchera, C., and W. Kang. 2014. "Easy Access to FBI Arrest Statistics 1994–2012." U.S. Office of Juvenile Justice and Delinquency Prevention. www.ojjdp.gov/ojstatbb/ezaucr /asp/ucr_display.asp.

Pyke, Karen D., and Denise L. Johnson. 2003. "Asian American Women and Racialized Femininities: 'Doing' Gender across Cultural Worlds." *Gender and Society* 17 (1): 33–53.

Raby, Rebecca. 2007. "Across a Great Gulf? Conducting Research with Adolescents." In *Representing Youth: Methodological Issues in Critical Youth Studies*, edited by A. L. Best, 29–59. New York: New York University Press.

Raeder, Myrna S. 2012. "Special Issue: Making a Better World for Children of Incarcerated Parents." *Family Court Review* 50 (1): 23–35.

Reichert, Michael C. 2000. "Disturbances of Difference: Lessons from a Boys' School." In *Construction Sites: Excavating Race, Class, and Gender Among Urban Youth,* edited by L. Weis and M. Fine, 259–73. New York: Teachers College Press.

Reynolds, Cecil R., Russell J. Skiba, Sandra Graham, Peter Sheras, Jane Close Conoley, and Enedina Garcia-Vazquez. 2008. "Are Zero Tolerance Policies Effective in the Schools? An Evidentiary Review and Recommendations." *The American Psychologist* 63 (9): 852–62.

Rhodes, Jean E. 2005. "A Model of Youth Mentoring." In *Handbook of Youth Mentoring,* edited by D. L. DuBois and M. J. Karcher, 30–43. Thousand Oaks, CA: Sage Publications Ltd.

———. 2002. *Stand by Me: The Risks and Rewards of Mentoring Today's Youth.* Cambridge, MA: Harvard University Press.

———. 1994. "Older and Wiser: Mentoring Relationships in Childhood and Adolescence." *Journal of Primary Prevention* 14 (3): 187–96.

Richie, Beth E. 2012. *Arrested Justice: Black Women, Violence, and America's Prison Nation.* New York: New York University Press.

Rios, Victor M. 2011. *Punished: Policing the Lives of Black and Latino Boys.* New York: New York University Press.

Robbins, Christopher G. 2005. "Zero Tolerance and the Politics of Racial Injustice." *Journal of Negro Education* 74 (1): 2–17.

Roberts, Dorothy E. 2004. "The Social and Moral Cost of Mass Incarceration in African American Communities." *Stanford Law Review* 56 (5): 1271–1305.

Rose, Tricia. 1994. *Black Noise: Rap Music and Black Culture in Contemporary America.* Hanover, NH: Wesleyan University Press.

Russell-Brown, Katheryn. 1998. *The Color of Crime: Racial Hoaxes, White Fear, Black Protectionism, Police Harassment, and Other Macroaggressions.* New York: New York University Press.

Sabol, William J., Claudia J. Coulton, and Jill E. Korbin. 2004. "Building Community Capacity for Violence Prevention." *Journal of Interpersonal Violence* 19 (3): 322–40.

Schaffner, Laurie. 2006. *Girls in Trouble with the Law.* New Brunswick, NJ: Rutgers University Press.

Schlozman, Bradley J. 2005. "Investigation of the Hawai'i Youth Correctional Facility, Kailua, Hawai'i." Memo reporting the findings of investigation of HYCF by the Acting Assistant U.S. Attorney General, Civil Rights Division of the U.S. Attorney General. www.prisonlegalnews.org/news/publications/cripa-kailua-hi-youth-corr-facility-investigation-findings-8-4-05/.

Shaw, Clifford R. 1930. *The Jack Roller: A Delinquent Boy's Own Story.* Chicago: The University of Chicago Press.

Shaw, Clifford R., and Henry D. McKay. 1942. *Juvenile Delinquency in Urban Areas.* Chicago: University of Chicago Press.

Shook, E. Victoria. 1985. *Ho'oponopono: Contemporary Uses of a Hawaiian Problem-Solving Process.* Honolulu: University of Hawai'i Press.

Siegel, Jane A. 2011. *Disrupted Childhoods: Children of Women in Prison.* New Brunswick, NJ: Rutgers.

Silva, Noenoe K. 2004. *Aloha Betrayed: Native Hawaiian Resistance to American Colonialism.* Durham, NC: Duke University Press.

Simon, Jonathan. 2007. *Governing through Crime: How the War on Crime Transformed American Democracy and Created a Culture of Fear*. Oxford: Oxford University Press.

Simpson, Sally S. 1991. "Caste, Class, and Violent Crime: Explaining Differences in Female Offending." *Criminology* 29 (1): 115–35.

———. 1989. "Feminist Theory, Crime, and Justice." *Criminology* 27 (4): 607–31.

Sing, David Kekaulike, Alapa Hunter, and Manu Aluli Meyer. 1999. "Native Hawaiian Education: Talking Story with Three Hawaiian Educators." *Journal of American Indian Education* 39 (1): 4–13.

Skiba, Russell J. 2000. *Zero Tolerance, Zero Evidence: An Analysis of School Disciplinary Practice*. Bloomington: Indiana Education Policy Center.

Skiba, Russell J., Robert S. Michael, Abra Carroll Nardo, and Reece L. Peterson. 2002. "The Color of Discipline: Sources of Racial and Gender Disproportionality in School Punishment." *The Urban Review* 34 (4): 317–42.

Snyder, Howard N. 2012. *Arrest in the United States, 1990–2010*. Washington, D.C.: U.S. Department of Justice, Bureau of Justice Statistics.

Snyder, Howard N., and Melissa Sickmund. 2006. *Juvenile Offenders and Victims: 2006 National Report*. NCJ 178257. Washington, DC: U.S. Department of Justice, Office of Justice Programs, Office of Juvenile Justice and Delinquency Prevention.

Sohn, Linda, and Nancy D. Harada. 2008. "Effects of Racial/Ethic Discrimination on the Health Status of Minority Veterans." *Military Medicine* 173 (4): 331–38.

Sommers, Ira, and Deborah Baskin. 1993. "The Situational Context of Violent Female Offending." *Journal of Research in Crime and Delinquency* 30 (2): 136–62.

———. 1992. "Sex, Race, Age, and Violent offending." *Violence and Victims* 7 (3): 191–202.

Stanko, Elizabeth A. 2003. *The Meanings of Violence*. New York: Routledge.

Stanley, Barbara, and Joan E. Sieber. 1992. *Social Research on Children and Adolescents*. Newbury Park, CA: Sage.

Staples, Robert. 1975. "White Racism, Black Crime, and American Justice: An Application of the Colonial Model to Explain Crime and Race." *Phylon* 36 (1): 14–22.

State of Hawai'i, Board of Education. n.d. "Hawai'i Administrative Rules, Title 8, Department of Education, Subtitle 2, Part 1, Chapter 19: Student Misconduct, Discipline, School Searches and Seizures, Reporting Offenses, Police Interviews and Arrests, and Restitution for Vandalism of Work." Hawai'i Board of Education, Honolulu. Retrieved January 4, 2015, www.hawaiiboe.net/AdminRules/Pages/AdminRule19.aspx.

State of Hawai'i, Department of the Attorney General. 2012. *A Review of Uniform Crime Reports*. Honolulu: Department of the Attorney General.

———. 2010. *Hawai'i Youth Correctional Facility Recidivism Study*. Honolulu: Department of the Attorney General.

State of Hawai'i, Department of Public Safety. 2008. *2008 Annual Report*. Honolulu: Department of Public Safety.

St. George, Donna. 2011. "More Schools Are Rethinking Zero Tolerance." *The Washington Post*, June 1. www.washingtonpost.com/local/education/more-schools-are-rethinking-zero-tolerance/2011/05/26/AGSIKmGH_story.html.

Stodden, Norma Jean, Robert Stodden, and Anona K. Nā'one Napoleon. 2000. *Ho'oponopono Curriculum and Educator Training Curriculum*. Honolulu: Alu Like.

Stoler, Ann Laura. 2006. "Intimidations of Empire: Predicaments of the Tactile and Unseen." In *Haunted by Empire: Geographies of Intimacy in North American History,* edited by A. L. Stoler, 1–22. Durham, NC: Duke University Press.

Stuntz, William J. 2008. "Unequal Justice." *Harvard Law Review* 121 (8): 1969–2040.

Sugai, George, Robert H. Horner, Glen Dunlap, Meme Hieneman, Timothy J. Lewis, C. Michael Nelson, Terrance Scot, Carl Liaupsin, Wayne Sailor, Ann P. Turnbull, H. Rutherford Turnbull, III, Donna Wickham, Michael Ruef, and Brennan Wilcox. 1999. *Applying Positive Behavioral Support and Functional Behavioral Assessment in Schools: Technical Assistance Guide.* Washington, D.C.: Special Education Programs, Office of Elementary and Secondary Education.

Tajfel, Henry. 1978. *Differentiation between Social Groups: Studies in the Social Psychology of Intergroup Relations.* London: Academic Press.

———. 1970. "Experiments in Intergroup Discrimination." *Scientific American* 223 (5): 96–102.

Tatum, Becky. 2002. "The Colonial Model as a Theoretical Explanation of Crime and Delinquency." In *African American Classics in Criminology and Criminal Justice,* edited by S. L. Gabbidon, H. T. Greene, and V. D. Young, 307–22. Thousand Oaks, CA: Sage.

———. 2000a. "Toward a Neocolonial Model of Adolescent Crime and Violence." *Journal of Contemporary Criminal Justice* 21 (1): 1–30.

———. 2000b. *Crime, Violence, and Minority Youths.* Aldershot, UK: Ashgate.

Taylor, Jill M., Carmen N. Veloria, and Martina C. Verba. 2007. "Latina Girls We're Like Sisters—Most Times!" In *Urban Girls Revisited: Building Strengths,* edited by B. J. R. Leadbeater and N. Way, 157–74. New York: New York University Press.

Tengan, Ty Kāwika. 2002. "(En) Gendering Colonialism: Masculinities in Hawai'i and Aotearoa." *Cultural Values* 6 (3): 239–56.

Terrell, Jessica. 2015. "Tongan, Micronesian, Hawaiian Students Most Likely To Be Suspended." *Civil Beat.* September 5. www.civilbeat.com/2015/07/tongan-micronesian-hawaiian-students-most-likely-to-be-suspended/.

Thorne, Barrie. 1999. *Gender Play: Girls and Boys in School.* New Brunswick, NJ: Rutgers University Press.

Thornton, Timothy N., Carol A. Craft, Linda L. Dahlberg, Barbara S. Lynch, and Katie Baer. 2000. *Best Practices of Youth Violence Prevention: A Sourcebook for Community Action.* Atlanta: U.S. Centers for Disease Control and Prevention.

Thrasher, Frederic M. 1936. *The Gang: A Study of 1,313 Gangs in Chicago.* Chicago: University of Chicago Press.

Tonry, Michael. 2004. *Thinking about Crime: Sense and Sensibility in American Penal Culture.* New York: Oxford University Press.

Torre, Maria E., and Michelle Fine. 2006. "Researching and Resisting: Democratic Policy Research By and For Youth." In *Beyond Resistance! Youth Activism and Community Change,* edited by S. Ginwright, P. Noguera, and J. Cammarota, 269–87. New York: Routledge.

Trask, Haunani-Kay. 2008. "Settlers of Color and 'Immigrant' Hegemony: 'Locals' In Hawai'i." In *Asian Settler Colonialism: From Local Governance to the Habits of Everyday Life in Hawai'i,* edited by C. Fujikane and J. Y. Okamura, 45–65. Honolulu: University of Hawai'i Press.

————. 1999. *From a Native Daughter: Colonialism and Sovereignty in Hawai'i*. Honolulu: University of Hawai'i Press.

Tsai, Jack, and Grace Kong. 2012. "Mental Health of Asian American and Pacific Islander Military Veterans: Brief Review of an Understudied Group." *Military Medicine* 177 (11): 1438–44.

Tseng, Wen-Shing, and John F. McDermott. 1981. *Culture, Mind, and Therapy: An Introduction to Cultural Psychiatry*. New York: Brunner/Mazel.

————. 1975. "Psychotherapy: Historical Roots, Universal Elements, and Cultural Variations." *American Journal of Psychiatry* 132 (4): 378–84.

Umemoto, Karen, James Spencer, Tai-An Miao, and Saiful Momen. 2012. *Disproportionate Minority Contact in the Hawai'i Juvenile Justice System, 2000–2010*. Honolulu: University of Hawai'i.

Ungar, Micheal. 2002. *Playing at Being Bad: The Hidden Resilience of Troubled Teens*. Lawrencetown Beach, NC: Pottersfield.

U.S. Census Bureau. 2014. Quick Facts. http://quickfacts.census.gov/qfd/states/15000.html.

————. 2010a. U.S. Census: Summary File 1. www.census.gov/main/www/cen2000.html.

————. 2010b. 2009–2013, 5-Year American Community Survey. http://factfinder.census.gov/faces/nav/jsf/pages/index.xhtml.

————. 2000. 110th Congressional District Summary File (Sample), Matrix P50. www.census.gov/census2000/110th.html.

U.S. Department of Education, Office for Civil Rights. 2014. http://ocrdata.ed.gov/StateNationalEstimations.

————. 2012. Civil Rights Data Collection, LEA Summary of Selected Facts, Survey Year 2011. http://ocrdata.ed.gov/Page/PrintPage?t=d&eid=29005&syk=6&pid=736.

U.S. Department of Education and U.S. Department of Justice. 2014. *Supportive School Discipline Initiative*. Washington, D.C: U.S. Department of Education and U.S. Department of Justice. www2.ed.gov/policy/gen/guid/school-discipline/appendix-3-overview.pdf.

U.S. Sentencing Commission. 2011. *Report to the Congress: Mandatory Minimum Penalties in the Federal Criminal Justice System*. Washington, D.C.: U.S. Sentencing Commission.

Venkatesh, Sudhir. 2008. *Gang Leader for a Day: A Rogue Sociologist Takes to the Streets*. New York: Penguin Books.

Verdugo, Richard R. 2002. "Race-Ethnicity, Social Class, and Zero-Tolerance Policies: The Cultural and Structural Wars." *Education and Urban Society* 35 (1): 50–75.

Vorsino, Mary. 2011. "DOE Seeks Ways to Cool Classrooms." *Honolulu Star Advertiser*. www.staradvertiser.com/hawaii-news/doe-seeks-ways-to-cool-classrooms/.

Wacquant, Loïc. 2014. "Marginality, Ethnicity and Penality in the Neo-Liberal City: An Analytic Cartography." *Ethnic and Racial Studies* 37 (10): 1687–1711.

————. 2009. *Punishing the Poor: The Neoliberal Government of Social Insecurity*. Durham, NC: Duke University Press.

————. 2001. "Deadly Symbiosis: When Ghetto and Prison Meet and Mesh." *Punishment and Society* 31 (1): 95–134.

Wakefield, Sara, and Christopher Wildeman. 2014. *Children of the Prison Boom: Mass Incarceration and the Future of American Inequality*. New York: Oxford University Press.

Wald, Johanna, and Daniel Losen. 2003. "Defining and Redirecting the School-to-Prison Pipeline." *Journal of New Directions for Youth Development* 2003 (99): 9–15.

Walker, Lorenn, and Rebecca Greening. 2013. *Reentry and Transition Planning Circles for Incarcerated People.* Honolulu: Hawai'i Friends of Justice and Civic Education.

Ward, Geoff, and Aaron Kupchik. 2010. "What Drives Juvenile Probation Officers? Relating Organizational Contexts, Status Characteristics, and Personal Convictions to Treatment and Punishment Orientations." *Crime and Delinquency* 56 (1): 35–69.

Ward, Janie Victoria. 2000. "Raising Resisters: The Role of Truth Telling in the Psychological Development of African American Girls." In *Construction Sites: Excavating Race, Class, And Gender among Urban Youth,* edited by L. Weis and M. Fine, 50–64. New York: Teachers College Press.

Watts, Ivan Eugene, and Nirmala Erevelles. 2004. "These Deadly Times: Reconceptualizing School Violence by Using Critical Race Theory and Disability Studies." *American Educational Research Journal* 41 (2): 271–99.

Weis, Lois, and Michelle Fine, eds. 2001. "Extraordinary Conversations in Public Schools." *Qualitative Studies in Education* 14 (4): 497–523.

———, eds. 2000. *Construction Sites: Excavating Race, Class, and Gender among Urban Youth.* New York: Teachers College Press.

Welch, Kelly, and Allison A. Payne. 2010. "Racial Threat and Punitive School Discipline." *Social Problems* 57 (1): 25–48.

West, Candace, and Sarah Fenstermaker. 1995. "Doing Difference." *Gender and Society* 9 (1): 8–37.

West, Candace, and Don. H. Zimmerman. 1987. "Doing Gender." *Gender and Society* 1 (2): 125–151.

White, Brent T. 2003. "Report on the Hawai'i Youth Correctional Facility," August 14. Memo to Hawai'i Attorney General Mark Bennett on ACLU findings of site inspections at the Hawai'i Youth Correctional Facility.

Whitehead, John, and Charles Lindquist. 1985. "Job Stress and Burnout among Probation/Parole Officers: Perceptions and Causal Factors, Part 1." *International Journal of Offender Therapy and Comparative Criminology* 29 (2): 109–19.

Wildeman, Christopher, Sara Wakefield, and Kristen Turney. 2013. "Misidentifying the Effects of Parental Incarceration? A Comment on Johnson and Easterling (2012)." *Journal of Marriage and the Family* 75 (1): 252–58.

Williams, L. Susan, Sandra D. Alvarez, and Kevin S. Andrade Hauck. 2002. "My Name is Not Maria: Young Latinas Seeking Home in the Heartland." *Social Problems* 49 (4): 563–84.

Willis, Paul. 1977. *Learning to Labor: How Working Class Kids Get Working Class Jobs.* New York: Columbia University Press.

Withy, Kelley M., Wayde Lee, and Ralph F Renger. 2007. "A Practical Framework for Evaluating a Culturally Tailored Adolescent Substance Abuse Treatment Programme in Molokai, Hawai'i." *Ethnicity and Health* 12 (5): 483–96.

Wun, Connie. 2014. "Unaccounted Foundations: Black Girls, Anti-Black Racism, and Punishment in Schools." *Critical Sociology* (Dec. 24, 2014):1–14. doi:10.1177/0896920514560444.

Zhou, Min, and Carl L. Bankston III. 1998. *Growing Up American: Vietnamese Children Adopt to Life in the United States.* New York: Russell Sage Foundation.

INDEX

Aaron (pseudo.), 90

Abrams, Laura S., 190n8

adolescents: colonial patriarchy perspective on, 148; role of peer groups in, 186n6; as a social construction, 13–14. *See also* youth

African Americans, 12, 19, 43–44, 157, 183n12, 189n4

Alexander, Jeffrey C. et al., 20

Alika (pseudo.), 128–31, 133–34

Anderson, Elijah, 7, 8, 10, 30, 74, 87, 89, 94, 100, 134, 140

Anderson-Nathe, Ben, 190n8

Andy (pseudo.), 171–72

Angel (pseudo.), 1–2, 40–41, 47–48, 49, 50, 62, 64–65, 77, 79–80, 81, 82, 83, 121, 122, 136–37, 142, 143–44

Anita (pseudo.), 119–20

Annabelle (pseudo.), 66–67, 72–73, 136, 138

Arlene (pseudo.), 52, 168–70

Auggie (pseudo.), 109–10, 111–12

Auntie Maile (pseudo.), 84

Benny (pseudo.), 3–4, 75–76, 89–90, 99–100, 102–3, 142, 144

Billings, Ramie and Marshall, 130–31

Blake (pseudo.), 24, 141

boys: ability to avoid housework of, 55–56; adherence to male hegemony is not helpful for, 152–53, 190n8; "being a man" concept of, 101–4; believe country is "jacked up," 86, 90, 153, 158; believe girls are not for friendship, 102; definitions of race of, 88–89, 154; difficult transition to manual labor or military of, 153; distance themselves from all things feminine, 81, 102, 150; dress codes for, 63; falling out with friends by, 141–42; are fighting multiple inequalities with few resources, 152; harsh criticism of girls by, 77, 81, 82; have no agreed upon moral code, 140–42; ideas about success as adults of, 142–43; idea that they go through "female" stage in adolescence, 156–57; independence of, in response to failure of adults and institutions, 138–41; not held accountable for wrongdoing, 69; "playing" girls by, 75–76; racialized gender compromises ability to survive as adults, 153; role in public arenas of, 152, 158; seen as less resilient than girls, 15; see survival in gendered terms, 103; sexuality of, not subject to same scrutiny as girls, 67–68; view of girlfriends of, 74

boys' violence: altruistic, 95; being fearless and fearsome, 87–88, 98–102; boys involved in may still have conventional goals, 190n6; distaste for "mobbing" in, 95; engineered by overarching consciousness of power and sense of masculine agency, 104; fears of, 152; interracial, 93–94; loose rules govern,